TENNESSEE: CRY OF THE HEART

DOTSON RADER

TENNESSEE: CRY OF THE HEART

DOUBLEDAY & COMPANY, INC.
GARDEN CITY, NEW YORK
·1985·

Portions of this book have appeared in *The Paris Review*, *Parade*, *Esquire*, and the *Evergreen Review*.

Some of the names of persons mentioned in Tennessee: Cry of the Heart have been changed to protect the privacy of the individual.

Photograph of Tennessee and his dog © 1985 Thomas Victor.

"Life Story" from Tennessee Williams' In the Winter of Cities. © 1956 by Tennessee Williams. Reprinted by permission of New Directions Publishing Corporation.

Lines from "An American Prayer" by Jim Morrison © 1968, privately published; trade publication © 1984, Zeppelin Publishing. Reprinted by permission of the B of A Company Trust.

Lines from "Fire in the Architecture Institute" from *Antiworlds and the Fifth Ace,* by Andrei Voznesensky, translated by Stanley Kunitz, edited by Patricia Blake and Max Hayward © 1966, 1967 by Basic Books, Inc.; © 1963 by Encounter Ltd., reprinted by permission of Basic Books, Inc.

The lines from "For the Marriage of Faustus and Helen" from *The Complete Poems and Selected Letters and Prose of Hart Crane,* edited by Brom Weber, are reprinted by permission of Liveright Publishing Corporation. Copyright 1933; © 1958, 1966 by Liveright Publishing Corporation.

DESIGNED BY LAURENCE ALEXANDER

Library of Congress Cataloging in Publication Data
    Rader, Dotson.
      Tennessee, cry of the heart.
    1. Williams, Tennessee, 1911– —Biography.
    2. Dramatists, American—20th century—Biography.
    I. Title.
PS3545.I5365Z524 1985   812'.54 [B]
ISBN 0-385-19136-7
Library of Congress Catalog Card Number 84-28556
Copyright © 1985 by Dotson Rader

FOR PATRICIA KENNEDY LAWFORD

Author's Note

DURING THE YEARS Tennessee Williams and I were friends, I kept, with his knowledge, notes, letters, journals, and other papers about my life with him. Also, from time to time, we would have conversations that we taped. With the exception of quotes that are indicated as having been written by him, his words as they appear in this book derive from my own papers, and, of course, from memory. I have tried to check my memory of his life by talking to his brother, Dakin, and reading his fascinating book, *Tennessee Williams: An Intimate Biography*, written with Shepard Mead.

But I have largely relied on friends. And here I want to acknowledge my debt to them, and to thank them: Tom Seligson; Philip and Joan Kingsley; my editor at *Parade*, Walter Anderson, whose support and guidance were invaluable; Eli Wallach and Anne Jackson; Truman Capote; Norman and Norris Mailer; James Kirkwood; Irv and Essee Kupcinet, two of Tennessee's closest friends, who stood by him through the good and the bad in Chicago; Liz Smith; Leoncia McGee; Brooks and Adriana Jackson; Bertha Weed; Gloria Jones; Frank Perry; Barbara Goldsmith; Jerzy Kosinski; Jane Smith; Vass Voglis; Catherine Kingsley; Jack Weiser; Lorraine Garland; and Alex Greenwood.

At Doubleday, I am deeply appreciative of the editorial work and support of my editor, Adrian Zackheim, and Mary Ellen Curley.

I want also to thank Morton Janklow and Anne Sibbald.

Finally, most important of all, I am grateful to Richard Zoerink, who lived it with me.

TENNESSEE: CRY OF THE HEART

PART · ONE

Death makes angels of us all
and gives us wings
where we had shoulders
smooth as raven's claws.

—JIM MORRISON

CHAPTER · ONE

I FIRST MET Tennessee Williams shortly after he got out of what he called Barnacle Hospital (actually Barnes Hospital) in St. Louis, where he had been confined by his brother, Dakin, in 1969. Tennessee had flipped out on copious amounts of Doriden, Mellaril, Seconal, Ritalin, Demerol, amphetamines, and too much sorrow in Key West. He thought his house was surrounded by assassins, rifles pointing at him through the thick foliage, terrorists lurking inside the walls. He feared that he was going the way of his friend playwright William Inge, who had his own horrific difficulties with booze and pills, and who also drifted in and out of the same paranoid fog now enveloping Tennessee.

"I felt like a sleepwalker in a nightmare, unable to wake up," he said later.

In a drug-induced stupor, he fell against a hot stove in his patio, knocking over a pot of boiling water, and badly burning himself. He felt nothing. Dakin was called in St. Louis, and flew to Key West, where he had Tennessee baptized a Roman Catholic at St. Mary, Star of the Sea Church—an event lost forever in one of the boozy black holes of his mind. Then Dakin hauled him to the nuthouse.

He was first settled in the hospital's posh Queenly Tower, a place aptly named, he remembered, given the sexual proclivities of some of the staff. When he tried to flee the asylum, he was forcefully transferred to the vio-

3

lent ward. Later he was locked in an isolation cell for fighting with other inmates over what they would watch on the communal television set. Tennessee liked soap operas, and the other loonies wanted to see game shows; a row ensued, and the orderlies dragged him off and shut him away in a padded cell. There he had a series of convulsions, suffered two coronaries, and nearly died. For all that and more he never forgave his brother, Dakin, and it inculcated in him a fear of going mad that never left him.

Years later, near the end of his life, when Tennessee did something particularly odd—dress in pajamas for a formal dinner or agree to marry another man or wander around town in a fright wig pretending to be his sister, Miss Rose—I would laugh and try as gently as possible to dissuade him, all the while knowing that when the peculiarity of his action finally sank in, he would take it as evidence that his pilot light was about to burn out and Barnacle Hospital lay ahead as the last stop on his trolley line.

Constant through the years I knew Tennessee Williams was his panic, which was as much a part of him as his poetic gifts or his sexual craving or his aching loneliness, waxing and waning with the critical fortunes of his work, with the amounts of chemical substances popped, shot, swallowed into his system. "My monkey," he termed it, "the monkey on my back, the one friend who never walks away."

When his panic hit, days would follow of convincing him once again that he was not going crazy or senile, that one brain cell too many had not been burned out by booze. Then he would seem momentarily on course again, the keel even, until my phone rang, and he said, "Baby, I don't know where I am. I'm all alone. I'm at the Sheraton."

When he said "Sheraton" I knew he was lost. If he didn't know the name of his hotel in some strange town he would firmly declare he was at the Sheraton because he was convinced, when his mind was confused, that every U.S. hotel outside of New York City was named Sheraton.

"Do you know what city I'm in, or what the hell I am doing here?" he would ask.

In one case, it was Indianapolis. Tennessee, with an engagement in Minneapolis, had boarded the wrong plane and ended up in Indiana when he was expected in Minnesota.

In another instance, he decided to throw a small party in New York. He called six friends and invited us to come to his suite at the Hotel Élysée. When we showed up that night, he wasn't registered. Rather he was across town at the City Squire Motor Inn waiting expectantly in his rooms for us to appear. In issuing the invitations he had again forgotten the name of his hotel.

Lapses like these occurred when he was by himself, one of the reasons he rarely permitted himself to be alone. Over a lifetime he hired a brigade, if not a division, of traveling companions, usually young, most often blond. Many were devoted to him for a time. Some were trustworthy. Some were not. On the final night of his existence it was the action—or rather the inaction—of Jon Uker, the last in the line of live-in companions, that weighed the balance against his life.

Two years before he died, Tennessee told me, "I'm happy I never had any children. There have been too many instances of extreme eccentricity and even lunacy in my family on all four sides for me to want to have children. I think it's fortunate I never did. Miss Edwina [his mother] went crazy. A year or so before Mother died, she believed she had a horse living with her in her room. She didn't like its presence at all, and she complained bitterly about this imaginary horse that moved into the place with her. She always wanted a horse as a child. And now that she finally had one, she didn't like it one bit. But when Mother didn't want to do something, she'd say, 'I can't, Tom. I have to go riding today!' "

The night I met Tennessee Williams, I had gone to the opening of an underground movie in Greenwich Village, a porno flick passing as a work of art. It was narrated by Allen Ginsberg and Salvador Dali, which gave it a certain cachet. Filmed in Greece, it featured sailors in tight trousers dancing together; an adolescent boy humping a poster of Jayne Mansfield and, in one especially memorable scene, making love to a honeydew melon with a hole cut in it. An altogether wretched piece of work, smarmy and pretentious at the same time, but what a crowd it drew.

The theatre was jammed with famous people, many of them writers and painters, something that surprised me because I didn't know then what I know now: common to the people who make our art is a passion for pornography. I have been with or bumped into more celebrated American writers in darkened smut palaces in Times Square than one meets at a publishing convention. To the degree that if you bombed five or six skin houses in Manhattan on any given afternoon, you'd probably wipe out half the literary establishment in the United States. I do not know why that is, nor why so many of our greatest artists—

painters, writers, poets, composers—are either gay or Jewish or both. But there you are.

After the movie I went to a party for the filmmaker in SoHo, a district that was not yet fashionable. The party was held in a filthy loft with dim red lights, votive candles, mattresses on the floor, Day-Glo posters, cheap wine, dope. The atmosphere was redolent with the stench of pot, and incense made from Indian sacred cow manure, a room freshener unaccountably popular then among the demimonde.

In attendance was the usual assortment of druggies, fetishists, whores of both genders, and other popular figures of the day. Also present in force was the Andy Warhol gang—actor Joe Dallesandro, director Paul Morrissey, poet Gerard Malanga, superstars Jackie Curtis and Candy Darling—plus a considerable number of uptown socialites—Mrs. William F. Buckley, Jr., director Peter Glenville, and Prince Egon von Furstenberg, still married to Diane, although the marriage would not survive once she hitched her wagon to the rag-trade star and floated away.

I spent some time speaking with Jim Morrison of the Doors, whose music I liked and whose poetry intrigued me. A handsome, tall young man, with long hair and haunted eyes, as deeply gifted as he was troubled. I had the conviction that night that he was as doomed as any man could be, but I did not guess how quickly death would find him naked and defenseless at twenty-nine in a bathtub in Paris.

I had met Morrison months before at the Bitter End, a Village bistro that offered new singers a platform. A few days later I saw him at a party on Fourth Street.

Jim Morrison was given to sexually displaying himself at gatherings, a lapse in manners that could epitomize as well as anything the sixties' aggressive egotism and solipsism, sex-as-shock-effect. Only nobody was shocked anymore, such behavior by then seeming almost quaintly tame in a city where to give a party meant possessing a thorough knowledge of how to react if your guests went into drug-induced comas.

At the party, Morrison—who, through me, met Tennessee—lay on the floor with his back propped against a wall. He was quite drunk, having a staggering capacity for liquor, not to mention drugs. Dressed in a dark shirt and brown corduroy pants, his fly open, his penis slowly being worked by his hand. Occasionally he lifted a bottle of booze to his mouth; from time to time someone slipped over and gave him head while I sat on the floor, making conversation as if nothing untoward were taking place. We talked of death, fittingly, because, like Tennessee, Morrison viewed sex and death as intimately related, as in *Suddenly Last Summer,* where cannibalism becomes the objective correlative of homosexuality. Morrison was intrigued, almost possessed, by death, like a bird facing a snake and paralyzed by fascination.

Later I followed him into the bathroom where we discovered Edie Sedgwick on her knees before another girl.

Morrison sat down on the edge of the tub, and Edie moved between his crotch and the girl's, pleasuring them in that blue-tiled room long ago.

In those rancid years, on the cusp of the decade, when the Age of Aquarius had finally found its killing ground, that was one of the ways of making the acquaintance of a rock-and-roll star. Or just about anyone else. Sex and/or drugs being a currency that could buy you a place in the center ring.

In their torment Jim Morrison and Tennessee Williams were much alike, as they were in their love of poetry, and in their ambivalent tango with death. For Tennessee the dance lasted longer, but the music was the same.

I suppose in looking back at the party in SoHo it seems curious that the greatest playwright of our age would be present, but we were in the lees of the sixties, when you discovered the most famous people in the most improbable places, at Maoist rallies, for example, or in the sex rooms of the Anvil. Fitzgerald said his was the lost generation. He was wrong. The lost generation was alive, unwell, dying in New York in that historical rabbit hole that was dug with the death of President Kennedy. And Tennessee Williams, who thought himself a radical, a revolutionary, had been physically incapacitated through much of the sixties and so had an intense, if belated, curiosity about the social, sexual, and political movements of the period, especially as they touched the young. He liked to slum, in part because he identified with the outcast, the loser, those up against it. And also, in being places where respectable people thought it unsuitable to be seen, he formed a kind of cockeyed solidarity with those who shared with him a hatred of the rich.

Perhaps because he was poor and unrecognized for so long, he laid responsibility for most of the world's troubles at the feet of the wealthy, the cake-eaters who despoil the poor, who eat the earth. And yet his relationship with the rich was ambivalent: he had enormous contempt for the *fact* of their wealth, and still needed them to invest in his plays.

He claimed to be a socialist desiring the abolition of the capitalist state while, in apparent contradiction, he had become one of the world's richest writers through the capitalist theatre and film industries.

On the one hand, he longed for the social acceptance of the beau monde, a trait his mother shared on a much smaller stage; on the other, he distrusted fat cats and was quick to take offense.

For example, Tennessee became fiercely angered when he learned that Irene Selznick was giving a party at her Hotel Pierre apartment in New York and had neglected to invite him. At the time he was staying in town at the Hotel Élysée, with Robert Carroll, his young companion. Irene was nothing if not rich, being the daughter of Louis B. Mayer, the first wife of David O. Selznick, and a successful theatrical producer to boot. She was also immensely gracious.

Tennessee called me in a rage. He had found out I had been invited to her party, and that a lot of other people he knew, including Cary Grant, were also on Irene's list. I told him I would call her, and ring him back.

"Irene says it's a seated dinner and she doesn't have room for two extra men. She can't fit both you and Robert in," I explained, after speaking with her.

"That rich Jewess! That rich bitch!" Tennessee exploded, his voice quaking, his Mississippi drawl thicker than usual. "Baby, all she cares about is her bank account! She doesn't have room for *me* at her table? She's so mean she'd spit in the face of the baby Jesus!" He was speaking about the woman who had produced *A Streetcar Named De-*

sire nearly thirty years before. "She is without love for artists. All she loves is the almighty dollar."

I said I'd call her back and see what could be done.

"You tell her I'll eat anywhere. I'll sit on the toilet with a fucking plate on my lap!" He paused, his anger exhausted. Then, quietly, sadly, "Irene never liked me, baby. All I ever was was just a meal ticket for her, and when she couldn't make a buck off me anymore she numbered me among the dead."

Regrettably, he believed that until he died.

Although Irene finally did invite Tennessee, and he did attend the party and had a grand time of it, too, he had been wounded, and he saw her money as the sole motivation for her having hurt his pride. Irene had "turned on him" because she was wealthy, and for no other reason. In point of fact, that had nothing to do with it. She was a hostess caught with too many extra men underfoot and not enough chairs.

In the seventies, this hatred of the rich and powerful, exacerbated by the commercial failure of his later plays, drew him further to the political left. In time, he came to include among his friends David Dellinger, the great pacifist leader, Eric Mann of the Students for a Democratic Society (SDS), and a wide number of youthful radical activists, especially one young man, Mark Kluz, imprisoned for opposing the Vietnam War, a conflict that reached its apex the night we met. Almost by default, Tennessee created a community of the heart, a gathering of fugitives, as it were, that did not include the rich or the many celebrated actors—Warren Beatty, Elizabeth Taylor, Marlon Brando, *et al.*—who had made their careers on his work. Increasingly seeing himself in the defeat of others, destiny reflected in the wreckage of lives, like a future unbound in a sediment of tea leaves, he drew to himself those who needed his compassion. Chief among them, the purest abiding passion of his life, was his sister, Miss Rose.

In 1971, Tennessee and I took Miss Rose to dinner in the Oak Room of the Plaza Hotel in New York. Miss Rose was sixty-one, two years older than her brother. She had undergone a prefrontal lobotomy in the 1930s, one of the first of those wicked procedures done in the United States. As a result she had a curiously becalmed disposition, and a mental age of about six. Nevertheless, to Tennessee she was the most beautiful creature on God's green earth. He treated her with immense affection and tenderness. With the exception of his late maternal grandparents, the Dakins, Rose was the only member of his family he ever loved. And with good cause.

At 6 P.M. I joined Tennessee and Miss Rose in his suite at the hotel. Rose was wearing a light blue suit Tennessee had purchased for her at Bloomingdale's that afternoon.

When he was in New York he usually spent time shopping for his sister, because he remembered her love of clothes as a young woman, before their mother had Rose's mind cut away, leaving her forever sealed in a kind of mental amber, a perpetual debutante of the Old South locked in timelessness. About her clung more than just the remnants of a faded gentility, like some ancient scent lingering in an airless room. She *was* that gentility itself. In every gesture, in her excessive politeness, in the feminine delicacy of her person, in the beneficence of her mournful eyes, Miss Rose expressed another time and place, long dead, like some animated museum piece periodically brought out for airing. One had the sense that the chambers of her mind were cluttered with memories, faint music still dimly heard that she was powerless to give voice to, mute inside the wrappings of the past.

Rose lived in her own world inside a private cottage at a sanitarium in Ossining, New York. Tennessee paid for her expensive care. Happily she liked the hospital, content to be away from it only a few days at a time. There were many young patients, teenagers, and these were her friends. Since she had no conception of her actual age, she continued to think of herself as a teenager as she gently advanced into her dotage. A few days away from Ossining and she would say, "I wonder how the children are?" It was the cue to take her home.

When I entered the suite, Miss Rose, standing next to Tennessee, cocked her head to one side, and said, smiling hopefully, "Merry Christmas!"

It was months after Christmas, early spring, to be exact.

I looked over at Tennessee. He laughed, delighted by my bewilderment.

"Merry Christmas!" Rose repeated, more emphatically this time. She stood with her shoulders hunched, her purse gripped firmly in both hands, her large head tilted to one side, gray hair cropped short in that humiliating, butch-dyke style common to institutionalized inmates everywhere. Still, she smiled, her green-gray eyes looking at me in expectation.

"Merry Christmas," I replied, kissing her on the cheek. Her skin felt dry, soda-y, smelling of talc.

"Miss Rose," I observed, "it isn't Christmas. Christmas is a long way off."

Tennessee giggled. "She knows that. Don't you know

that, Rose? She's no dummy. She wants a Christmas present, Dot."

"Dot" or "The Big Dot" were his nicknames for me.

I told Rose I planned to buy her a present downstairs in one of the lobby shops. That settled, we set off for the restaurant.

We made a kind of royal progress from the elevator, through the lobby, past the Palm Court, down the hall to the Oak Room. There were lots of people about. Rose moved with practiced dignity, her handbag dangling from her left arm, while with her right she waved slowly at the people, a monarch acknowledging her subjects, stopping every now and again to give a small wave and sweet smile to a child. Nothing entranced her heart as did small children.

"Rose believes she's the Queen of England," Tennessee remarked. "Lovely Miss Rose. She once signed a photograph of herself to me, 'Rose of England.' I don't know how she got that particular bee in her bonnet, but when she won't answer me, I now have to say, 'Your Majesty' and make a correct little bow before she is willing to reply. She believes Queen Elizabeth is an impostor and the *real* Windsor pretender is dining in the Oak Room tonight. I can only think of one person who will support Rose's claim to the British throne. Wallis Windsor!" He cackled.

Tennessee had a very loud laugh, a cracked, machinegun-like, firecracker bark that exploded often, unexpectedly, not infrequently at the most inappropriate moments, say during the most serious scenes of a play. Actors sometimes dreaded his attending a performance of his own work because, like clockwork, at the most dramatic moments, from the center of the house would come his cackling laugh. It pierced walls, a strange noise radiation, like Superman's X-ray vision. You couldn't avoid it. It was always pretty easy to keep track of him at a party or in Key West: you heard his laughter rooms or blocks away. His most famous line from *A Streetcar Named Desire*—"I have always depended on the kindness of strangers"—invariably broke him up. In fact, during the New York rehearsals he had fought with Elia Kazan, the director, to have the line cut from the play, complaining that it never got a laugh. Kazan insisted it stay in, and won. "I wrote it as a laugh line, it never works," he groused when we left yet another performance of *Streetcar* where once again he was the only member of the audience to hoot at Blanche's parting line.

We sat together at a banquette in the back of the Oak Room, Miss Rose in the middle. The place was practically deserted.

Tennessee asked his sister what she wanted for dinner.

Rose, staring firmly at the menu, declared, "An ice cream sundae with chocolate sauce."

He tried to convince her to order something sensible, but she wouldn't budge. So while we ate steaks, Rose happily spooned down her sundae, like a child at a birthday party.

After dinner, Rose turned to me, held out her hand, and said, "Cigarette, please?"

I was advised to ignore her. But Rose insisted, asking again and again, unperturbed that the cigarette wasn't immediately forthcoming, her patience regal in its serenity.

Tennessee gave way, as he always did with her. "Let her have one, let her be happy, dear Rose. She has known so little happiness in this world," he said, leaning toward her, looking at her lovingly, his hand lifted slowly, gently caressing her wrinkled cheek.

Her doctors had ordered her off cigarettes and her rather tough Irish nurse, not on the scene that day, thank God, followed orders with a vigor that would make a Teuton proud. Tennessee loathed the nurse, was continually discharging her; she blithely ignored the dismissals and went on imposing her tyranny on Rose.

"Rose smokes too much," he admitted. Tennessee had been a chain-smoker himself, until his lover, Frank Merlo, died of cancer and he gave it up. "Rose enters a restaurant and asks, 'How many packs of Chesterfields do you have? *I'll take them all!*' Or she'll ask in a store, 'How many bars of Ivory soap do you have? That all you got? Well, I need at least twenty!'

"One night," Tennessee continued, "Rose went with me to Mrs. Murry Crane's as a dinner guest. This old dowager was the heiress to the Crane toilet-bowl fortune, and I was trying to get her to invest some of her toilet millions in a production of one of my plays. Rose had a huge reticule with her. Do you know what that is? It's a huge embroidered bag. Rose was very sly, as schizophrenics often are. You have to watch them every minute or they'll walk away with the store. All during dinner, after each course, or even when people were eating, Rose would turn to Mrs. Crane, this stately dowager to her right, and say, 'Have a cigarette, dear?' " Tennessee imitated Rose's voice. "And Mrs. Crane would reply, 'Oh, I don't smoke, Miss Williams. I do not smoke! And I fear that you're smoking too much, Miss Williams!'

"Well, Miss Rose took umbrage at that. So after dinner she excused herself. There were four or five lavatories in this duplex apartment, and Rose was gone for a *remark-*

ably long time. When she came back her reticule was absolutely packed like Santa Claus's bag. She'd cleared the house completely out of soap and toilet paper! It was the biggest haul since the James brothers. Needless to say, we didn't get a return engagement there."

After dinner we walked Miss Rose to her limousine, waiting in the hotel's carriageway to return her to Stoney Lodge, the sanitarium.

"You have to go home now, Rose. It's bedtime," he told her.

"No," she said.

"Please get in the car, Rose."

"No." She refused to move. Gripping her large purse, she stood her ground with the rigid stubbornness of children everywhere at bedtime.

"Dotson will buy you a pack of cigarettes for the return journey if you sit in the car. I'll see you again in a few weeks," he pleaded, torn by her having to leave when she desired to stay. He had to fly to the Coast in the morning. There was no choice in the matter.

I ran and bought her cigarettes, a pack of Larks. When I returned she was seated in the limousine. I handed her the cigarettes. "Merry Christmas!" she thrilled, delighted.

When she was gone, Tennessee said, "I love her, you know. For a person like Rose who spent many years in a state asylum, as she had to do before I got money, living is a constantly defensive existence. The stubbornness, the saying 'No!' flatly to things is almost an instinctive response. If I say to Rose, 'It's time for you to go home now,' her instinct is to say, 'No!' Or if I say, 'Don't you think it's time for you to get some rest?' she'll answer, 'No!' That is her only defense. But then, you know that all too well."

One of the things I shared in common with him and his sister was that I, too, had been an involuntary guest at an insane asylum.

One night Tennessee and I went barring in New York, something we always did when together. It was a diversion he had indulged in since he first came to Manhattan in 1939, cruising the meat-rack bars more for the company than for sex. A lonely man, he resisted going home to bed when he knew the bed was empty.

We ended late at night at the Haymarket, a sinister saloon on the Minnesota Strip off Times Square. It was a hustler bar of the lowest rank—two large rooms where male prostitutes, no longer able to turn a trick on Third Avenue or score with an escort service, found themselves shipwrecked. A dangerous place; fights took place, knifings sometimes happened, yet Tennessee enjoyed coming here, sitting in the back room on a bench, wearing dark glasses and a black ship captain's cap, laughing and chatting, teasing and generally dallying with the youths who drifted over from the pool table in the center of the room. Like eager young actors at an audition, they posed and strutted for our attention, thinking we might be their ticket out. Many of them were drug addicts who sold the very bodies their habits were killing.

Tennessee had a lifelong fascination with prostitutes, and never did understand why bringing a hooker to a fancy dinner party wasn't good form. He enjoyed listening to their life stories. From them he got a good deal of vicarious experience that went into his short stories and plays. He *felt* for them, and championed their right to be just as they were. But then, he viewed American society as an unjust and unequal arrangement that compelled most people to be whores of one form or another, selling their virtue to the rich. In short, prostitution was a metaphor for the American system.

About an hour after we arrived, Tennessee got up to go to the bathroom. When he didn't return, I became concerned and went looking for him.

I found him in the john, kneeling on the floor by the urinal. Lying on the wet pavement, wearing only blue jeans and sneakers, was a boy of perhaps eighteen, with closed eyes, pasty, pimply skin, a small tattoo on his shoulder, blond hair, long and matted. A hypodermic needle hung at an odd angle from his arm.

"Tenn," I said, "we should leave."

He looked up at me. "Call for medical assistance! An angel has fallen!" he said, his voice breaking dramatically.

"He's a goner, Tenn. There's no help for him now."

Tennessee reluctantly stood up, and we left, after having the barkeep call an ambulance.

At lunch the next day, Tennessee talked about the boy—or rather fantasized about who he must have been, making up a biography for a body seen lying in its own urine on a toilet floor.

He assumed he was a Southerner lured to the big city by "dreams of fame, dreams of love," only to be reduced by the crush of youth and circumstance to prostitution and addiction. He may have been right. In any case, the more he talked the more the elements in the biography resembled his short story, "One Arm." That is, he was telling the story of how his own life might have turned out if he hadn't been a writer struck by Fortune's lightning.

"He died of dreams!" he claimed. "Dreams are the poison that kills quickest!"

Here was another death, another sadness for him to claim. Sorrow activated his poetic sensibility in the way speed excites an addict.

"What's wrong with dreams?" I wanted to know.

He gave me a sharp look, and snapped, "They never come true!"

So dreams kill, and he saw dreams at the heart of the sixties.

"The sixties were a decade of great vitality," he remembered more than a decade later. "The civil rights movement, the movement against war and imperialism. When I said to Gore Vidal, 'I slept through the sixties,' I was making a bad joke. I was intensely aware of what was going on. Even in the violent ward I read the newspapers avidly. Then we had brave people fighting against privilege and injustice. Now we have the Oscar de la Rentas. They are the Madame du Barrys of our time! I find them an outrageous symptom of our society, the shallowness and superficiality, the lack and fear of any depth that characterizes this age, this decade. It appalls me."

The sixties, as he certainly knew—and they stretched well into the early years of the seventies—were also about a boy running out of gas in a filthy ginmill with a needle in his arm.

The sixties were about death.

At the party in SoHo the night we met, Candy Darling, a drag queen and Andy Warhol superstar who would later play in Tennessee's *Small Craft Warnings*, one of his most beautiful works, came up to me. I had known Candy since she first appeared on the scene a few years before. She was a tall man, in her early twenties, with dark eyes, heavily lashed; long platinum hair; high cheekbones; a thin nose; and a full, sensuous mouth. There was a certain resemblance to Marilyn Monroe in her appearance, although her face was longer and thinner and, being a man, she lacked Monroe's bust. That night she was wearing high heels, pink-tinted panty hose, a tight black halter, and a fetching black monkey-fur evening jacket. As always, her makeup was heavy.

Normally, Candy Darling spoke in a breathless whisper, like someone who had just run up several flights of stairs, but when she was angry her voice suddenly became sharp and manly, and the effect of being snarled at in a hoarse longshoreman's voice by this stunningly beautiful "woman" was quite unsettling.

"Tennessee Williams is here," she hissed angrily, in her asthmatic way. "He wants to meet you!" She was jealous.

I said, "I thought he was *dead.*" I thought that because he had disappeared from public view. In the sixties people dropped like flies right and left, and if you didn't hear about somebody for a time you assumed they had succumbed.

"No, no," she boasted, "he's my *date.*"

He was. (This strange friendship lasted until Candy Darling died of cancer seven years later. A few days before her death, Tennessee and I went to visit her. She lay pale, weak, terribly thin, almost lifeless in a private hospital room that Warhol provided for her. She was wearing a white satin chemise that could not disguise the ravishment of her body by disease and chemotherapy. When Tennessee finally said good-bye, she reached up and pulled a

handful of platinum blond hair from her head, like someone picking lint off a sweater. She handed it to Tennessee.
"I have nothing left to give—only this," she explained to
her horrified friend. She played out her part to the foul
end.)

Candy Darling brought me over to meet Tennessee. I
was dressed in a black leather jacket, leather Frye boots,
and a black cowboy hat, which was the costume I affected
then.

Tennessee was wearing a gray suit, a multicolored
silk scarf, and the most hideous tie I had ever seen—a sort
of fluorescent rainbow of clashing colors that Eighth Avenue pimps adore. I was amazed by how tiny he was: five
feet eight, weighing about 150 pounds. I was six feet four.
(When his body was carried out of the Hotel Élysée in a
black plastic bag and lifted into the morgue wagon, I was
again reminded in the most terrible way of how little a
man he was; so much brilliance came from so small a
flame.)

Although he had read one of my books and some of
my magazine stuff, he pretended to take me for a hustler.
It was the only pass he ever made at me, and in the years
to come I realized that if I had consented it would not
have worked, because his sexual taste was so specific and
so completely delimited by his memory of the body of
Frank Merlo that any sexual engagement between us
would have been unhappy. For it was through sex that he
sought to bridge the distance between himself and his late
lover. It was Merlo's death that shattered him, and in the
years that remained he tried to overcome the loss; but he
never did.

"Frankie was so close to life!" he once told me. "I was
never that close, you know. He gave me the necessary con-

nection to day-to-day and night-to-night living. To reality. He tied me down to earth, baby. And I had that for fourteen years, until he died. And that was the happiest period of my adult life."

So the night I met him, Tennessee Williams grinned at me and asked, "How much do you get a night?"

"One hundred bucks," I replied, playing along.

He paused, rolling his blue eyes at Candy, his heavy, black-rimmed glasses slipping down his nose. "Well, baby, what do you charge to escort an older gentleman to dinner?"

"Fifty bucks."

Feigning shock, he felt in his pockets for money, pulled out a few bills. After making a great show of counting his cash, he looked up and asked, "Do you suppose we could settle for *lunch?*"

He was fifty-nine, and I was twenty-six, but to me we both seemed so much older than we were.

The next day I met him for lunch at the Plaza Hotel, where he had a suite overlooking Central Park. All I knew about him was that I, like every other writer who came after him, was irrevocably affected by his work. You couldn't get away from him because he had changed the way writing was done. With *The Glass Menagerie, A Streetcar Named Desire, Cat on a Hot Tin Roof, The Rose Tattoo, Sweet Bird of Youth, Orpheus Descending, Summer and Smoke, Camino Real, Suddenly Last Summer, The Night of the Iguana,* and other plays, he married poetry to naturalism and opened drama to subject matter never before touched upon in our theatre: incest, homosexuality, cannibalism, impotency, drug addiction, cancer, madness, sexual frenzy, ineffable loss and longing, all redeemed and beatified by poetic gifts for dialogue and scene construction unmatched by any other writer. He ended the puritan sensibility in American theatre and liberated it, poetically and thematically, from the moralism and falseness and middle-brow smugness that held it bound. In so doing, he helped free us all and ushered in an age when, among other things, the opening of a pornographic movie could be a social event. Tennessee Williams forever changed America's knowledge of herself, opening up to light the darkest corners of her psyche, and thereby forced her to accept truth she did not want to confront.

I ended up staying three days with him in his suite. There were piles of unread manuscripts and galleys sent to him by publishers hoping for a blurb in praise of their products. Manuscript pages lay scattered about the place, words typed on hotel stationery. For some unfathomable reason he was loathe to buy paper; instead he wrote on the back of commercial stationery. That may have been purely because of convenience; more likely it was due to his tightness with a buck. When it came to money he had a very original approach. If he paid for something with a credit card or check, the amount never bothered him. If it was with cash, he could be stubbornly tightfisted. It was as if credit cards and checks weren't really money, only cash was.

Several years after we met, I was staying with him in Key West. He asked me to clear out the downstairs guest-room bureau because a friend of ours was coming to stay. In the bureau drawer I found over twenty thousand dollars in unused airline tickets in his name. I brought them to him and told him to cash them in.

"I don't want them. Just throw them out. They're worthless."

I explained that they were the same as money, and he should send them to his accountant for refunding.

He screwed up his face, shook his head no. I left them on his bed. I assume he tossed them away.

During those three days in New York with him, living in a suite that, like all his dwellings, smelled of Listerine, I quickly became used to his routine. He arose early and made himself a martini, ordered a pot of coffee, and with a bottle of red wine in hand toddled into the living room and sat down at his portable typewriter, a battered Royal manual, and worked until noon. Then we went to lunch and later took a swim. He maintained the same schedule until he died.

He swam at the West Side YMCA, although he had guest privileges at the New York Athletic Club. However, he wouldn't go there because the members made anti-gay remarks about him and it reminded him too painfully of his father, the shoe salesman, who would cruelly call him "Nancy" in front of his friends when he was a boy.

"They're all the same. Shoe salesmen with a bad territory and wives they can't abide. So they take it out on us," he said.

During those first brief days of our friendship, I came to love him. A curious thing about love is that you can often pinpoint the precise moment of its birth, or at least the point in time when your consciousness was made aware that your heart was captive to a new affection. That was true with Tennessee.

On the second day I stayed with him we left to go to lunch with Audrey Wood at the Italian Pavilion. Audrey had been his literary agent since 1939. He was nervous about the meeting as he no longer trusted her.

Tennessee believed that Audrey was making deals behind his back, selling him out. She had utterly lost his confidence, and he saw her as part of a wider conspiracy to destroy his career, a monstrous intrigue "led by the sinister Gelbs at the New York *Times*, " as he menacingly put it, and having its seed in the perceived rivalry between himself and the late Eugene O'Neill. Audrey, of course, was in the thick of it, yet he was afraid of confronting her head-on, something he carefully avoided that day at lunch.

"Audrey is too powerful now, although I made her career." Tennessee declared. "She thinks I'm about to die. She thought I died in the nuthouse, and it delighted her! She wants me to expire so she can control and pervert my work. Well, baby, even old crocodiles have a wicked bite! I still have a trick or two up my sleeve, you know."

At that point, I had no idea who Audrey Wood was, had not as yet met her, and thus I took what Tennessee told me at face value, particularly when he said it in a conspiratorial tone of voice. I also did not know that I was witnessing for the first time his paranoia, a condition that would increasingly distort his perception of reality.

The previous night we had gotten quite drunk, and now we were hung over like sick dogs. Tennessee's eyes were bloodshot; his hands trembled.

Despite that, he dressed smartly for lunch, wearing a handsome beige suit, white shirt, blue tie, and a panama hat. He loved hats and adored dressing well.

As we walked down the steps of the hotel, I was shocked to see his left sleeve soaked with blood. I made him return to the suite. He was not in the least alarmed, being blithely indifferent to the bleeding. He dismissed it by remarking that it happened all the time.

Upstairs he took off his coat, and then his heavily bloodied shirt. I washed his upper arm where the capillaries had burst. Over time he had so abused his body that sometimes when he was tense the smaller veins couldn't withstand the blood pressure and broke. It was something I saw many times.

In washing him, in pressing cold hand towels against his skin to stanch the bleeding, I was at once conscious of his mortality, fragility, the very preciousness of his body. How vulnerable he was, and how childlike and dependent in his quietly protesting submission to my nursing him and my hectoring warnings about drinking too much. It was in that moment, in the simple act of physically caring for him, that I was overcome by the dearness of his person. I knew I loved him and always would.

With love came tolerance. I became used to his falling down; his drug haze; his drinking; hysterical laughter, rage and remorse; the web of self-destructive habits that would undo him in the end. But in some unknown way the spirit that bequeathed the world Blanche DuBois and Stanley Kowalski, Chance Wayne and Alexandra del Lago, Big Daddy, Amanda Wingfield, Sebastian and Mrs. Venable, One Arm, and more was, by their very creation, so depleted of defense, rendered so exceptionally vulnerable, that it required the "ministrations," as he would say, of drugs and liquor to make it through the night. When I met Tennessee Williams I became witness to the beginning of his irreversible decline, when he could no longer keep his torment under control.

CHAPTER · TWO

THOMAS LANIER WILLIAMS was born on March 26, 1911, in Columbus, Mississippi, in the rectory of his grandfather's Episcopal church, a few miles from the Alabama border and less than a hundred miles from New Albany, Mississippi, where William Faulkner, the South's other great writer, was born.

He spent his first eight years in Mississippi, and they left impressions and memories that not even the torment of his later life could eradicate, eight years that forever hallowed the Deep South in his imagination and made it the home and refuge of his fugitive heart. He always remembered his childhood as one of unalloyed happiness and innocence, a secure time and place where, with his sister Rose, he collected broken shards of colored glass bottles which they kept in crystal bowls of water and held up to the sunlight to see a rainbow captured there. He raised white rabbits, cut paper dolls from Sears catalogs, made paper boats to sail and dreamed they were real, and at dusk hunted fireflies to light a Mason jar.

The family's black maid, Ozzie, was a favorite. She had been part of the Williams household since she was sixteen, an illiterate girl, the daughter of desperately poor sharecroppers. Grandmother Dakin and his mother, Edwina, taught Ozzie how to read and write; and she read to Tom as he played with toy fish in a bathtub and told him stories of witches and spooks, and tales of the Old South before the Yankees came with Billy Sherman to rape and kill and despoil and rend what was never to be again.

Edwina held classes at home for Tom and Rose. "Rose was always faster than Tom in acquiring knowledge in the little classes I conducted at home," Edwina wrote. "Sometimes we would hear her scream and Tom would be pulling her hair angrily and saying, 'She's too proud of herself!' "

He was immensely shy, and fearful of strangers. When he went off to kindergarten at age five he enjoyed working in clay, making animals, elephants mainly, as long as his mother was in the room. But the minute she left, he would begin to scream and keep it up until she returned. His first poem, written as a child, was titled "Kindy Garden," about playing with colored beads and being jealous of Rose because she knew the multiplication table and he didn't.

As a child, with the exception of his sister, the people closest to him were his grandparents Dakin: Rose, whom he called "Grand," and Walter.

Rose was of German descent, the daughter of rigidly pious Lutheran parents, and to escape them she married, at sixteen, Walter Dakin, a short, slight, kindly man, the first eligible bachelor she had met. He was an accountant, but he had heard the Call of the Lord and made up his mind to enter the Episcopal priesthood, a decision that came as an unwelcome surprise to his new bride. She bent to his will. "Grand" was a musical woman who, as a girl, had had ambitions for the concert stage, dreams that were not to be realized. She played the violin and the piano, practicing daily all her life, and years later, when her grandson Tom was trying to achieve success as a writer and had no money and little prospects of any, she supported him by giving lessons on piano and violin and sending the money to him.

There is a snapshot of Tom as a baby sitting on a quilted chair with a fanlike back, much like the wicker throne chairs he loved so much as an adult. He is wearing a white dress, white baby shoes; his sparse blond hair is combed forward, his eyes wide, his smile crooked, and he is looking terribly pleased with himself.

When he was five his grandfather was sent by the bishop to a new parish in Clarksdale, in western Mississippi on the Tallahatchie River. Tom, his sister Rose, and Edwina followed his grandparents to their new home, without his father, Cornelius, who had fallen into the pattern he would hold until he died: driving his Model T Ford over rural roads selling shoes to country stores, womanizing, drinking, and staying away longer and longer, until one year he did not come home for a single visit.

Cornelius was one of those men who are defeated by life before they begin. Even though Tennessee always remembered him as a hated figure, terrifying and cruel, depriving his son of elementary affection and regard, he can be seen as a pathetic man, a marginal American loser worthy of sympathy. His childhood was ghastly, his own father a tyrant who squandered the family wealth on a succession of mistresses and a seemingly endless and unsuccessful campaign to be governor of Tennessee. (Among his ancestors was Thomas Lanier Williams I, chancellor of the Southwest Territory, as the state of Tennessee was known before it was admitted to the Union; John Williams, the state's first United States senator; and John Sevier, the first governor of the state of Tennessee; altogether a distinguished band of forebears.) Cornelius's mother, the beautiful Isabel Coffin Williams, whom he adored, died from tuberculosis when she was only twenty-eight.

Cornelius had attended the improbably named Bell-buckle Military Academy, where he was thoroughly miserable, spending most of his time in the guardhouse, surviving on a diet of turnips. Then he went on to join the Army and fight in the Spanish American War, an unfortunate career choice, because he caught a wicked case of typhoid fever and as a result went completely bald. Yet when he met Edwina the fact that he had a head like a darning egg didn't faze her in the slightest; she saw him as handsome and young, a dashing Southerner from a distinguished, if temporarily impoverished, family. She felt that way about her husband until his drinking bloated and flushed his face and his womanizing broke her heart.

He went through life secretly knowing he was a loser, waking each day comparing himself unfavorably to his ancestors, never measuring up; each day he was home, listening to Edwina hector him about money, nag about keeping up appearances, living as their social station demanded. He turned to booze and easy women on the road, carrying his sample cases from one rural hotel to another; in hotel rooms with turning ceiling fans, boasting to the boys over whiskey, crowing to the other itinerate tradesmen about the big orders placed, the ladies in each town awaiting him, the solid gold watches a grateful shoe company gave to their hot-shot salesman, all the while knowing it wasn't true. Unable to face himself, he was increasingly unwilling to face the harpy he had married and the children he did not know how to talk to anymore. So he physically abandoned the marriage and psychologically abandoned his kids.

In 1916, at the age of five, Tom nearly died from diphtheria, or so his mother diagnosed the sickness. She nursed him herself, having him sleep in bed with her, for nine days changing the ice packs placed on his throat to break the fever.

"On the ninth day," she wrote, "I looked down his throat and noticed that his tonsils, which had become enlarged by his illness, had completely disappeared. I called the doctor in panic. He came over, examined Tom, and said he must have swallowed his tonsils."

Of course, he didn't and couldn't swallow his tonsils, although Edwina insisted he had until the end of her life. But whatever the disease, he couldn't walk, nearly died, and badly damaged his kidneys and his eyesight. For two years he pulled himself about on a small handcar, and this boy, physically active though shy, who had loved rough games, became reclusive, dominated by an overly solicitous mother, who shielded him from other children whose germs or strong play might harm her son. Gradually he withdrew into an imaginary world, and made up stories about knights and kings, animals and magic forests, to overcome his shyness; he invented playmates and secret protectors only he could see. Except when he was with Rose, he played alone. At seven he read *The Iliad* and with playing cards ordered Greek and Trojan armies across fields of carpet.

In July 1918, his father was made sales manager of the Friedman-Shelby branch of the International Shoe Company in St. Louis, and the happiest years of Tennessee's life came to an abrupt end.

When he was thirteen he suffered his first nervous breakdown. And four years later, on a trip to Europe with his grandfather Dakin, while visiting Paris, he suffered another.

They set sail from New York on the *Homeric,* once the flagship of the Kaiser's passenger fleet. On their first day out, Tennessee, still known as Tom, had his first taste of alcohol, green crème de menthe, and his palate discovered one of its passions. It was the summer of 1928. Tennessee was a thin, handsome youth, with slightly curly, dark brown hair, deep blue eyes, a handsome, strong nose, and a wide, soft, sensuous mouth. His hands were thin, his fingers long and elegant, and they moved with the slow, sublime, patrician gestures that became a trademark of his person. Though he had only spent eight years in the Deep South, they were critical years; his accent was a profound Southern drawl that never changed; his voice was deep, his diction precise, his vocabulary courtly and oddly dated, even Victorian, in its elaborate euphemism and polite conceits.

At seventeen, aboard ship, he met, flirted with, and danced with a dancing teacher, a woman of twenty-seven. It led nowhere, but he never forgot the waltzes.

One day in Paris, walking alone, he was suddenly aware that he was thinking; he was self-conscious to a frightening degree, he couldn't stop thinking about thinking, helplessly pondering the processes of thought, becoming depersonalized, his thinking the object of his own thought, as if he were standing outside himself observing himself. It sent him into panic. He believed he was going mad.

At the cathedral in Cologne, where they traveled on their tour of the Continent, this terror of his own process of thought reached its climax.

He was breathless. He knelt to pray, and he felt an

"impalpable hand" upon his head and in that instant his terror, his phobia went away.

"At seventeen, I had no doubt at all that the hand of our Lord Jesus had touched my head with mercy and had exorcised from it the phobia that was driving me into madness."

Later he would say, "I always feel that I bore people and that I'm too ugly. I don't like myself. Why should I? I'm quite aware of being mad. I've always been mad."

Tennessee Williams started writing in adolescence, primarily short stories, occasionally poetry. In 1935, when he was twenty-five, he turned to drama and saw his first play hit the boards. *Cairo! Shanghai! Bombay!* was produced by the Garden Players, an amateur group in Memphis. A year later he enrolled at Washington University in St. Louis, his hometown, and two of his one-act plays were presented by little theatrical companies in that city.

By 1937, he had dropped out of Washington University and matriculated at the University of Iowa. There, in a play-writing class, he worked on his first full-length play, *Not About Nightingales,* a highly depressing drama, as the title indicates. The action takes place in a prison complete with a "hot box" punishment cell that functioned much like an oven. Needless to say, the warden is the heavy in the piece, a corrupt sadist who, among other indignities, insists on feeding the prison population rotten meatballs and spaghetti everyday. Enough is enough; the cons rebel. The heroine is a woman prison administrator (a novel idea at the time) who falls in love with an inmate, and together they struggle against the evil warden. In addition to shoveling out lousy grub, the warden has permitted the death of a number of prisoners in the "hot box." The play is very earnest, and not very good.

What is significant about *Nightingales* is that it shows, quite early on, Tennessee's deep concern with social issues, and the influence of Clifford Odets and other left-wing playwrights of the day on his developing dramatic sensibility, an influence he never acknowledged. In this first three-act play his desire was to expose, and thus end, a very real social injustice.

Tennessee has often been criticized for not having any consistent political views, or having no politics at all. In the seventies, when for the first time he spoke out in public against the Vietnam War, he was attacked as being an intellectual lightweight seizing an issue because it was chic. His detractors insinuated that he hadn't the vaguest notion what he was talking about. He had simply lost his head.

Gore Vidal in particular took that tack, warning me against filling Tennessee's head with a lot of leftist nonsense he had no capacity to understand. He thought Tennessee was making a fool of himself. I thought at the time that Gore's advice to Tennessee that he cool it, politically speaking, was self-serving, having more than a little to do with his fear that Tennessee might upstage him as a writer on the left. Gore had, after all, made a career for himself on the talk-show circuit as a smirking left-wing curmudgeon tweaking the American Establishment, and I don't think he wanted any competition.

Tennessee was a politically committed man of the left, as I think *Not About Nightingales* indicates, as do many of the plays that would follow. And as does his vote for Norman Thomas, the Socialist candidate for President in 1932, the first and only vote he ever cast. He was always on the left, never losing his interest in political life. And he was, for what it's worth, one of the few Americans who could sing the revolutionary workers' anthem, "L'Internationale," and get the words right.

While he was at the University of Iowa, where he was a good student, *The Fugitive Kind* was produced by the Mummers in St. Louis, a semiprofessional ensemble that quickly ran out of money and promptly fell apart. The group had formerly produced his *Candles to the Sun* to good notices.

Also while a student at Iowa he wrote *Spring Storm*, a two-acter about sexual relations between two sets of lovers. It is not the most flattering look at making love, but it is, up to that point, his most direct dramatic comment on a subject that was to occupy his creative imagination all his life.

Doubtless the inspiration for the play was his affair with a girl whom he described as a "genuine nympho and alcoholic." She is the only woman with whom he ever claimed to have consummated a sexual relationship. There is no question that he did have a flirtation with a morally loose rumhead in the snows of Iowa. Whether actual intercourse took place is another matter, given his feelings of physical revulsion for female sexual anatomy. In any case, I don't think it much matters.

The actual act of heterosexual sexuality seemed to him a slightly ridiculous enterprise, distasteful to his senses. Although he understood better than most why some people might like it, he didn't. Fundamentally, heterosexual intercourse lacked the grace that he perceived in homosexual engagement; also it was resistant to romantic overlay. His attitude of mind was typical of homosexuals of this time and place: the Greek ideal of masculine love as interpreted by an entire tradition of homoerotic art and commentary. There *is* such a thing as the homosexual imagination, and Tennessee certainly possessed it and respected its conceits, even while denying its existence.

Nineteen thirty-eight found Tennessee living in New Orleans without money or work. He was a "gentleman of remittances," surviving on small checks sent by his grandmother Dakin and his mother. It was a very hand-to-mouth life, precarious indeed, because often he went days without eating. And yet he was happy.

He rented a room in a boardinghouse in Vieux Carré, a seedy establishment managed by three old Southern ladies of limited means, members of the deracinated Dixie gentry, down on their luck, a class for whom he had an abiding affection. His landlady slept on a cot in the front hall to keep the movements of her tenants under strict supervision and to prevent them from stiffing her with the rent. She was subsequently induced by Tennessee to permit him to open a small restaurant in her boardinghouse as a means of paying for his lodging. It was his only entrepreneurial venture, and it was a hopeless idea. It lasted a week, did no business to speak of, and shut its doors. He soon wrote a short story about the rooming house, "Alcove," which he turned into *Vieux Carré*, one of his better plays of the seventies.

Tennessee loved New Orleans, and the Queen of the Delta remained his favorite American city, even if he liked to whine about the poverty he had known in the Quarter. He required a cigarette to begin work in the morning. Before he could sit down at the typewriter—one he eventually hocked to pay for his passage out of town—he went into the street and importuned passersby for a smoke. It was in the bumming of butts in those days—depending on the kindness of strangers—that he remembered whenever he heard Blanche DuBois's famous exit line. The idea for *A Streetcar Named Desire* was germinated then.

From New Orleans Tennessee traveled with a friend, Jim Parrot, by car to Los Angeles, checking in at the YMCA. At that time, he was still living off handouts from his family. He and his friend got a job house-sitting a chicken ranch near Laguna. They were paid nothing, merely allowed to live in a shack close to the chicken run. Tennessee came as close to starving as he ever would, making do by stealing food, mainly avocados. He got around by bike. One day the chickens began to drop dead from some pestilence, perhaps the heat, and the jig was up.

Several months before he arrived in Laguna, he had mailed off a bundle of short plays *(American Blues)* to the Group Theatre in New York to be entered in their drama contest. The first of the candidate plays was *Moony's Kid Don't Cry*, about an outdoorsman trapped in a dead-end factory job and trying to break free. The character was to become a stock figure in Tennessee's canon. *The Case of the Crushed Petunias* concerned a gay young man who inadvertently tramples a woman's flowers and then trots off with her to a cemetery, of all places, to have sex. The last of the three plays tells the story of an Italian girl who has been knocked up, much to her mother's embarrassment, and is kept hidden out of sight. It's entitled *The Dark Room*. None of the plots are particularly inspired, but the language often is.

On March 29, 1939, four days after his twenty-eighth birthday, Tennessee received a telegram from the Group Theatre:

> THE JUDGES OF THE GROUP PLAY CONTEST ARE HAPPY
> TO MAKE YOU A SPECIAL AWARD OF ONE HUNDRED

DOLLARS TO YOU FOR YOUR THREE SKETCHES IN AMER-
ICAN BLUES.

It wasn't first prize, but Tennessee was deliriously happy. His mother, not always known for her faith in his career, almost collapsed on hearing the news. She had more or less written her son off as a failure. And his father, Cornelius, responded with the authentic instincts of a shoe salesman who has won three gold watches: he sent Tennessee a note of congratulations and a pair of shoes.

As a result of his winning the Group Theatre prize, he came to the attention of Audrey Wood. Audrey, with her husband, Bill Liebling, ran a theatrical talent agency in New York, Liebling/Wood. Audrey wrote to him, saying she was impressed by his work and wanted to represent him. Tennessee enthusiastically agreed, and thereupon began a creative relationship that lasted thirty-two years and changed the theatre of the world.

Audrey was a tiny woman. She was about his age, with reddish-brown hair that she styled in an improbable beehive precariously sitting on top her head to give her diminutive stature the illusion of greater height. She had a wide face, with a thin mouth that gave her a rather hard, imperious appearance, and wonderful, large Bette Davis eyes. Tennessee immediately became dependent on her for encouragement, advice, and the means to keep body and soul together.

In 1943, when he began work on *The Gentleman Caller* (later *The Glass Menagerie)*, Audrey Wood got him a screenwriting contract with MGM for the then princely sum of two hundred and fifty dollars a week; it rescued him from his seventeen-dollar-a-week job as a movie usher in New York City.

Years after, he recalled, "In the 1940s I had a glorious time in Hollywood because I was fired almost at once from the MGM project I was working on and they had to continue to pay me. That was in my contract. For six months they had to pay me two hundred and fifty dollars a week. This was in 1943 when two hundred and fifty dollars was equivalent to about a thousand dollars now, I would guess. They had to pay me whether I had an assignment or not.

"First they put me on *Marriage Is a Private Affair* for Lana Turner. Well, they expressed great delight with my dialogue, and I think it was good. But they said, 'You give Miss Turner too many multisyllable words!' So I said, 'Some words do contain more than one syllable!' And Pandro Berman, who loved me very much—Lana Turner just happened to be his girlfriend at the time—he said to me, 'Tennessee, Lana can tackle two syllables, but I'm afraid if you go into three you're taxing her vocabulary!'

"Then they asked me if I'd like to write a screenplay for a child star, one named Margaret O'Brien. I said, 'I'd sooner shoot myself!' By that time I knew I'd get the two hundred and fifty dollars regardless. So I lived out in Santa Monica and had a ball until the money ran out."

For those delightful days in Hollywood he was indebted to Audrey Wood. As he was for much else because she was more than simply his agent—she was one of his best friends, his first critic, chief defender, playing the roles of nurse, protector, psychologist, even mother.

An example: when Tennessee decided to end his relationship with his longtime lover, Frank Merlo, Audrey Wood was brought in as mediator between the two estranged men. She played the same function when he split up with Bill Glavin, another companion.

But it was as critic that Audrey was most essential to Tennessee. Her opinion, along with that of Elia Kazan's, counted most with him.

Since *Slapstick Tragedy* (two short plays) in 1966, Audrey had not really liked any of his plays and had discouraged him from seeking to have them produced, going so far as to refuse to help find backers for them. Tennessee thought that Audrey, like his mother, believed he should give up writing and find a new career. What she actually felt was that he was temporarily burnt out, emotionally exhausted, and needed a long rest from writing and, more critical, from the pressures of theatrical production. She may have been right, but to suggest such a course of action to Tennessee was, to his mind, asking him to hang up his dancing shoes and die. Writing and life were synonymous.

When Audrey did act on behalf of his plays she did so with a great measure of reluctance that he sensed and bitterly resented. Soon her name was permanently added to the growing list of "saboteurs" in league to destroy him, the whole cabal informed and directed by the "sinister Gelbs of the New York *Times*."

In looking back, I don't believe he would have broken with Audrey if he had not been under the stress of a new production, his first since being released from the violent ward. Or if that stress had not been exacerbated by drink and drugs, and if his suspicions had not been reinforced by insinuations against Audrey made by close friends, notably Maria, Lady St. Just (née Britneva).

In any event, Audrey Wood was out of the picture for good.

CHAPTER THREE

IN THE SUMMER of 1971, Tennessee Williams was staying at the Ambassador East Hotel in Chicago. His new play, *Out Cry*, was having its first production at the Ivanhoe Theatre.

Very late one night, about 4 A.M. New York time, Tennessee phoned me from Chicago, asking me to join him there. Drunk or drugged or both, very agitated and unhappy and not entirely coherent, he rambled on about how the play was being sabotaged; his Boston bulldog, Gigi, was most likely being slowly poisoned because her hair was falling out in clumps; complained about his failing health, bad room service, the press, the play's director, on and on, pouring out a bellyful of bile. As usual during the early production stage of a new play, his nerves were shot, his paranoia roaring out of control, his judgment unbalanced by fear.

"I'm surrounded by barracudas here!" he shouted. "I have to protect my play from sharks and philistines. Audrey is trying to destroy the play. She has been packing the house with elderly ladies hired to snicker and cough during the performance!"

I made a weak attempt to defend Audrey Wood. It didn't work.

"You're on her side?" he demanded suspiciously. "Well, baby, I just *fired* Audrey. I've cut off the serpent's head."

He had sacked her that night. I was surprised, like

everyone else. I had thought his anger with her would pass. He owed a great debt to Audrey Wood because she had, in a real sense, discovered him, supported him, and nurtured his talent when nobody else paid him any mind.

I got into Chicago on a hot, sunny day, arriving at the Ambassador East Hotel around 5 P.M. Entering his suite, where I was to stay, I found Tennessee alone and still asleep. Around eight he awoke, showered, and dressed, and we went off by taxi to the Ivanhoe Theatre to see *Out Cry*.

There was a restaurant at the theatre where we had dinner, the whole operation being a kind of dinner theatre that offered a meal to people who purchased tickets, not the most favorable situation in which to present a play as anguished and delicate as this. By showtime, most of the audience was half in the bag.

Tennessee was in a surprisingly chipper mood. He flirted with the waiter, who reminded him of Montgomery Clift, quite a handsome creature to be serving one dinner. During that period Tennessee was continually seeing the dead walking about in other people's bodies, as if he had consciously put out of mind the fact of their demise. It was both eerie and poignant, his inability or unwillingness to come to terms with death. Perhaps finding the dead strolling among the living may have been an accommodation with the longed for and lost.

"You're right," he said, squinting at the waiter, his hand making a languid gesture in his direction. "It couldn't be Monty. Poor Monty was prettier than that boy."

Tennessee was on his third martini, which was unusual, because he normally limited himself to one, going on to red wine for the remainder of the evening.

He talked about Montgomery Clift, whom he had first met at a party in New York during the run of *The Glass Menagerie.*

"I was beguiled by his very feminine beauty. Monty was the loveliest man in the world then, and he was considered the finest young American actor until he threw it all away. I think Marlon [Brando] broke his heart. Before Marlon became a star, Monty had no competition among young actors. But after?" He shrugged.

"When I met him, he was quite drunk, baby. Not mean drunk. *Blind* drunk! He made no sense at all, but I was mesmerized by his eyes. They were like a wounded bird's.

"I stayed at the party for about an hour. I left when Monty fell on the floor, out cold, and people just walked over his body like it wasn't there. Apparently they were accustomed to his collapsing. I was terrified.

"People say he liked to go into the back rooms of gay bars and pass out and anybody could fuck him. I don't think that's true. I could believe it of some people. But Monty was too refined, you know." He paused, and then laughed. "Well, maybe not!"

I asked Tennessee if he had ever had sex with Clift.

He was offended by the question. "I have never been to bed with an actor, baby!" he indignantly replied. "That is not professional behavior. Actors have wanted to go to bed with me but I have always declined. When I was in Puerto Rico with Marion Vacarro, you know, the banana queen?"

Marion Vacarro was a friend from Key West whom he called the banana queen because she was married to an heir to the Standard Fruit Company fortune.

"She and I were in the casino gambling. She was playing blackjack, and I was playing roulette. All of a sudden a waiter came up to me with a little glass of milk on a silver platter, and said, 'A gentleman has sent this to you.' I said, 'I don't appreciate this kind of sarcasm!' So I went on playing roulette.

"After I had lost the amount of money I allow myself to lose, I started to leave. And there standing grinning at the door was Warren Beatty. 'Tennessee, I've come to read for you,' he said. He was very young then, a really handsome boy. He wanted the part in *The Roman Spring of Mrs. Stone,* and somehow had discovered where I was and flown to Puerto Rico. I didn't know Warren's work, and I thought the role in *The Roman Spring of Mrs. Stone* should be played by a Latin type, since the role's a Roman gigolo.

"I said, 'But why, Warren? You're not the type to play a Roman gigolo.'

"And he said, 'I'm going to read it with an accent, and without. I've come all the way from Hollywood to read for you.' His career was in temporary decline then.

" 'Well, that's lovely of you,' I said. And Marion and I went to his room, and he read fabulously. With an accent, and without. And I said, 'You have the part, Warren.'

"I went up to bed. There was a knock on my door. When I opened it, there stood Warren in his bathrobe. I said, 'Go home to bed, Warren. I said you had the part.'

"Warren has no embarrassment about anything. Whenever he sees me he always embraces me. What an affectionate, warm, lovely man. I've found actors to be lovely people, although there are a few of them who have been otherwise."

Tennessee continued to reminisce, sipping his martini.

"Warren is very handsome in a masculine way. But

Monty was pretty, like a young girl. He had a very small cock, like many pretty men do. That seems to be true about most truly beautiful men.

"I remember Ned Rorem once invited me back to his room. He lived in one room then. Oh, Ned was very drunk. Now he doesn't drink anymore and so isn't as interesting anymore. Some people are very interesting when they are drunk, and total bores when they're sober. Ned was so beautiful when he was young. I stared at him all night long. So when he invited me to his room I thought I'd hit the jackpot! He pulled off his clothes and lay down on the bed and pretended to pass out. I just caressed him for a few minutes, and then I went home. There wasn't much to work with, you know.

"Monty played the pilot in *You Touched Me* [1946]. He was very good even if the play wasn't. Then Elizabeth Taylor got him to do *Suddenly Last Summer*, probably the worst movie ever made of my work. I was in Hollywood and I visited the set. Poor Monty's beauty was gone, I mean his physical beauty. And he seemed to want to die. A strange boy.

"He had a mother much like Miss Edwina, tyrannical and crazy. Monty's father's family was from Tennessee, like the Williams family. His horrible mother had dreams of grandeur, an aristocrat on a pauper's income. She believed she had fabulously rich relatives who had stolen a king's ransom from Monty and his sister. It is the kind of fantasy many frigid women have. Monty could never escape his mother.

"Even when she wasn't around he had female companions who acted as mothers for him. Katharine Hepburn was one who loved him very much, and was very kind to him. And Elizabeth Taylor. Elizabeth was in love with him. I think she still is. She wanted to marry him and never really believed he was gay. There are many women like that who fall in love with a gay man and can't admit the truth about him."

I asked Tennessee when he last saw Montgomery Clift.

"The last time?" He considered the question a moment. "In the fifties. I had dinner with him in New York. I wanted him to play in *Cat on a Hot Tin Roof* with Elizabeth. Audrey was with me in some restaurant I had never been to before nor braved since. Well, Monty was about an hour late, and so drunk he could hardly stand up. He came into the restaurant staggering like a passenger on a ship caught in a gale, only it wasn't a ship and there was no gale-force winds blowing. What it was was a stuffy restaurant whose elderly, rich patrons did not cotton to drunken actors who staggered through rooms!

"Monty sat between Audrey and me. He said to Audrey, 'Do you have any reds?' She pretended not to hear the question. Audrey was very good at pretending not to hear what she did not care to hear. He turned to me and asked if I had any yellows. I said, 'Later, baby.' I was not about to allow myself to be arrested slipping him controlled substances across the table in a restaurant resembling an elephants' graveyard!

"It was impossible to hold a conversation with him, so we tried to get through dinner as fast as we could. We ate like bread thieves swallowing the evidence! About midway through that unfortunate meal, Monty slid off the banquette onto the carpeted floor. He just collapsed under the table! Audrey hissed, 'Just ignore him!' She hates public displays of any sort, which is one of the reasons I think she is definitely in the wrong profession!

"Well, I could hardly ignore Monty because his head was on my crotch under the table, and he was trying with little success to unzip my fly, an undertaking never before known to be difficult!" Tennessee laughed. "I sat there with the plaster-faced propriety of a nun at mass. We finished our dinner in silence.

"By the time we left, Monty was unconscious. We had to pay waiters to carry him into a taxi and see him home. Audrey said, 'I don't think he's up to playing eight shows a week on Broadway, dear!'"

Tennessee and I left the restaurant and went into the theatre to see *Out Cry*. The play is a dark, harrowing discourse on panic, written directly out of Tennessee's ordeal with drug-induced psychosis. Terrifying in many respects, it is a nightmare within a nightmare, a world where all the boundaries of reality are unstable; characters travel unknowingly into a state of unreason, never aware that they have crossed over its frontiers. The play's two protagonists, a brother and sister, are actors deserted by their own company of players, abandoned in a "state theatre in an unknown state." Each character represents a side of the playwright's conflicted soul.

Tennessee said this about *Out Cry:* "I think it is my most beautiful play since *Streetcar,* and I've never stopped working on it. I think it is a major work . . . It is a *cri de coeur,* but then all creative work, all life, in a sense is a *cri de coeur.*"

The Ivanhoe Theatre is small, its seats uncomfortable, although it has an ample stage, good sight lines, and fine acoustics. We sat in the center of the house, Tennessee holding a writing pad and penlight to make notes for the director, George Keathley. As was his wont, throughout the performance he cackled at the most heartrending lines, interrupting monologues in midsentence with his barking laughter, like lightning breaching an autumn sky.

Halfway through the first act a portly gentleman, sitting with his equally plump wife on my left, leaned over and said, "Shhhh!"

Tennessee ignored him and continued to laugh gaily away.

The man shushed him several more times and finally out of patience said, in a loud whisper, "Will you please *shut up?* The little woman and I paid good money for these seats!"

Tennessee, not the type of person to bow to the outrage of a paying member of the audience, went on laughing.

"I said shut up! Shut up!" The man was becoming unhinged.

"Call the manager!" his wife demanded.

Tennessee drew himself up in his seat, leaned forward, glared at the couple, and in a booming voice asked the offended man, "Do you know who I am?"

"No, but be quiet or I'll have you thrown out on your ass!"

"My name is Tennessee Williams, and I wrote this play!" He was furious.

"Well," the man sniffed, "you ought to be *ashamed* of yourself."

The following day Tennessee slept late. I didn't know then what drugs he was using. All I knew was that when he got out of bed and stumbled into the living room he could barely walk and seemed disoriented. Alarmed, I asked if I should call the hotel's doctor.

"Are you trying to destroy me, too?" He slurred his words. "Have you been in secret communication with Audrey Wood?"

I replied that I was worried about his health.

He snorted. "Call a doctor? Get it in the newspapers, on all the front pages! They reserve space in every edition to announce my demise. Tell the newspapers I'm sick and we'll *have* to close the play!"

He grabbed an opened bottle of red wine left over from last night, staggered back into his bedroom, and slammed the door.

A few minutes later I knocked and, getting no answer, went into the room. He was asleep on the bed, out like a light, and I couldn't rouse him. I touched his skin. He was very hot.

I called Donald Madden, the actor who starred with Eileen Herlie in *Out Cry*. Tennessee was in love with Madden, and I trusted him. I told him Tennessee had passed out, I couldn't wake him; should I call a doctor? Madden advised me to let him sleep it off.

On his bedstand were a dozen empty bottles of pills, their contents dumped on the table—tranquilizers, sleeping potions, speed, blood-pressure capsules, pills for pancreatitis, a rainbow of chemical hues scattered about within easy reach. I had spent a good deal of my life around people who used and abused drugs—I used them myself—but I had never seen quite such a variety in one place before.

Tennessee, who had had a series of cataract operations and could barely see in one eye and was going blind in the other, had fallen into the habit of having someone open all his pill bottles so he could dump their contents on whatever table was closest to the bed. He did this because he could rarely open medicine bottles; after safety-lock caps were introduced, it was completely beyond him. He couldn't read the labels, in any case, although he did recognize the tablets by their colors.

One of the principle reasons he was forever trying to scrounge pills was because a large percentage of what he was able to obtain was spilled as he struggled with the bottle caps or lost as they rolled to the floor. Most were wasted because he carried handfuls in his trouser and jacket pockets and he'd forget to retrieve them when the clothes were dispatched to the cleaners.

Another reason, of course, was that doctors—the honest ones, and there weren't that many—were aghast at the amounts of medication they were prescribing. After a while, when it had sunk in that they were dispensing enough pills to satisfy the needs of a small city, they refused to renew prescriptions unless a reasonable period of time had elapsed, a period that was entirely unreasonable to Tennessee. He got around this by having as many doctors as possible treating him in any given town, each sawbones blissfully unaware of the others. He had staffs of physicians dishing out the goodies. I know of at least six doctors in Manhattan alone who were on his case at the same time. We used to do a Doctor's Day, an entire afternoon exclusively devoted to traveling by taxi to various East Side medical waiting rooms, collecting prescriptions, the most valued being the Federal Schedule 2 forms that unlocked the apothecary treasury and dropped the real hard stuff into our hands, the pharmacological equivalent of winning the Irish Sweepstakes. Tennessee was, like most alcoholics and addicts, extremely sly, skillful, and inventive when it came to coaxing drugs from recalcitrant medicine men.

In the late sixties, when he was working on *The Eccentricities of a Nightingale,* he was gripped by unrelenting depression, a black despair greater than he had ever known before, and he could not break free of it. A friend, trying to be helpful, took him to visit the infamous Dr. Max Jacobson ("Dr. Feelgood") who had a stable of celebrities as patients in New York.

This is how Tennessee remembered it: "There was a lovely young guy at New Directions [his publisher] named Robert MacGregor, who's dead now. He'd been a patient of Dr. Max Jacobson. He only took little pills that Jacobson gave him. I was in such a state of profound depression that he thought anything was worth trying, so he took me to Jacobson. It was through this Robert Mac-Gregor that I had those three years of Jacobson shots that he mailed to me in various parts of the country."

What Dr. Max obligingly gave him was a complex shot, a lot of vitamins, especially B's and E, laced with amphetamine that contained the firepower of the battleship New Jersey. Tennessee was hooked. In time, the doctor provided his new patient with his own syringe and vials of the drug, a kind of traveler's companion, so Tennesee could shoot himself up and not have to bother coming to the office every day for his fix. What complicated his addiction to speed was that he continued to drink heavily and take Mellaril, Doriden, and other drugs. It's a wonder he didn't die.

"I did find Max Jacobson's shots marvelously stimulating to me as a writer," Tennessee said. "And during those last three years of the sixties, before my collapse, I did some of my best writing. People don't know it yet, but I did.

"My collapse was related to the fact that I continued to drink while taking the shots. I was not supposed to. I had a bad heart. Dr. Max Jacobson never listened to my heart. Never took my pulse. Never took my blood pressure. He would just look at me. He was really sort of an alchemist. He would look at me for a long time. He had all these little vials in front of him. He'd take a drop from one, and a drop from another, and then look at me again, and take another drop or two . . . Of course, the primary element was speed. And after I had a shot, I'd get into a taxi and my heart would begin to pound, and I'd immediately have to have a drink or I wouldn't be able to get home. I'd have died in the cab otherwise."

To give Dr. Max Jacobson his due, at that time the danger in the abuse of amphetamine, principally in the form of Dexedrine, was not clinically proven. The drugs were easily available, relatively inexpensive, and widely prescribed for weight reduction, languor, depression. What was quite literally lethal was to mix amphetamine (speed) with alcohol or other drugs, something Tennessee did with enthusiastic abandon. This practice of shooting himself in the hip with a syringe full of the doctor's elixir, and then hitting the bottle and swallowing barbiturates inevitably led to psychosis and a padded cell.

It took years before Tennessee had enough self-confidence to feel he was able to write without the morning wake-up call provided by speed. Perhaps it wasn't a renewal of self-confidence; probably it was due more to the fact that he gradually came to claim as his own the critics' diminished expectations of what he was still capable of writing, and so he didn't care much anymore. The critics always bellow that their reviews don't affect, psychologically, a writer's ability to create. That isn't true. Critics have killed more writers than liquor. They certainly defeated Tennessee. One of the few times I saw him cry was when he read a review about his work by John Simon, entitled, "The Sweet Bird of Senility."

In the end, writing became something he did more by rote than out of a desire or need; producing small plays, knowing from the beginning of their creation that they wouldn't find an audience, certainly not in New York, and New York was what counted. He wrote out of habit, like an old priest who has lost his faith and continues to pray to a God in whom he no longer believes because he doesn't know what else to do with himself.

Writing became a way of paying ritualistic homage to a Muse who had already packed her bags and left town.

Tennessee told me that artists—by that he meant writers, for he rarely referred to them by any other term —spend their lives dancing on a high wire without any protective net beneath them, and when they fall it is sudden and final. Only his end wasn't sudden. It was protracted and painful, lasting more than a decade during which he saw himself held up to public contempt. Finally, he came to dread every new production, feared a capricious public, and, except for Claudia Cassidy and Clive Barnes, hated the critics. When I first knew him he delighted in being recognized in public. By the end of his life, it mortified him, because he felt like currency debased, like an old ham who had become a caricature of himself.

However, in Chicago, and lasting until the critics demolished all hope with their gang assault on *Out Cry* in New York in 1973, was the belief that great work re-

mained in him. "I still have a trick or two up my sleeve."
He was right. But where he was wrong was in believing
he needed a department store of drugs to be able to create.

An incident comes to mind.

In 1972, the first time I was with him in Key West, he
ran out of Nembutals and Dexedrine spansule, both
tightly controlled Schedule 2 drugs. I dutifully went to a
doctor, a simple thing to do in Key West then, and got
prescriptions for myself because there wasn't a doctor left
on the island who had not washed his hands of Tennessee's habit. Even the quacks had turned surly. My prescriptions were supposed to last me a month. Tennessee
went through them in about a week. Once out of the stuff,
he became impossible. Accusatory. Unable to work. To
sleep. To have sex. He was desperate, and I couldn't take it
anymore.

Things soon reached a nasty pass, and he started plotting to get himself admitted to the hospital, not easy to do
when you've been blackballed by the local medical establishment. To show you the degree of his despair, he had
strongly warned me *never* to come down to Key West unless I was in the best of health. To get sick on the island, he
declared, was to forsake life. No one entered the local hospital and left it alive. Once, he said, a friend of his named
Edmund had checked into the hospital to be circumcised.
All his friends warned him of the danger to which he was
recklessly exposing himself, begging him to get his affairs
in order, update his will, make his final farewells to his
loved ones. Still, like some helpless compulsive, Edmund
checked in for the minor surgical procedure. By mistake,
the doctors castrated him. On another occasion, Tennessee
said, some fool entered the local medical slaughterhouse

complaining of severe headaches. They removed his left lung.

Unfortunately, things had reached the point where even he was willing to brave the hospital in hope of getting drugs.

To forestall that desperate act, I started hunting in the local bars for a pusher. In Key West that normally should be as simple a task as finding a wino in Bryant Park. The chief, though unofficial, industry on the island is smuggling, primarily drugs. On Key West people wear T-shirts reading: SAVE THE BALES!, a reference to the tons of marijuana that float like manna to its shores as shrimpers, spotted by the Coast Guard, unload the evidence into the sea. I had the damnedest time finding a dealer in prescription drugs. Then luck hit.

One afternoon in Captain Tony's Saloon, then a gay establishment, I met a handsome young doctor who was stationed at the naval base. I bought him a drink, and as we talked I quickly caught on that he was an addict. That was good news. From what he told me, he had been discovered by the Navy selling pills to patients up North at a naval hospital where he had been on staff the previous year. For some unaccountable reason—perhaps the shortage of physicians during the Vietnam War—he wasn't sacked on the spot. Rather he was sent to Key West as punishment, ordered to undergo drug rehabilitation while he continued to practice, and that's probably the word for it, medicine on the unwitting military sick in his charge.

Telling him I had a friend who was out of pills and going bonkers, he agreed to stop by Tennessee's house after his tour of duty at the naval hospital that night.

Tennessee was thrilled. Around 11 P.M. the pill doctor

arrived; blond, looking very smart in his Navy whites. Except for a noticeable slur in his speech, he looked every inch the ideal of American medicine. I eyed his black bag with undisguised expectation, for it was sure to contain the means to set Tennessee's trolley back on the tracks.

Earlier that afternoon Tennessee and I had agreed on a scenario to convince the good doctor to release unto us a large, perhaps endless supply of mind-altering drugs. When the physician arrived, I was to act suitably frightened by Tennessee's condition, the fragility of his health; in short, to create a deep sense of doom about his present state. Then I was to usher the anxious and prepped Dr. Kildare into his bedroom where Tennessee would do his best to enact the death scene from *Camille*. The problem was that it was a pointless farce, as I pointed out to him, because the young doctor was an addict/pusher. Tennessee refused to change the game plan. The plot had worked before. He wasn't in the mood to take any chances since the sailor was our only pigeon, and God only knew when another patsy would come along. *Camille* it would be.

Before the Navy entered the house, Tennessee scurried into his bedroom and shut the door.

I told the doctor I thought Tennessee was dying, suicidal at the least, and unless he received some medical reinforcement, he was a goner for sure.

"It's in your hands," I pleaded, appealing to his compassion, "I'm at the end of my rope, and Tenn's at the end of the road!"

The doctor, properly horrified, entered the bedroom and closed the door.

A half hour or so passed. Finally he emerged with his patient, both grinning broadly.

I made the doctor a drink. Doc sat on the sofa, opened

his bag and counted out a hundred precious pills, fifty Nembutal, fifty Dexedrine spansule. "They're five dollars each," he announced. He was a bad businessman. Tennessee would have paid ten times that.

Tennessee rushed off to get a check.

When he returned, beaming, the Navy said, "I can't take a check. It has to be cash."

"Cash?" Tennessee's face collapsed, panic filling his eyes. "It's midnight. Where the hell can I cash a check at *midnight?* This is not a frivolous matter, doctor. It is life or death! I'm at death's door!" Whereupon Tennessee promptly toppled to the floor, right on cue, completing the last act of *Camille.*

Now the Navy was scared. Tennessee played dead better than anybody. To increase the pressure, I rushed to the phone and announced I was calling the police.

"My God! Don't!" the doctor yelled. With that, the young physician, seeing the jailhouse door swinging open before him, gave up. He quickly agreed to pick up the cash the next day. He never did.

In the summer of 1982, ten years later, Richard Zoerink and I stayed with Tennessee in Key West. After a few days it was clear that he was again having serious problems in procuring drugs, once more unable to persuade the local sawbones to write him a prescription. There was also a crackdown by drug-enforcement agencies in southern Florida on pushers of federally controlled substances, and pills became harder to find than a Baptist virgin, as Tennessee would say.

I was little help because I had the same problem with

Key West doctors as he. His only hope was Richard, who had never been to a doctor in Key West.

Tennessee told Richard of his need for Valium. "I seem to have misplaced my prescription."

"Oh, I have one with me," Richard said, "from my doctor in New York. He prescribes them for my nerves."

Tennessee's face lighted with joy. And Richard went off to get his prescription filled. When he returned, Tennessee took the large bottle from him, saying he would keep it in his own bedroom where it was safe from larcenous hands, meaning the hands of most of his Key West friends.

Now Tennessee could never remember from one minute to the next whether he had taken his pills or not, which was why he so often seemed drugged. He was, but it was unintentional. After a week, he had gone through all of Richard's Valium. He woke one morning, reached for a pill, and discovered the bottle was empty.

He was in a foul mood from this discovery, and he came into the patio, where we were having coffee, and said, "There's a thief in the house. A *pill* thief, the lowest type imaginable!" Since we were the only people staying in the house, he meant one of us.

I told him he was full of crap, since he had obviously taken the pills himself and wasn't aware of how often he took them.

He didn't say a word, merely turned on his heel, and walked out of the compound and got on his bicycle. I went running after him because he was at the age where he couldn't balance very well on a bike, and sooner or later the wobbling conveyance and he would fall into the street, often in heavy traffic. I made it a point to ride with him, on another bike, always at his back. I stayed about three feet farther into the traffic behind him, so that cars passing us would have to swerve away to avoid hitting me and thus pass safely by him.

He refused to let me come along.

He rode his bike to McCrory's five-and-dime on Duval Street. When he returned home, he was peddling erratically down Duncan Street, a steel box in his bike's basket. It was a small safe, weighing about fifty pounds.

He staggered into the house under his burden, wheezing as he did, and stumbled into his bedroom, kicking the door shut behind him. There was a loud clunk as he dropped his steel box to the floor. And then I heard the door lock.

Richard and I looked at each other.

"He's gone over the edge again," Richard said, laughing.

Then we heard what sounded like furniture being moved about. Tennessee was hiding his safe.

At dinner that night he was very pleased with himself, having found the solution to all those thieving dopeheads coveting his precious stash.

We went to bed early. About one in the morning I heard Tennessee wearily climbing up the steps to my bedroom, where I was reading.

He stood in the doorway, looking sheepish, like a child about to receive a scolding.

"What's wrong?" I asked.

"You know that safe I bought this afternoon? Well, I hid it in my room, and I can't remember where. And I hid the key to the safe, and I can't find that either."

I went into his room and found the safe hidden behind a pile of books in the bookshelves. The key he had hidden under a bar of soap in the bathtub's soap dish.

That was the last we heard of his plan to thwart larcenous hands. He never used the safe again because he knew if he hid it he couldn't find it, and if he misplaced the key he couldn't open it. And what use was an unlocked safe in plain view?

In December 1944, *The Glass Menagerie* opened in Chicago. The play starred the legendary actress Laurette Taylor playing Amanda Wingfield, whose crippled daughter, Laura, awaits her Gentleman Caller, a visitation arranged by her brother, Tom. It is a memory play, decidedly the most autobiographical of all Tennessee's dramas.

Amanda is based on his mother, Miss Edwina, although she always refused to concede the similarity, perhaps because of a remark made to her by Laurette Taylor. When Miss Edwina met the great actress after the opening night performance, she asked her why she wore bangs.

"I have to wear them playing this part," Miss Taylor explained to Mrs. Williams, "because it's the part of a fool and I have a high, intellectual forehead!"

"I am *not* Amanda," Mrs. Williams countered. "The only resemblance I have to Amanda is that we both like jonquils!"

Nevertheless, she *was* Amanda, as everyone except her husband, Cornelius, and herself readily admitted. Still, she thought it was a good play, if not a great one, and she quickly accepted the loot when Tennessee gave her half ownership of the work. She lived very nicely on the royalties for the rest of her long life.

The Glass Menagerie was created out of Tennessee's anguish and powerlessness before the unraveling of his sister, Rose, into mental confusion and the destruction of her mind under the surgeon's blade. The decision to have her undergo a lobotomy was completely her mother's. And what precipitated it was an incident where Rose told her mother that at the convent school the girls used altar candles for self-abuse. This revelation sent Miss Edwina into hysteria and she demanded that the doctors cut this filth out of her daughter's mind. They obliged. There is no question that Rose was suffering emotional disequilibrium, a mild hysteria most likely caused by her loneliness and her mother's oppressive Victorian attitudes. Edwina Williams was anything but a liberated woman, disliking even the mention of sex and, when she engaged in it with her husband, she didn't lie back and think of England, she screamed. Tennessee never forgot his mother's wails resounding through the house, and until he discovered the facts of life himself he thought what went on behind closed doors between his parents was brutal and violent. That must have had an effect on his own sexual development.

Miss Edwina's sexual intolerance, the repugnance she felt for human intimacy, had the effect of driving her husband from her bed and into the arms of a long series of other women; and it affected Rose. She was always an emotionally delicate creature, and her mother's revulsion when Rose awakened to sex helped trigger her emotional collapse. As for the lobotomy, Tennessee, who was away at school, tried to stop it but couldn't. He never forgave his mother, because he believed it was unnecessary, cruel, an act of willful spite against Rose. His attitude toward the lobotomy and his mother's role in its occurrence is most clearly seen in the person of Mrs. Venable in *Suddenly Last Summer*.

Tennessee worked on *The Glass Menagerie* for years, its

genesis being his short story, "Portrait of a Girl in Glass," except that the Laura of that piece wasn't physically crippled, as she would be in the play; in the short story Laura is mentally paralyzed by fear. She was Rose.

He finished the first draft of the play while sharing rooms with Bill, a law student at Harvard, whom he had met in Provincetown. He and Bill maintained a sexual relationship, off and on, for a number of years until Tennessee met Frank Merlo. Bill was not really to his taste, being a compulsive peeping Tom—he had a map of Cambridge with all the best peep sites marked—and he was an alcoholic of increasingly frightening proportions. Bill died quite young, decapitated as he drunkenly leaned out of a subway window in New York, shouting good-bye to friends as the train sped away.

The character Tom in *Menagerie* is, of course, Tennessee, whose christened name was Thomas Lanier Williams. He was known as Tom to his family. As the play's narrator, Tom is able to poetically express Tennessee's own unexpiated guilt and unpurged grief over his sister's fate. When the play ends we know that Laura (Rose) will continue to wait for another Gentleman Caller, who will never come. She is locked, crippled, in a cell of loneliness from which there is no escape.

"Blow out your candles, Laura—and so good-bye . . ." Tom says in closing the play. She blows them out, and it ends.

Again, *The Glass Menagerie* is a memory play, and in its break with strictly naturalistic conventions, in the poetry of its speeches—most notably the narrative monologues of Tom—it was received by the public as an avant-garde work, somewhat experimental and confusing to the audiences first exposed to it. Remarkable as it now seems, there was considerable audience resistance to it, despite lavish praise given it by the Chicago critics. The audience's discomfort was over the play's shifts back and forth from one time and place to another, and over Tom's stepping in and out of the play to speak directly to the audience and comment on what they are watching. Tom's narration is an awkward, self-conscious device, not wholly successful, something Tennessee himself admitted when *Menagerie* was later done as a television play with Tom's monologues edited sharply back with no perceptible damage to the work as a whole.

After the first week, the box office began to weaken. To the rescue came Claudia Cassidy of the Chicago *Tribune*, the city's most influential critic, and Ashton Stevens of the *Herald-American*, who made the survival of *Menagerie* a crusade. It worked. They kept the show running to capacity audiences, and Tennessee started collecting more than a thousand dollars a week in royalties and was swiftly on his way to becoming a rich and famous man. In Chicago, decades later, this is how he remembered his first success:

"It all began for me here in Chicago in 1944. I've had some of the happiest times of my life here. We were in Chicago for three and a half months with *The Glass Menagerie*. We opened in late December, and played until mid-March. And I had a lovely time. I had ten dollars a day in expense money. It seemed a lot then. And I swam every day at the Y. I knew a lot of university students, you know?

"So I associate the success of *Menagerie* with the Chicago critics Claudia Cassidy and Ashton Stevens. They really put it over. The opening-night audience had never seen this kind of theatre before, and their response was puzzlement. And I suppose the play would have died here if Claudia Cassidy and Ashton Stevens hadn't kept pushing and pushing and pushing. They compared Laurette Taylor to Duse, which was a good comparison, I think. Miss Cassidy is very elderly now, but her mind's as sharp as a whistle!

"Edwige Feuillère [who starred in the French production of *Sweet Bird of Youth*], Anna Magnani, Geraldine Page, and Laurette Taylor are the greatest actresses in my plays, but Laurette was the greatest of them all.

"*Menagerie* got to New York in 1945. It was sold out three and a half months before it opened. People would stop off in New York to see it because they knew it was a new kind of theatre, and they knew about Laurette's incredible performance, though the rest of the cast was pretty run-of-the-mill.

"The sudden success? Oh, it was terrible! I just didn't like it. If you study photographs taken of me the morning after the huge reception it got in New York, you'll see I was very depressed.

"I'd had one eye operation, and I went into the hospital for another one I needed. Lying in the hospital, unable to move for several days, people came over and read to me, and I recovered some sense of reality.

"Then, after *Menagerie*, I went to Mexico and had a marvelously happy time. I went alone. Leonard Bernstein was there. He introduced me to Winchell Mount, who gave weekly Saturday night dances. All male. And I learned how to follow! I was the belle of the ball because I could always dance well, but I gave up that career for writing.

"Before the success of *Menagerie* I'd reached the very, very bottom. I would have died without the money. I couldn't have gone any further, baby, when suddenly, *providentially, The Glass Menagerie* made it when I was thirty-four. I couldn't have gone on with those hand-to-mouth jobs, these jobs for which I had no aptitude, like waiting on tables, running elevators, and even being a teletype operator. None of this stuff was anything I could have held for long. I started writing at twelve. By the time I was in my late teens I was writing every day, I guess, even after I was in the shoe business for three years. I wrecked my health, what there was of it. I drank black coffee so much, so I could stay up nearly all night and write, and it exhausted me physically and nervously.

I asked Tennessee where plays come from; how, for example, did he get the idea for *The Glass Menagerie?*

"The process by which the idea for a play comes to me has always been something I really couldn't pinpoint," he replied. "A play just seems to materialize; like an apparition, it gets clearer and clearer and clearer. It's very vague at first, as in the case of *A Streetcar Named Desire,* which came after *The Glass Menagerie.* I simply had the vision of a woman in her late youth. She was sitting in a chair all alone by the window with the moonlight streaming in on her desolate face, and she'd been stood up by the man she planned to marry.

"I believe I was thinking of my sister, because she was madly in love with some young man at the International Shoe Company who paid her court. He was extremely handsome, and she was profoundly in love with him. Whenever the phone would ring she'd nearly faint. She would think it was he calling for a date, you know?

"They saw each other every other night, and then one time he just didn't call anymore. That was when Rose first began to go into a mental decline. From that vision *Street-*

car evolved. I called it at the time, *Blanche's Chair in the Moon*, which is a very bad title. But it was from that image, you know, of a woman sitting by a window that *Streetcar* came to me.

"Of course, the young man who courted my sister was nothing like Stanley. He was a young executive from an Ivy League school. He had every apparent advantage. It was during the Depression years, however, and he was extremely ambitious. My father had an executive position at the time with the shoe company, and the young man had thought perhaps a marriage to Rose would be to his advantage. Then, unfortunately, my father was involved in a terrible scandal and nearly lost his job. At any rate, he was no longer a candidate for the board of directors. He had his ear bit off in a poker fight! It had to be restored. They had to take cartilage from his ribs, and skin off his ass, and they reproduced something that looked like a small cauliflower attached to the side of his head! So any time somebody would get into the elevator with my father, he'd scowl, and people would start giggling. That was when the young man stopped calling on Rose. He knew the giggling had gone too far and gotten in the newspapers.

"The idea for *The Glass Menagerie* came very slowly, much more slowly than *Streetcar*, for example. I think I worked on *Menagerie* longer than any other play. I didn't think it would ever be produced. I wasn't writing it for that purpose. I wrote it first as a short story called "Portrait of a Girl in Glass," which is, I believe, one of my best stories. I guess *Menagerie* grew out of the intense emotions I felt seeing my sister's mind begin to go."

In Chicago's Loop, under the El, was an Italian restaurant where Tennessee used to dine with Laurette Taylor after rehearsals for *Menagerie*.

"Laurette Taylor did not seem to know her lines as Amanda Wingfield," he recalled in his *Memoirs*, "hardly a fraction of them, and those she did seem to know she was delivering in a southern accent she had acquired from some long-ago black domestic. Her bright-eyed attentiveness to the other performances seemed a symptom of lunacy, and so did the rapturous manner of dear Julie [Haydon], who played Laura."

While watching rehearsals, and the curious performance of Miss Taylor, he speculated on what menial occupation was next in store for him, since it was plain that *Menagerie* would be dead in the water come opening night.

"Everybody thought Laurette didn't know her lines because she was drunk. After her husband died she went on a binge that lasted thirteen years, which must be some sort of world record. I used to go to an Italian restaurant with her after rehearsals, and she got drunk and laughed. She was so gay all the time, and I couldn't understand it because I was certain the play would be a flop. The closer we got to opening night the happier Laurette was. I thought, Laurette's happy because she's drunk all the time and doesn't appreciate the calamity that awaits her at the hands of the critics! I'd already made plans to sneak out of town on the first available conveyance."

Laurette Taylor, on opening night, knew her lines and gave one of our theatre's most luminous performances.

In Chicago, twenty-six years later, Tennessee insisted on going back to the restaurant where he and Miss Taylor drank together in the days when he thought he was finished as a playwright before he had really begun.

"I know the owner very well, baby," he assured me before we left the hotel. "He was a friend of Al Capone. He brought his gangster pals to see *Menagerie*." He grinned in recall.

We showered, and as I was dressing, Tennessee called me into the bedroom.

He handed me a rather large leather case, like a presentation case. He asked if I knew how to use what was inside?

In it, lying like a silver dagger on a purple satin cushion, was a shiny, enormous stainless-steel syringe, like the kind used to knock out horses. With it were a dozen vials of fluid.

I asked what the drug was.

It was Demerol, he replied. He explained that he had had a toothache in New York and a doctor there had given him a traveling kit with a shooter and a dozen crystalline bullets to ease the pain. Only he did not have a toothache, that being merely a ploy to procure a drug to deaden a more harrowing pain, that of the heart.

He took back the case, loaded the syringe, and handed it to me. Standing in front of the dressing table, he pulled down his jockey shorts and slapped his right buttock. I injected him there.

When I pulled out the syringe, he started to bleed. I put a Band-Aid over the spot.

Then he inquired if I wanted an injection. I had never used Demerol and I wasn't sure exactly what it did, but he assured me that it was perfectly safe and provided a blissful feeling of euphoria, much like morphine, only it wasn't addictive.

I dropped my shorts, bent over, and he shot me up. Demerol was as he advertised it, gently pulling one into a state of sweet contentment. Nothing mattered anymore. With that initial shot began a dependency on the drug that kept me bound for two years. He wasn't to blame. Given what those two years were to deliver up into my life I would have found my way to it without his help.

Both of us high and happy, we set off to find the Italian restaurant in the Loop where he and Laurette Taylor had drunk away their fears a quarter of a century before. It was not an easy place to find. Tennessee's recollection of the streets of Chicago did not in any way conform to the real map of the place. He couldn't remember the restaurant's name. It started to rain, and our tour by taxi stretched into nearly an hour until at last we arrived at the establishment he remembered as having been Laurette's watering hole.

I think his insistence on going there—despite the rain and time lost in finding it—was out of a desire to relive the past, to touch base with former glory. Here in Chicago success had found him; now he had a new play on the boards, *Out Cry*, and while he hoped for a success to match *Menagerie* it was obvious from the audience response that it was not to be. His rage with Audrey Wood was that she could not or would not cover her pessimism about *Out Cry*. She advised against bringing it to New York. In admitting the truth as she saw it, she outraged Tennessee because she stripped from him the illusion of hope.

The restaurant was a large, musty-smelling place, dank and rather dark, and had several dozen round tables covered with checkerboard oilcloth, each with an empty wine bottle in a straw basket with a candle stuck in its snout. Sausages hung from the ceiling.

We were met at the door by a fat, short man dressed in a soiled tuxedo.

"Guido!" Tennessee exclaimed, embracing the man, who was thoroughly confused by the bearhug. "I haven't seen you in twenty-five years."

"This is Tennessee Williams," I interjected, since it was obvious the man didn't know him from Adam.

"Welcome! Welcome!" The light dawning, the man glowed in recognition. He looked to be about fifty, with a flushed, rotund face and tiny, closely placed eyes. He panted heavily, like an old dog in the sun or a child molester spotting a sandbox in the park. "But I'm not Guido, Mr. Williams. I'm Joseph, Guido's son. My father passed away a long time ago, God rest his soul." He crossed himself.

Tennessee, now confused, mumbled commiserations as Joseph showed us to a table. Suddenly the place came alive as he ordered waiters about, bringing a clean, white cloth to cover the stained oilcloth, obviously a rare honor given only to very special guests. Glasses and red wine were produced, and Joseph joined us in a toast to his dead father and, uninvited, sat down at our table. He rattled on about his father and his gangster pals, the old crowd dead and gone; about how he knew most of Tennessee's plays by heart, particularly the role of Stanley Kowalski. When he said that, I groaned. Trouble ahead. He was an actor who loved the theatre, he passionately declared, but, alas, there wasn't any theatre in Chicago worthy of his large talents, gifts such as his deserving a wider stage. For that reason he planned to sell his restaurant and head for New York and the Great White Way. Tennessee suggested he set his sights a little lower, like getting us something to eat.

"Leave it to me," he said, getting up and rushing off.

Moments later he returned leading a line of waiters carrying two enormous platters piled high with spaghetti with meat sauce; salads, bread and butter, cheese. He hovered near us as the food was arranged, and then hovered some more. Finally, Tennessee asked if we could have a little privacy.

Joseph was nothing if not thick-headed. Rather than moving off, he asked Tennessee if he could read for him.

"Anytime, baby," Tennessee generously replied, hoping that would get him out of the way.

We were left more or less alone for about a half hour during which Tennessee picked at his food, feeling suddenly despondent, morose now that someone else from his past had been wiped from the board. The restaurant he had remembered with such fondness, Laurette's old stamping ground, was drab, nearly deserted, run by a man with a sixty-watt brain. And if this evening's clientele was any indication, the joint would soon be closing its doors. (Which is what happened. When we visited the place ten years later, don't ask me why, all that remained was an empty lot, the whole structure having been demolished. It looked like a bomb crater. Tennessee, staring at the desolation, remarked, "The food was bad, baby. But not *that* bad!")

The day before Tennessee had spoken to me about finding an agent to replace Audrey Wood. He didn't want to leave International Creative Management (ICM), the vast theatrical agency that had swallowed Liebling/Wood and for whom Audrey now worked. He wanted a young man, preferably Southern and gay, to represent him. So I had called Lynn Nesbit, who was my agent then, to help him. Lynn was in the Hamptons, eight months pregnant, awaiting the birth of her child. I gave her the essential picture: Tennessee would under no conditions return to Audrey Wood.

He was now claiming—and he held to it until he died —that Audrey had secretly negotiated with ABC television to sell the rights to *all* his plays at a ridiculously low figure contingent, of course, on his death, something Audrey expected momentarily. After his death ABC planned to lift the various characters—Big Daddy, Brick, Blanche, Chance, Stanley, etc.—and put them together in a television series, a World of Tennessee Williams soap opera that would commercialize, cheapen, and defile his vision and life work. As I understood it, the point was to produce a show that was "The Beverly Hillbillies Go to Peyton Place," with a little *Baby Doll* thrown in. I could see why he was incensed.

As if that wasn't bad enough, the clever Miss Wood was also deep into secret negotiations with various unnamed land developers to build in the South—again after his death—Tennessee Williams theme parks, literary Disneylands, if you can imagine such things, where, in place of Mickey Mouse and Dumbo, Donald Duck and Goofy, you would have Stanley and Stella, Sebastian and Mrs. Venable, and so on. As crazy as that sounds, Tennessee was adamant in his belief that such were the evil designs Audrey had on his work, a conspiracy he had discovered and exposed in the nick of time. *That* was why he had fired her. And while the confrontation, which took place in Donald Madden's dressing room, had been exceedingly unpleasant, it had been necessary to make her face the music.

"I cursed her, and I shouldn't have. I try always to be a gentleman," he said. "I called her a thieving cunt, and she said that if her husband were alive and in the room I wouldn't dare to use such language in her presence. I regret it, but she had to go."

Now he needed someone to take her place, someone congenial and trustworthy.

That someone, Lynn Nesbit suggested, should be Billy Barnes. He was young, southern, and good-looking, and new to the agency, having joined ICM a few months before. Previously he had worked for the formidable Otto Preminger, the director, and anyone who could survive employment by Otto ought to be able to handle Tennessee Williams. Lynn, however, believed that in time, when things cooled down, Tennessee would patch things up and return to Audrey. I didn't see it that way. In any event, she was anxious to keep Tennessee in the ICM stable because the agency's 10 percent fee on his royalties represented a hefty chunk of its profits.

I emphasized to Lynn that things were getting sticky in Chicago. Tennessee was stoned most of the time, often incoherent; he was depressed, fearful, a little out of control. What's more, the town was quickly filling up with freeloaders, total strangers to me, who checked into the Ambassador East, charged their rooms and meals to him, and appeared at our door, usually early in the morning, demanding to see him. I would wake him and watch him stagger out of bed, greet whoever was calling, sullenly listen to their request for funds, and then hunt for his checkbook. Exhausted, he'd sign the check, hand it to them and tell them to fill it in, and struggle back to bed. I finally took control of that particular situation by refusing anyone admittance before he was well up and alert, and by keeping his checkbook hidden. It didn't do much good, because they waylaid him in the lobby or the bar or at the Ivanhoe Theatre.

It was a circus the likes of which I had never seen before. Simply put, I had never before observed human sharks in a monetary feeding frenzy before. Anything not nailed fast to the floor was fair game. They not only walked off with money, credit cards, and jewelry, they took my camera, tape recorder, bath towels, books, bottles of wine and vodka, ashtrays, anything that struck their fancy or could be pawned. It was total anarchy. They nagged, cajoled, importuned, threatened, cried, did everything short of beating him over the head with a club to get their hands on the money. And he gave in because he was too tired and too distraught to put up a fight.

These old friends. The only people who really loved Tom, as they repeated endlessly. They loved him the way a fox loves a chicken. I wanted to send the lot packing. But Tennessee would say, in his tired way, "What does it matter, Dot? She can't meet her rent." Or, "She was a fine actress once. Now the poor thing lives in a welfare hotel with her crazy brother." Or, "He was kind to Rose once." Or, "She's related to me, distantly." Or, "He means well, only he suffers from terminal brain cancer and can't help himself." Half the crew of bloodsuckers were suffering from one fatal disease or another, according to him. That was fourteen years ago and every one of these terminal cases outlived him. To a man.

This descent of camp followers I was to witness for many years in many parts of the world; Tennessee was hounded and bled not by creditors but by deadbeats, losers, no-talents, people who refused to do a lick of work because they were "artistes" to whom the world (read: Tennessee Williams) owed a living. Labor was mysteriously beneath them, an affront to their delicate and artistic sensibilities. Many of them were actors who had appeared years ago in one production or another of his plays and who never let him forget what he owed them for these performances in some regional theatre in the boondocks. Or they were unpublished writers, usually poets well advanced in years. He was a pushover for any old wretch who claimed to be a poet. He would lavish them with praise and money, perhaps because he saw what he might have been in their circumstance. He was being manipulated, and I don't think he much cared. I thought it appalling.

So at dinner at the Italian joint in Chicago I told him what I knew about Billy Barnes, his agent-to-be. It seemed to cheer him up. He decided to go to New York to meet Billy, and work things out. I was as anxious as he was for it to be a successful relationship. I hoped Billy would be able to take things in hand, clear the decks, and allow him the space and quiet he needed to create.

" 'Take a look at yourself in that worn-out Mardi Gras outfit, rented for fifty cents from some rag-picker!' " Joseph, Guido's son, appeared at our table gesticulating madly, shouting loudly, giving us his rendition of Stanley Kowalski from *Streetcar*. " 'And that crazy crown on! What queen do you think you are, Blanche?' "

"Oh God," Tennessee groaned, dropping his head in his hands.

" 'I've been on to you from the start! Not once did you pull any wool over this boy's eyes! You come in here and sprinkle the place with powder and spray perfume and cover the light bulb with a paper lantern . . .' "

"Thank you, baby," Tennessee said, peeking at Joseph

from between his fingers that now covered his face like grillwork. "You read very well."

" '. . . and lo and behold the place has turned into Egypt and you are the Queen of the Nile! Sitting on your throne and swilling down my liquor! I say *Ha! Ha!*' " he shouted, shoving his face near Tennessee's, who started to visibly shudder.

"I said thank you, baby. Enough is enough!" Tennessee tried to stand.

" 'I say, *Ha! Ha!* Do you hear me?' " Joseph bellowed in a voice to wake the dead. He was totally consumed by the role, and did not seem to notice that Tennessee was standing up, unsteady, and trembling either from rage or nerves.

"*Ha! Ha! Ha!*" went Joseph.

Tennessee's head fell back, his eyes rolled in his head. "I can't take it anymore!" he said, as he fell forward, like a mummy falling from its box, and crashed onto the table, knocking it over. He landed on the floor, plates of spaghetti, wine, tablecloth in a pile on top of him.

He played dead, always his ploy of last resort. I got him into a taxi and carried him home.

In bed, he ruefully said to me, "Don't ever be a playwright, baby. The occupational hazards are too great!"

CHAPTER · FOUR

WHILE IN CHICAGO with Tennessee, July 1971, I used the opportunity to talk to him about the antiwar movement and about his speaking at a fund-raising event for the People's Coalition for Peace and Justice at the Cathedral of Saint John the Divine in December. The People's Coalition was an organization whose function was to raise money to protest the Vietnam War. I was vice chairman of the group, David Dellinger was chairman, and Tom Seligson was treasurer. Tennessee was incensed about the war and frustrated because he knew of no way to engage himself in the antiwar movement. He desired to catch up with history, for somewhere he had lost the sixties. He would find them, the sixties, after they were over, gathered in a cathedral in New York City months later.

On July 25, my birthday, Tennessee asked me to be sure I was back at the hotel room by 9 P.M. But my roommate, Jack Weiser, had called from New York and told me that a friend of mine had died from an overdose of speed. It busted me up, so I went out and got smashed.

I returned to the hotel after midnight to find Tennessee lying exhausted on the sofa, still dressed, a gray hotel blanket thrown over him. Before him, on the cocktail table, was an enormous birthday cake, the candles burned down to the frosting, the edges of it eaten.

"Baby," he said, "you missed your party. It's over. We waited so long for you."

I sat down on the far corner of the sofa and took a

bottle of vodka from the table and drank from it. I looked over at several actors in the room. Everyone was very quiet. I avoided looking at Tennessee because his eyes expressed the disappointment he felt over my nonappearance at the small celebration. He loved me and had tried to do something for me, and I had let him down.

"You shouldn't drink so much, Dot," he said, funereally, his voice tired and hoarse.

I looked at him. "Jeremy died."

"*Who? Who* died?" he said, alarmed.

"Remember Jeremy, the boy we kissed at Max's Kansas City the night Jean Genet was there?"

He nodded, remembering Jeremy coming in and joining us at a table in the back room of Max's Kansas City, a bar on Park Avenue South that was for a decade the place where "underground" painters and writers and junkies hung out. We were sitting with Mickey Raskin, who owned the joint, and Eric Emerson, one of Warhol's actors, and Jeremy came and sat between Tennessee and me. And Jean Genet came in with three big, mean-looking black hustlers, taking a table near us. All evening they stared at us, saying not a word. Tennessee waved at Genet, who couldn't speak a word of English, and sent over a bottle of wine.

"He's into black trade, baby," Tennessee informed us, "trade" being gay argot for an ostensibly heterosexual male who likes gay men to fellatiate him. "*Rough* trade, from the looks of it," he said. "Rough trade" being an ostensibly heterosexual male who beats up the fairy after getting his blow job.

He went on to talk about Yukio Mishima, the Japanese writer who would later die decapitated by his lover. "Mishima used to fly to the States from Japan for a blond fix. I knew him. I met him through Truman [Capote], and a few years back he came to San Francisco while I was there and we went cruising for young blonds. Baby, that was his ticket."

He stopped, and looked over at Genet's table, at the three blacks glowering at us for reasons never determined. "Kiss me," he said to Jeremy. He did, several times, I think to show off in front of Genet. A small thing but it has stuck in my mind because I loved Jeremy, Tennessee knew it, and he was trying to pick him up and failed. But then he spent his life with me trying to pick up whomever I happened to love. And often he succeeded, until after a time I didn't much care anymore. I figured that we are all big boys now and know what we are doing.

I had met Jeremy a few nights before his first encounter with Tennessee at Max's Kansas City. He was about twenty years old; with dark, wavy brown hair; pale blue eyes set above ruddy cheeks; tall, well-built, with a glorious ass. It was through Andy Warhol that I came to know him. I had gone down to the Factory, Warhol's studio, to have dinner. A group of us—Andy, Joe Dallesandro, Paul Morrissey, Bridget Polk (née Berlin), and Jeremy—went to a restaurant off Union Square. We also had a chimpanzee with us, dressed in a bullfighter's sequined suit. I remember we stopped on the way to buy the New York *Daily News*, a newspaper the chimp was fond of perusing over dinner.

At the table Warhol, as usual, had his tape recorder going. We ordered an ice cream soda and a straw for the chimp, who sat contentedly sipping his drink and turning pages of the *Daily News*. He talked of sex, much of the conversation spent on speculation about what Billy Graham liked to do in bed, an area of knowledge I was considered expert in because I had known the evangelist for many years through my father, who is also a Fundamentalist preacher.

I sat next to Jeremy and couldn't take my eyes off him or later keep my hands off him. He was a kid from Long Island, who had been taken up by the Warhol gang because of his beauty, and that alone was enough to insure his doom.

He wanted to be a bricklayer because as a boy he had seen pictures in *Life* magazine of Winston Churchill building a serpentine wall at Chequers, his country estate.

I came to love him, and then he died.

In Chicago, Tennessee asked me how Jeremy met the Grim Reaper. Tennessee was always keenly interested in the exact details of the death of someone he knew, as if the knowledge would somehow give him a clue as to how to avoid a similar fate.

"He died at the Hotel Chelsea," I explained. Jeremy lived in the Hotel Chelsea on Twenty-third Street in Manhattan, a somewhat seedy establishment that has been home to many great artists, Dylan Thomas and Virgil Thompson among them. "Some of Warhol's people were making a movie in the hotel. There was a bubblebath scene in the film, and during the shooting they ran out of bubblebath. They were also out of money, so they rang up Jeremy and said they needed twenty bucks for bubblebath, and if he gave it to them they would give him some speed."

"Poor child. I didn't know he was a druggie," Tennessee remarked, shaking his head disapprovingly. He had caught the clue: drugs kill.

"Jeremy had never used drugs," I said. "But he handed over the money and took a syringe and vial of speed in exchange. He shot himself up, or was shot up by someone else, no one knows for sure, and the shock of the speed was so great it stopped his heart dead in its tracks."

Tennessee's eyes filled with tears; he looked away, saying nothing. For a few minutes everyone was silent while he composed himself. I swigged the vodka.

"I told you not to drink so much, baby. It'll kill you," he finally said sternly. It was obvious I was looped, and he was angry, not wanting to lose me.

He started talking about boys who died young, of whom he claimed to have known many, and he had. And he went on to talk about the young soldiers dying in Vietnam, the anguish of battle in a cause not worthy of a young man's death. Full of his discourse on the war, he turned to me, as I guzzled the booze, and said, "How can you stop a war if you are bombed all the time?"

A good question. You couldn't, I supposed, not half in the bag all the time, you couldn't stop anything. But I did not answer. I had been an activist in the antiwar movement since 1967, when I joined the Students for a Democratic Society at Columbia. I had been arrested in demonstrations many times, teargassed and beaten, the usual discomforts that came with the territory. And the war went on, and I was trying to enlist Tennessee in the movement against it, and I did drink too much. But then, I thought, so the hell does he.

"Baby," he said, "these people do not understand revolutionaries!" He meant the collection of deadbeats and old hams drinking his booze. "I've *always* spoken for the oppressed!" It was as if knowing my desire to have his cooperation—I had been hounding him for weeks about appearing at the antiwar benefit in December—he had devised this little speech to say to me at my birthday party as a gift. The party had not happened, so he was saying it now. "And now I've decided to do something. Dot, it's time for me to do something for the movement. It is *past* time! I must speak out! Maybe it's time for the movement to pick up the gun!"

Pick up the gun? The movement couldn't pick up lunch for two at Nedick's. It was broke, divided, infiltrated by G-men, harassed, battered, and nearly broken by Nixon and Company.

"We're in trouble, Tenn," I remarked, stating the obvious. "I think it will get a lot worse before it gets any better."

"But the movement will win," he replied, trying to counter my depression. "It has *history* with it."

I didn't believe him then, but he was right.

I think what drew Tennessee to the antiwar movement, what made him accept my invitation for him to speak at the benefit in December—his first public protest against the war in Vietnam—and what finally pulled Norman Mailer and Gore Vidal and other writers was a romantic conception of the young and of history itself, the sense that there was the imperative for direct, active participation in the struggles of the left if you were to maintain any credibility among the rising generations.

Sartre had recently said that intellectuals who did not take to the streets in support of workers and students, who stayed at their typewriters, were guilty of "bad faith." He stated, "In my view, the intellectual who does all his fighting from an office is counterrevolutionary today, no matter what he writes." I sensed that was true, that at least some sort of public act was required of the writer beyond his craft, that one's body physically had to be put on the line.

As I told Tennessee, it seemed increasingly clear to me that demonstrations and legal protests were ineffective and, as the years passed, more and more they seemed exercises in futility and self-indulgence. The benefit that I was organizing, while it might have little or no effect on the war itself, was necessary because it was imperative that the movement get out of debt. We expected to raise a minimum of sixty thousand dollars at the benefit. People whose freedom depended upon movement resources were in jail for the lack of money to spring them.

Among the things that attracted Tennessee to the antiwar movement, beyond his profound hatred of war, was the fact that young people, most especially those committed to media-centered action, made him feel alive, in contact with history, in a way that books and theatre did not. And, of course, there were profound moral and political reasons for the involvement of Tennessee and Mailer and Vidal and other writers on the left, however distant that engagement was. Tennessee especially felt a sense of deep, almost irrational solidarity with the victims of oppression. His motives seemed absolutely clean to me. He loved the beaten, the lost, the put-upon, the disregarded, the outsider, the revolutionary. And, as a romantic, the figure of a young man up against it, the young male eager to "pick up the gun" had enormous sexual and emotional appeal to him. It was irresistible. When he spoke of revolution and of "going to the mountain," by which he meant facing death, I took him quite seriously.

Tennessee finally agreed to speak at the benefit on December 6, 1971, at the Cathedral of Saint John the Divine in Manhattan. He also later wrote a poem for us ("Ripping Off the Mother") which we sold to *Evergreen Review,* and an article ("We Are Dissenters Now") that was published in *Harper's Bazaar*, the money given to the People's Coalition. And during the months preceding the Remember the War Benefit, as it was called, Tennessee opened himself to wide contact with movement people. He was changed by that experience.

Two days before I left Chicago for New York, where I lived, Tennessee's paid companion, Michael, arrived at the Ambassador East to take over my watch. Tennessee had met Michael a few years before at a motel in Florida where Michael was night clerk. They became lovers, and until Robert arrived on the scene in 1972, Michael was, after Frankie Merlo, the longest-running romantic engagement of Tennessee's life.

Michael was very blond and very handsome, with blue eyes as big as a cow's. To put it kindly, his brain was not the brightest bulb in the chandelier. He didn't know how to read very well and had a small boy's love of chemistry sets, gadgets, toys, although he was in his early twenties. Tennessee called him "Mary Poppins" because of his pollyannaesque innocence and his unshakable optimism in the face of all evidence to the contrary.

Tennessee owned a small apartment house at 1014 Dumaine Street in New Orleans that he had bought with the profits from *Streetcar*. It was a stately old townhouse, broken into six or eight flats, with a courtyard, small swimming pool, and a former slave quarters in the rear that held several more rooms. This property, like the house in Coconut Grove, Florida, was owned as a tax shelter. He rarely visited the Coconut Grove place, and often in New Orleans he stayed in a hotel rather than at his apartment. And I can see why, because his one-bedroom

flat was gloomy, airless, with dark red walls, heavy draperies, and awkward, unmovable, ugly Victorian furniture. It
had the feeling of a Harlem funeral parlor.

Tennessee had given Michael the job of building su-
perintendent, an unwise decision, since Michael was con-
genitally incapable of collecting rent or leasing rooms to
tenants Tennessee considered suitable. Recently Tennessee had shown up in New Orleans without prior notice.
Walking into the courtyard he noticed that the pool was
surrounded by lesbians taking the sun. Tennessee, outraged, stood in the center of the courtyard screaming,
"Out, dykes!" at the top of his lungs.

He then stormed upstairs to find Michael naked and
asleep on the bed.

"Baby," he later told me, "it was painfully obvious
Mary Poppins had been entertaining the fleet! I woke him
up and demanded to know the precise number of tricks
he'd daily had parading across my bed in my absence! It
was clear from the state of complete neglect of building
maintenance that Mary had occupied his time with en-
deavors of the flesh. Mary jumped out of bed and heatedly
denied giving himself to anyone. He stamped his foot,
shaking the floor, and a tub of Vaseline the size of a milk
pail rolled out from under the bed! He had used every
ounce of it. Not only has he allowed the place to be overrun with muff-divers, but he has turned my bedroom into
the venue for twenty-four-hour gangbangs!"

As usual he forgave Michael, putting the blame for
his actions on the boy's stupidity. Michael was trusting to
a fault, which made him one of the most bedable boys God
ever gave life to, was loyal as a puppy, and once asked me
how long was the bus ride from New York to London,
England, having no idea where England was. Yet Tennes-

see loved him very much, and when he went away for good Tennessee missed his kindness and his simple, open ways, and at the end of his life, when he was more or less alone, Tennessee tried to find him again. All we knew was that Michael was married, and working as a night clerk in some motel back in Florida. We tried but couldn't find him.

"Mary Poppins loved me," Tennessee said then. "He was good to me. I never should have let him go." He shrugged and smiled that sad, crooked smile of his, the smile he presented whenever he acknowledged loss.

Part of the reason Michael had to leave was because Tennessee was afraid to fly with him anymore, and that is a definite handicap: a traveling companion you're wary of traveling with. Tennessee's alarm was caused by an incident. They were leaving New Orleans for New York. They went to the airport, checked their baggage, and headed for the metal detectors on their way to the gate. There had been a number of airline hijackings in recent weeks, and, more to the point, airport guards had caught via the metal-detecting machines a number of would-be hijackers attempting to slip on board planes with guns, knives, and other such weapons secreted on their persons. So security at the New Orleans airport was now extremely tight.

"We were late for the plane," Tennessee said, "and I was the first to go through the metal detector. Then Mary Poppins walked through. Alarms, bells went off! People yelled, guards pulled their guns! I practically had a heart attack. They wouldn't let us board the plane. They took us off to a little room where they searched Mary. They ordered him to take off his trousers and there, taped around his legs like medieval armor, was aluminum foil! When they asked him why he did it, he said he wanted to see if the metal detector machines really worked! He's got six less than a dozen upstairs, baby."

Tennessee never flew with him again.

Michael came to Chicago because I had to leave and somebody had to watch out for Tennessee, who was not, as I have said, in the best of shape.

The night before I left, Tennessee had been invited to a party on Lake Shore Drive. That afternoon I reminded him we were expected to be "at a party given by some old queens on the lake."

Around nine o'clock we got into a taxi. Tennessee was wearing a white suit, panama hat, and sunglasses. His eyes were bothering him. He was stoned on something, Demerol perhaps, and he sat in the cab between Michael and me, clutching a towel under his arm. I asked him why he was carrying a bath towel to a party.

"My swimsuit's inside it," he replied.

Why are you bringing a swimsuit? I asked.

"You said we were going to a party on the lake!" he indignantly answered.

(When he was in Chicago during the rehearsals of *Menagerie*, decades before, he had little money. He couldn't find a swimming pool, and he loved to swim. Early one morning, around dawn, a friend found him sitting on the steps of the Art Institute waiting for the doors to open. When he asked him what he was doing there with his towel and swimsuit, Tennessee said, "This is an art museum. They *love* artists. Surely they have a swimming pool!")

The party was in an apartment on one of the top floors of a very tall skyscraper apartment block. We took the elevator up, and entered a very modern, very overdecorated flat done up by some fussy, prissy, and pricey decorator. Our hosts, two aging queens who had seen better days, took Tennessee's towel and swimsuit and ushered us into a room filled almost entirely by effeminate homosexuals of roughly the same age and class.

Tennessee asked me to get him a triple Scotch on the rocks, a surprising request, since I had never seen him drink Scotch before. He was trying to fortify himself for the boredom that so plainly lay ahead.

Soon he was surrounded by gentlemen making small talk, chatting him up with the relentless singlemindedness of fans he had experienced before in other times and places. From time to time he would catch my eye across the room, and roll his eyes in feigned desperation as if to say, Save me! A few minutes later I noticed him making eyes at a blond kid of about twenty across the room. Tennessee made little waves in his direction, winked repeatedly, pursed his lips and popped his eyes to capture the youth's attention.

I turned away, and moments later I heard a crash and looked to see Tennessee lying flat on his back on the floor before a horrified and somewhat hysterical gaggle of queens. I went over with Michael, and we lifted him onto a sofa. I thought he might have had a heart attack, and knowing his paranoia about the press and his repeated warnings that any bad news about his health would close his play and destroy what was left of his career, I decided to get him out of there fast, before the word was out. I told someone to call a taxi, and then I tore open his shirt and put my ear to his chest and listened to his very strong heartbeat. I then sat up and felt his forehead, and as I did he opened his right eye almost imperceptibly and winked. Michael and I and the blond kid he had been flirting with carried his limp body out the door past the flabbergasted guests, mumbling apologies and excuses as we left. We laid him on the floor of the elevator; his body was still. When the door closed, and the cab began its descent, Tennessee sat up and started cackling loudly, mightily pleased with himself.

"You cunt!" I was furious. "How could you do that to me? I was worried sick!"

He shook his head, and the greatest playwright of the age said, "Dotson, I was so *bored*. I had to leave, and I couldn't think of an exit line!"

In New York, I took Tennessee, Michael, and a hustler/pusher we had picked up the night before at a bar called Cowboys to Abbie Hoffman's apartment in the Village. Tennessee was anxious to meet Abbie, who was, with Jerry Rubin, founder of the Yippies and perhaps the most famous American antiwar activist alive.

Tennessee and Abbie embraced warmly, and Abbie introduced him to his wife, Anita, who was nursing their new baby, America.

"America!" Tennessee exclaimed. "You gave him a whole country and all I've got is one Southern state!"

We smoked grass and Tennessee drank wine and the hustler/pusher who was with us sat on the floor, stoned on Quaaludes, a boy very much Tennessee's type, blond, very young; his face sweaty, fixed in a perpetual zonked smile . . . undoing his pink fluff shirt, his hands playing with his nipples; and Michael, introduced as Tennessee's secretary, showed Abbie magic tricks, the kind you buy at the toy counter at Woolworths: a peeper where you look to

see a naked woman and instead get an electric shock, card
tricks, mind reading, kid stuff . . .

The entire encounter held an element of the absurd,
even of the pathetic, as Abbie and Tennessee talked of
revolution and, later, of Cuba. It was an apparent incon-
gruity to be speaking of revolution while a hustler sat
stoned on the floor playing with his tits, magic tricks were
displayed, and jokes were cracked throughout; but under
it, beneath the ego flush Abbie experienced in meeting
Tennessee Williams, a celebrity like himself, and beneath
the mindlessness of the pot and the Third Avenue sexuality on the floor, was Tennessee's very real concern to learn
where the hell the movement was going, what, in fact, the
antiwar movement was. And so he came to Abbie Hoffman with a naïveté and a sincere desire to be part of the
struggle, a movement that Abbie, accurately or not,
through his books and public acts, had come to represent
in Tennessee's mind.

It was difficult to get the conversation on a serious
level given Abbie's attention span (about that of a six-year-
old) and his penchant for telling jokes, entertaining. They
talked of Cuba, Tennessee angered by the regime's perse-
cution of homosexuals and writers. It was a question—
why intolerance in the revolution?—that Tennessee would
ask again and again.

"I met Fidel Castro only once," Tennessee said, "and
that was through Hemingway. The time I met Hemingway was the time I met Castro. I was in Havana during
the first year of Castro's regime. Castro would have remained a friend of the United States except for that bastard John Foster Dulles, who had this phobia about anything revolutionary. He apparently thought that Mr.

Batista—a sadist who tortured students to death—was great fun.

"I met Hemingway through Kenneth Tynan at the restaurant Floridita in Havana. Tynan was known as Lord Slap-Slap because he was always beating up women. Hemingway and I had a very pleasant meeting, and he gave us both a letter of introduction to Castro. Hemingway said this was a good revolution. And if Mr. Dulles hadn't alienated Castro, it might have been.

"Castro was a gentleman," Tennessee declared. "An educated man. He introduced me to all the Cuban Cabinet. We'd been waiting three hours on the palace steps for this emergency cabinet meeting to end. When he introduced us, Castro turned to me and said, 'Oh, that *cat!*' and winked. He meant *Cat on a Hot Tin Roof,* of course. I found that very engaging. What a beautiful man! He *embraced* me! Uhhh, this powerful man, this revo*lu*tionary said it was an honor to meet *me*. What a gentleman. I am certain he does not know what is going on in his prisons or he would instantly put a stop to it!"

Abbie shrugged. He was high. Abbie gave Tennessee copies of his books, and we all signed a poster on Abbie's bedroom wall. And it had very little to do with the left or politics, although Tennessee was pleased to be in a room with Abbie, seeing in him a symbol of rebellion in the decade, so he did not notice or did not mind the absurdity of the situation. If it was not decadent, that group of us babbling of revolution amidst wine and pot and hustler and other indulgences of the privileged class, it was certainly unserious and most assuredly ironic. We were free men discussing the bondage of others, and getting stoned doing it.

As we were leaving, two radical types in blue work

shirts and combat boots who had sat silent throughout the meeting on Abbie's Danish modern couch said, "You bourgeois rip-off artists!"

Tennessee was confused. But then he had a right to be. So he rose on the balls of his feet and said defensively, "Abbie's a *saint!* Such courage. Magnificent. He has accepted his death. He's been to the mountain!"

"I don't wanna die!" Abbie wailed. "What do you *mean,* man? I don't wanna die!"

"You've been to the mountain, baby," Tennessee repeated.

All that night Tennessee rode high on the encounter with Abbie Hoffman, for it was to him an encounter with the history of the New Left. Of course, it was nothing of the kind.

Late at night we stood in a parking lot in the East Village after having been to a show and a number of gay bars cruising for boys and lucking out. Tennessee and I pissed against a wall, Tennessee singing at the top of his lungs, "Mary, sweeter than you know . . ." And I pointed out the graffiti sprayed on the wall: ROCKEFELLER MURDERED! AVENGE ATTICA! Governor Rockefeller had ordered in troops to end the inmate rebellion and occupation at Attica State Prison. The troops had opened fire, and many inmates had died. That was the reality, not the meeting with Abbie. At that time in America, Attica was what the real left was about.

Tennessee said, "God bless the movement!" and then shyly, "Off the pigs!" He was trying on the argot to see if it fit.

I took Tennessee to a demonstration against the Attica Prison massacre. We waited at Rockefeller Center with Betty Peterson, Dave Dellinger's wife, for the demonstrators to arrive from Union Square. As far as I know it was the first public political protest Tennessee had ever attended.

As the leading pacifist in the United States, Dellinger had spoken downtown and then led the protesters to Rockefeller Center. As they reached us, people in the line of march recognized Tennessee and raised their fists in greeting, a raised fist then being a symbol of resistance to oppression. He returned the salute. It was two days after Attica.

We waited for Dave Dellinger, who was bringing up the rear of the march, plodding along at the end in his rumpled beige tweed jacket and brown corduroy trousers, carrying a package of books under his arm. He had brought along copies of his book *Revolutionary Nonviolence* for Tennessee and me.

"Dave!" I yelled happily, and he jogged over, grinning, and embraced Betty, and then threw his arms around Tennessee and me.

We strolled through the crowd of demonstrators on Fifty-second Street decrying Nelson Rockefeller as an assassin, and while the speeches droned on I pointed out to Tennessee various friends in the crowd, among them former Weatherman Brian Flanagan. He had been tried for attempted murder in the paralyzing of Mayor Daley's counsel during the Weatherman "Days of Rage" violent protests in Chicago.

"He looks Irish," Tennessee said. "When I was young the Irish became cops."

Then Julian Beck and his wife, Judith Malina, came

over, hugging everybody. We were astonished to see them, none of us knowing that they had returned from imprisonment in Brazil. The Becks had founded and directed The Living Theatre, a radical, experimental, left-wing ensemble that went all over the world and got into trouble everywhere it went.

Betty, Judith and Julian, Dave, Tennessee, and I left the demonstration, joined by Tom Seligson, the writer. We ended up at a bar in the RCA Building.

Tennessee was in high spirits, and he kept mugging, laughing loudly, cracking jokes. He asked Judith Malina, whom he had known for twenty years, about her imprisonment in Brazil.

"It was unbelievable. We requested a room for the company to rehearse in at the prison." Judith spoke very quietly, twisting a napkin between her fingers. She is a tiny person, with jet black hair and enormous eyes. She spoke so softly we all leaned forward to hear her.

"They gave the room to us. It was next to the one in which they tortured the men. We could hear them screaming, political prisoners, young, young men screaming and crying as we tried to rehearse a theatre piece in the next room. Oh, my God, it was . . ." She started to cry, sniffing and coughing. I found it laughable. Why the hell anybody with half a brain would want to rehearse in prison and then be surprised when the sadists running the can put them next to a torture chamber?

Judith went moaning on about their ghastly time in Brazil, about Julian being beaten and thrown down a flight of stairs by the guards after interrogation. I don't know, there was something about her, her black hair and wild eyes, the refusal to give way to age, her tininess and insistent sexuality.

Tennessee stared at her, his mouth open in disbelief at the performance she had given. Like me, he didn't know whether to laugh at her or cry with her.

We returned to the subject of Cuba. "What about the arts in Cuba?" Tennessee asked Dave Dellinger, who had visited the island five or six times and knew Castro. "And what is the role of art in revolution, of the artist, baby?" He took Judith's hand, speaking intensely, dramatically: *"It is to do what he does best!"* He grunted. "To do his work."

It all came back to work with Tennessee. Work gave definition and meaning to life, and therefore it must be what gave meaning to revolution. He was like a fisherman whose life was little more than catching fish, who smelled them, knew the feel of their bodies as he knew the texture of his hands. And that chore of fishing, that constant intimacy with his prey, was the fisherman's only disciplined passion. Words were Tennessee's fish. And if the fish died out?

Dellinger interrupted him. "There are two tendencies in Cuba. The bureaucratic socialists aligned with the Soviet Union, they are repressive of the arts and of homosexuals, of sexual liberation in general. And then there are . . ."

"What does it matter!" Tennessee was being histrionic. He knew about as much about Cuba as he did about Upper Volta, about which he knew absolutely nothing, but he had already made up his mind. He was not going to countenance criticism of Cuba, not after Hemingway had told him its revolution was good.

"It does matter," Dellinger said. "The other tendency is Fidel's, which is open to experimentation. For a while the arts flowered in Cuba."

Seligson spoke up: "But unlike the state, the arts wither away."

Tennessee looked at Tom. "What is the importance of art?" he said, shrugging. The remark was sad rather than cynical.

"It has *great* value."

"How can you place value on art," Tennessee flared, "when there are guns pointed at your country's throat!" He jabbed at his throat with his hand. "The missiles! The Soviets, the Cubans, they are surrounded, baby, they are under siege! There are more important things than art. When the imperialists have you surrounded . . ." I don't think he believed a word of what he was mouthing. He got carried away grandstanding for a group of left-wing friends. Art was the single most important creation of man to him.

"Tennessee . . ." Dellinger tried to interrupt. Tennessee was outflanking him on the left.

I jumped in. "It's social fascism, Tenn, what the Cubans and Russians do to homosexuals and artists."

Dellinger: "It's *bureaucratic* socialism." We were both trying to think up some label to apply to official intolerance in a socialist state to remove it from our conceptions of true socialism. In those radical days, everything socialist was good. The bad was something else entirely. All excesses could be explained away. It was self-delusion of a high degree indeed. But what we did not understand was that Tennessee had no need of explanation. He went ahead with his defense of the revolution while we, ridiculously, tried to make too precise definitions to mitigate revolutionary responsibility for crimes.

Tennessee, turning on me, demanded, "What do you expect? The revolution isn't won!"

"No, it is betrayed!"

"They are *encircled*, baby!" He shrugged. "Who are we to judge? They think us decadent. Dissipated. Look at yourself." He was speaking to me, waving his hand theatrically. "Just *look*. As artists and revolutionaries your task is to do your work. To make art, baby. Who are we to judge the men who die? But I will go to the mountain," he said mournfully. "I have gone before, Dotson. Many times."

In November, a few weeks before the benefit at the cathedral, Tennessee returned to New York from Rome, where he had seen Gore Vidal.

We had lunch at a pancake palace near his hotel, the City Squire Motor Inn, a real dump.

He said he had met Hiram Keller in Rome. Now Tennessee had been trying to meet and get into the sack with Hiram ever since he saw Fellini's *Satyricon*, a movie in which Hiram starred. He was from Georgia, the son of a state supreme court justice, an immensely charming, sexy young man with drop-dead good looks.

"Gore knows him," Tennessee explained. "So I called the boy and asked him to lunch. He said he could come if he could bring one or two friends and if we could go to the best restaurant. I arrived early, and Hiram was late, and when he finally appeared on the scene he was accompanied by *twelve* of his friends. They ordered bottles of the best champagne. The bill, baby, would break the Bank of England! However, my chagrin was tempered somewhat by the fact that this beautiful boy was returning with me to my hotel for cocktails. However, before we left the restaurant Hiram made a phone call, and I believe I know to whom. Not five minutes after we entered my room at the hotel, the phone rang. The caller informed me that he had neglected to tell me that the boy had the clap! You know how venereal disease horrifies me! I hustled the boy out fast! And I've been thinking about that horrendous lunch check ever since." He laughed.

Hiram, of course, did not have the clap.

Tennessee had first met Vidal in the early spring of 1948 at a dinner party. Vidal had just published *The City and The Pillar*, one of the first American homosexual novels of any literary consequence. He had stayed in touch with Vidal ever since.

"Gore said I shouldn't trust you, Dotson, that you're irresponsible. That you are leading me on, baby. He said he knows you well," Tennessee narrowed his eyes and repeated, *"He knows you well."*

That surprised me, since I had never clapped eyes on Vidal in my life.

"I never met the man," I said.

"That you try . . ."

"I never met the man."

"It doesn't matter," he said, not believing me. "Revolutionaries have to use every means. Even their *best friends,*" he ominously informed me. "Revolutionaries are fugitives."

In the last month or so he had taken it into his head that he was a revolutionary, and I was one. He was serious!

"Gore is full of shit," I said.

I met Vidal the following month under appropriate circumstances: at the *Screw* magazine anniversary party at Max's Kansas City, where Vidal received a bronze statuette in the shape of an erect penis for his political work.

He was standing with Howard Austin, his companion of many years. I went over to be introduced, and Gore said to Howard, "Oh, this is the little cunt you've been telling me about!"

And I said to the friend I was with, pointing to Gore, "And this is the big cunt you've been telling *me* about."

We laughed, but it's been downhill ever since.

In December, Gore was to tell me that he no longer recognized Tennessee. "We've been friends a long time. He's changed. And you haven't been any help, Dotson, leading him down the garden path. He doesn't know anything about politics! For Christ's sake, you've filled his head with a lot of radical crap!"

After lunch we sat around in Tennessee's room and had a few drinks, and he talked about moving to Italy for good, getting a small farm with some goats and geese and a handsome shepherd to be his companion.

I learned to be wary whenever Tennessee talked about settling in Italy or, more typically, retiring to Bangkok.

"I'm restless. I like traveling," he said. "When Frank Merlo was living, he being Sicilian, we spent four or five, sometimes six months out of the year in Rome. I love Italy, I love the Italians. Some of the happiest times of my life were spent in Italy with Frank and Anna [Magnani]. She was wonderful as Serafina in the movie version of *The Rose Tattoo*, my love-play to the world."

He went on reminiscing about Magnani and his dead lover, Frankie, both Italians who, he thought with some envy, had temperaments very different from his own. While he was shy, they were open, direct, unselfconscious.

In Rome, he and Frank would arrive at Magnani's apartment about 8 P.M. The apartment was a penthouse atop the Palazzo Altieri, near the Pantheon; the terrace overlooked the Vecchia Roma. Sometimes they would wait more than an hour in her living room, drinking until she joined them, filling the room with her exuberance. She and Frank would chatter away, and Tennessee would listen, entertained, happy.

"The evening would never let down. It was centered around dinner, but after the coffee, Anna would demand a great sack of leftovers. And then we would start our midnight course about Rome, visiting all those places where hungry stray cats were waiting for her to feed them, the Forum, the Colosseum, under certain bridges, in Trastevere, in parts of the Villa Borghese."

The cats fed, the trio would return to her apartment and collect her dog, a big black German shepherd, and haul it off to the Villa Borghese for its nightly walk along the bridle paths under the moonlight. That done, they would end the evening with nightcaps at Rosati's on the Via Veneto. Late at night the Via Veneto would be crowded with people strolling, and with the paparazzi crowding about Tennessee and Magnani, taking endless pictures.

"I think I'll live out the few years left to me in Italy," he concluded.

I once asked him why he traveled so damn much. "Because it's hard to hit a moving target," he replied, laughing.

As I said, whenever he talked of settling in Italy or running off to Bangkok, I was wary, because it meant he was edging into panic and about to run. But he spent a lifetime on the run, and while he wasn't a revolutionary he was a perpetual fugitive, chased by the hounds of remorse and loss and the terror of going crazy. Many times, at nine or ten in the morning, he would call me up, knowing I usually slept until noon, and say, "Baby, I didn't wake you, did I? I've got a two o'clock flight out of Kennedy. I'm all alone. Can you come over and help me pack my gear?" I would get up, because this man, who knew thousands of people, had no one else he could count on.

When Tennessee spoke of traveling to Italy or Bangkok, those specific places, it usually meant his alarm had gone off and he sensed danger. For those places were, in his mind, a kind of final refuge from the world of theatre, from perceived failure, because that was, more and more, what he thought himself to be.

Italy, because it occupied a place of such loveliness and joy in his memory, associated as it was with Frank Merlo and Anna Magnani and the period of his greatest success.

Bangkok had a more despairing meaning. He wanted to die there, it was as simple as that. He was convinced that it was a haven for the old.

"Older gentlemen," he assured me, "are treated with kindness there. Oriental boys revere gentlemen of a certain age."

Although, as far as I know, the last time he went to Bangkok was a disaster because when he left the city he held a press conference claiming that he was near death and had been operated on for breast cancer, of all things, a claim that I never believed, since I knew his chest as well as my own and never saw the slightest scar indicating a surgeon's scalpel had touched him there. That, too, was part of his panic and insecurity, forever claiming he wouldn't live through the night, that he had suffered too many coronaries, had cancer of this or that organ, or had come down with some fatal, unpronounceable disease he had heard or read about somewhere and had adopted as his own. His hypochondria—for that is what it was—was a means to test one's love for him, to force acts and statements of concern. But he overdid it, using it as a ploy in the most absurd situations—for example, with street boys who didn't know Tennessee Williams from the Tennessee Valley Authority. He would collapse on a sofa or bed, groan, declare he was dying, and plead that the boy come and kiss this man moments before he slipped into eternity. And the play would go on from there. The sad, sad irony is that he died not of an illness, unless despair can be called a disease, but of choking to death. Poor Tenn.

A few years before he died he made one last attempt to return to Bangkok. Before he left with his companion, Robert Carroll, to board a cruise ship in Los Angeles bound for the Far East and, he declared, his permanent retirement, we had a tearful farewell, promising to write each other, that I would try to visit him every year; I tried to change his mind, but he was adamant: his karma, that tyrant of fate, had determined that Bangkok it would be.

Off they went by ship. I was astonished two weeks later when he called me in New York to inform me, somewhat sheepishly, that he was back in Los Angeles.

"What happened to Bangkok?" I asked.

"We got off the boat in Honolulu. Oh, baby, it was so *boring!* There was nothing to do on board but play shuffleboard and watch burials at sea!"

In addition to Tennessee, the other people I was able to convince to join the Committee for the Remember the War Benefit were Julian Beck, Malcolm Boyd, Jimmy Breslin, Ossie Davis, Rennie Davis, Willem de Kooning,

Martin Duberman, Jules Feiffer, Paul Goodman, Nat Hentoff, Norman Mailer, Episcopal Bishop Paul Moore of New York, Jack Newfield, Richard Poirier, Susan Sontag, and Gloria Steinem.

Several weeks before the Benefit Committee was completed, sometime in late November, Tennessee and I went down to Rip Torn's house in Chelsea to visit his wife, Geraldine Page. The place was absolutely filthy, the kitchen piled high with garbage. It looked as if no one had taken a cleaning rag to the dump in years.

Abbie was there. We had not seen him since the evening at his apartment months before. Abbie told Tennessee, who was beginning to suffer some prebenefit jitters, that he had had it with the antiwar movement. "I ain't going to be around for the benefit, Tennessee. I ain't even going to be around for the [national political] conventions. Shit, no! They ain't going to pin *that* on me, not this time. They beat me up enough, broke my nose, busted my back. I don't like *pain*, Tennessee. I want to *live*, man. Me and Anita, we're going somewhere warm. We leave the streets to you people."

On hearing that, Tennessee was very depressed.

"This benefit is crazy, Dotson. That shit don't work no more. Don't be so fucking dumb," Abbie said.

We passed around a joint.

"You seen old Gus lately?" Abbie asked me. Gus Hall was head of the Communist Party U.S.A., and I had done an article about him for *Esquire*. "You still pal around with old Gus? Ha! Ha! You know, those Commies, they're pretty *old*. All they're interested in is good plumbing. That's what the Commies want. When me and Anita were in Yugoslavia, that's what they showed us, *plumbing*. When we arrived in Rome we saw *Satyricon*, and I turned to

Anita and said, 'God, give us *decadence!*' It ain't boring anyway. But the Commies . . ." Abbie shivered. "Man, what do they got you want? Huh? They got *cards*. You ever *seen* them cards, huh? They say they got cards, but nobody ever seen them cards they carry. Man, did you ever see them cards?"

Tennessee, unhappy, went upstairs to see Geraldine Page.

Abbie left, telling me he was going to Florida to sit on a beach with fat, blue-haired Jewish ladies having nose jobs and try to figure out what the hell happened to all of us.

"The sixties, like, they came so fast. We don't even know what hit us. We're still spinning. We have got to figure out what the hell we are and what the fucking future is. Can't play the same shitty games no more. It ain't in giving benefits. It ain't there. We're freaks. That's what we are. *Freaks!* I don't even understand my oldest boy. The movement's finished. It's over."

I didn't know it at the time, but he had hit the nail on the head. It was finished.

I went up stairs and found Tennessee in Geraldine Page's bedroom. She was sitting in a rocking chair, slowly rocking; dressed in a bathrobe and nightgown she stared at the ceiling. Tennessee sat on the edge of the bed, leaning forward, his elbows resting on his knees, holding Geraldine's hand in his while she rocked. I stood in the doorway for about ten minutes and watched this tableau—Tennessee who had written the greatest roles that she had ever played, in *Sweet Bird of Youth* and *Summer and Smoke;* Geraldine, among his greatest stars. They did not exchange a single word, silent as two wax figures.

On December 8, the day of the Remember the War
Benefit at the Cathedral of Saint John the Divine, it
rained. In the afternoon I went to the Plaza Hotel to collect Tennessee. Tennessee was dressed in a gray Confederate uniform, a curious choice of garb for his first public
speech against the Vietnam War. He was high and happy,
although I sensed some nervousness. His agent, Billy
Barnes, was with him. There was also a television crew
from the Canadian Broadcasting Company who were filming a special on his appearance at the benefit.

While the crew filmed us, I briefed Tennessee on the
latest statistics from the war: the dead and wounded, the
bomb tonnage, troop numbers, the count of the antiwar
Americans still in jail, and so on.

"Hmmmm . . ." He was writing the figures down on
hotel notepaper as I gave them to him. "Am I the only one
who's going to give statistics? Because I don't want someone else to, uh, you know, steal it! Now let's get this rea-
sonably accurate, if we can, approximate at any rate."

"They're correct," I assured him. "I got them from
Dave Dellinger."

"Fifty-four thousand American death toll?" he asked,
stunned. "North and South Vietnam and Cambodia and
Laos, over a million death toll, mostly noncombatant.
Nearly four hundred thousand wounded American boys."
He took off his reading glasses, sighing. *"Four hundred thou-
sand."*

"Now I will tell you, Tenn. There are going to be
boys from various veterans hospitals brought to the cathedral tonight. They'll be near the stage. We want the television cameras to see them."

He put his glasses back on. He was suddenly terribly serious, writing. "Paraplegics and amputees . . . double and triple and quadruple, no, they can't be quadruple amputees. Two million wounded Asians? *Two million?* Good Lord in Heaven! And when they say wounded you don't know how badly wounded they really are. Some of them would prefer to be dead, I should think. And when does it stop? By whose secret schedule does this mass slaughter end, this shamefully criminal war stop?"

As Tennessee spoke, I went and sat beside Miss Rose on the sofa. The cameras filmed him. The room was very silent, just the hum of the cameras, and the low, Southern drawl of Tennessee's voice.

He continued, "Will it only be when another war begins and when it's begun? What does the military-industrial system depend on? Why do we allow profit in death and money made on the killing of innocents? Where is Kilroy's way out? And yours and mine?"

He began writing again, mumbling to himself. "Young Americans . . . and American dissenters and American war protesters? In prison on war-related offenses, baby?"

He paused, and looked over at me, perplexed.

"And that means resisting the draft, refusing to register," I said, "arrested for conspiracy to duck the draft, and that is why Mark Kluz is standing trial, for assaulting an officer and conspiracy to commit riot, conspiracy to oppose the draft."

He didn't catch the name.

"*Kluz*, remember? The blond kid I brought by the hotel the night we saw Geraldine Page? He took a shower in your room," I prompted.

He nodded, smiling in recall. "Such a gentle creature with such lovely eyes. How old is he?"

"Twenty-five. He's facing a possible life sentence. Did I tell you about him, Billy? About Mark Kluz?" I turned to Billy Barnes, Tennessee's new agent. "He's a kid who was arrested, he sold the *Berkeley Barb*, at Merritt College in California, which is where Huey Newton and Bobby Seale [of the Black Panthers] went to school. He was arrested at a bus stop carrying his newspapers under his arm with half a brick in his pocket, which he used to hold down the papers in the wind. He was arrested for assaulting a police officer with a deadly weapon, possession of a deadly weapon, the same half brick. In California he faces an indeterminate sentence of two years to life."

Tennessee was writing as I spoke. "Mark *Kluz* is the name of this child? How do you spell it?"

"K-l-u-z."

"I remember him quite well." Tennessee smiled. "We got him out of jail, didn't we? Temporarily, at any rate."

Tennessee had sent him bail money at my urging before he actually met Mark. Fifteen hundred dollars, as I recall.

"And what was he charged with?" he asked.

"Possession of a deadly weapon." We were back on the same routine again and I was beginning to have real doubts whether or not he was up to speaking in public in a few hours. He couldn't get his facts and names straight. The Confederate uniform was bad enough, but if he really had an off day and started ranting against the wrong war or the wrong side in the right war he would be a laughingstock on national television.

"Possession of a deadly weapon?" he repeated, puzzled.

"A half *brick!*" I was getting exasperated. "Brick. Like the character in *Cat*."

"What the hell has *Cat* got to do with it? I want to know what was the deadly weapon?" Now he was becoming frustrated and angry, and the whole absurd exchange was being filmed for Canadian television. The crew was starting to laugh.

"*The half brick in his pocket to hold down the newspapers!* That was what the police said was his concealed, deadly weapon."

He still didn't understand. I was ready to throw in the towel.

"There must be something else beside that, isn't there?" he said. "It doesn't make sense, jailed for half a brick?"

I explained it again, at great length, and he finally got the confusion more or less straightened out and started scribbling fast. "Waited a year . . . arrested at a bus stop . . . for carrying half a brick," he mumbled to himself.

"For carrying a half a brick *in his pocket, concealing,* concealing a deadly weapon was the charge against him." I was beginning to believe that perhaps Gore Vidal had been right about Tennessee's political sophistication. "And the jury in Marin County, California, where Mark is going to trial, the jury will be all redneck whites. He won't be judged by his peers—he'll be judged by the people who hate what he stands for and his long hair."

Tennessee glanced at me, and nodded. "Then you would say it was a . . . uh, statutory injustice? In Reagan country?"

"Right! And part of what we are doing tonight is trying to raise money for his defense."

Tennessee and Tallulah Bankhead in New York, December 15, 1955. They are at the City Center where *A Streetcar Named Desire* would open two months later, with Bankhead playing Blanche DuBois. Because of the antics of the largely gay audience, and Bankhead's excessive use of liquor and drugs, the play was a failure. Most of the audience, including Tennessee, couldn't understand half of what she said. *Credit: UPI/Bettmann Archive*

Tennessee and his longtime agent, Audrey Wood, January 1963. *Credit: UPI/Bettmann Archive*

Tennessee and Anna Magnani on the set during the filming of *The Fugitive Kind*. Credit: *Springer/Bettmann Film Archive*

Tennessee in the living room of his Key West house. Prowling to his right is Cornelius, the resident terror, a beast that nearly drove us from house and home.

Behind Tennessee you can see the breakfront with his collection of mismatched wine and martini glasses; his phonograph; and a framed picture of Eugene O'Neill that was the cover of the playbill from a festival of O'Neill's plays. *Credit: Thomas Victor*

He wrote it down. "We are trying to raise money to defend young Americans like him, like Mike Kluz . . ."

"No, Tenn. *Mark*. Mark Kluz."

He finally got it right, and we left, forty minutes late.

We arrived about six-thirty, an hour before the benefit itself was to begin in the cathedral, but an hour after the press reception had started. We went immediately to the Synod House, a small building directly across from the cathedral, where the Benefit Committee was giving a press party. Tennessee, who had no great love for Norman Mailer, said he would only stand by him a minute so the photographers could do their stuff, and that was all. Mailer was to speak that night and then present forty-five minutes from his play *D.J.* Tennessee was worried Mailer would use dirty language and embarrass the bishop and those assembled in his cathedral. Having had a grandfather who was an Episcopal priest, Tennessee retained a huge residual feeling of respect for the Episcopal Church, even though, as he put it, he had been "baptized under extreme duress into Mother [Catholic] Church!"

"If he uses a dirty word I'm going to punch him in the nose!" he declared, spotting Mailer. "The movement can't afford that kind of publicity, not now, not in the church!"

I told him I thought Mailer would respect the place in which he spoke. I was surprised by how adamant Tennessee was on the subject, I had never before known him to blanch at the utterance of locker-room terms.

There was a large press contingent, several hundred from the United States and Europe, and most members of the Benefit Committee were there, as were the performers: the Chambers Brothers, Charles Mingus, Edgar Winter and White Trash, Tuli Kupferberg, Phil Ochs. Richard

Avedon had set up a studio area and was hauling various celebrities before his camera. He immediately grabbed Tennessee and Norman Mailer.

The Cathedral of Saint John the Divine is the largest Gothic cathedral in the world and, after Saint Peter's in Rome, it is the largest church on earth. It joins its neighbors Columbia University, Barnard College, Union Theological Seminary, and Riverside Church in dominating the palisades of Morningside Heights. Below it lies the Harlem valley. An extraordinarily beautiful structure, it was filled to capacity with about five thousand people. It was an often unruly crowd. Welfare Rights Mothers carried placards, as did a group of squatters feuding with the Episcopal Church over church-owned apartments; a group of crazies with NLF flags stood in front of the enormous temporary stage built in front of the high altar and waved the Vietnamese Communist flags in front of the network television cameras; Gay Lib activists passed out leaflets; and a group of Puerto Rican Young Lords stood on the far side of the stage staring defiantly out at the crowd, the buttons on their jackets catching the lights. The Young Lords were, to put it diplomatically, a New York street gang from Spanish Harlem who had adopted a left-wing political coloration by which they attempted to defend their acts of "expropriation" of other people's stereos, gold chains, cars, and other property. But it was a time when young radicals considered shoplifting records at Woolworth an act of revolutionary "liberation."

Into this madhouse I brought Tennessee Williams.

Bishop Moore, a tall, handsome, gaunt man, opened the program by welcoming us, as representatives of the entire peace movement, to his church, an act of Christian hospitality that later brought a firestorm of criticism down on the poor cleric's head. He was followed by a tape recording made by a Vietnamese soldier/poet that had been smuggled to us the day before via Eastern Europe. It was especially recorded for the evening and was utterly unintelligible because the man couldn't speak a syllable of English beyond a somewhat hesitant "okay."

Tennessee and I sat in the fourth row at the foot of the stage with Peter Glenville, a British director who had directed a number of Tennessee's plays. He was a close friend of both of us. We listened to Charles Mingus play, followed by Edgar Winter and White Trash. Rock music was not Tennessee's forte, his musical tastes having been arrested in the late forties. He liked the big-band sound, jazz, blues, country-western, classical music. He was also wild about hymns, and since we were in church I think he was astonished and disappointed to find himself captive to rockers. He kept his hands cupped over his ears until I asked him to stop because the cameras were shooting him.

After what seemed an eternity, we climbed half deaf to the stage, the sound system being more than adequate for Yankee Stadium.

We stood while Dave Dellinger spoke of the war and of the young people across this country in prison for draft resistance and antiwar activities for whom the collection was being taken.

Tennessee was introduced. He walked alone across that enormous stage. The cathedral was dark except for a spotlight focused on him. He seemed terribly small and vulnerable.

He spoke about the heavy responsibility of all Americans for the war in Vietnam. He spoke of Mark Kluz and others who resisted, and got it right. "There is no business as usual with this evil, immoral war. We must not stop the protests until it is ended. Until all the peacemakers are free and the war is over. Now I am too old to march anymore"—the audience yelled No! No! and Tennessee raised his hand to silence them—"but I will march on paper!"

He got an ovation.

On the way off the platform I introduced him to Gloria Steinem, who had preceded Dellinger and Ossie Davis in speaking. He did not know who she was. I explained that she was a very influential feminist writer.

He looked at her, smiling, "My, and so young!"

When we were back in our seats in the audience, I asked him if he had been nervous?

"Nervous?" He laughed. "Oh, baby, I've had many opening nights!"

Norman Mailer followed Tennessee. He stood on stage with his hands thrust in his pockets, jacketless, his legs spread, his stance very provocative. Now I had known Norman for a number of years, and I loved him very much, and as he started to speak I prayed he would not begin with a dirty joke, as he so often did. It would set the crowd into an uproar and send Tennessee fleeing for the door.

There was great tension as Norman spoke, and he was heckled and booed at points, but I thought he spoke well and truly, and I think Tennessee agreed.

"Now we have to face into the future," he concluded, "which is curious, because the mood of revolution has come upon the young in America, and when that war in Vietnam is over, you have to ask yourself what you will do next, what are your values going to be, what your desires are going to be when there will no longer be a war in Vietnam to boo. And I tell you it is a good reason to pause and reflect and try to say to yourself what indeed is that

revolutionary future going to bring? . . . The more we
go in for self-righteousness and piety beyond this point,
the more we are in danger of becoming left-wing total-
itarians. That is the danger when all of us get together."

That revolutionary future? It brought us Ronald Reagan, but if anyone had said it that night we would have
laughed in stupefied disbelief.

There was some light applause and some heckling for
Norman. Then he turned and introduced his cast: Beverly
Bentley, Rip Torn, and Paul Gilford. He left the stage.

The play lasted about forty-five minutes, and about
every tenth word was "motherfucker" or something
worse, and Tennessee got angrier and angrier. Somewhere
in the middle of it he got up in a rage and stomped out of
the nave, followed by reporters. "An outrage! To use bathroom language in a church. Mr. Mailer owes the church,
the peace movement an apology for bringing such filth
into a place of worship! I am wiring the bishop an apology
tonight!"

We went out into the rain. I got him a taxi and told
him I would meet him later at Joe Allen's bar downtown.
He was too upset to speak.

I waited until the end of Mailer's play, and then slipped
out through a side entrance, avoiding the press, and
headed for Joe Allen's on Forty-sixth Street between
Eighth and Ninth Avenues.

Tennessee was sitting at a table with Dave Dellinger,
who left soon after I arrived, Burt Shevelove, a New York
director who had co-written and directed *A Funny Thing
Happened on the Way to the Forum*, and other plays, and Lord

Snowdon, who was in from London on a magazine assignment.

Joe Allen's is in the theatre district and it attracts actors and others connected with show business to its red brick rooms. It was a favorite restaurant of Tennessee's, partly because he was always guaranteed to find friends there.

When I sat down he was still ranting about Mailer's play, the disgrace of it, the embarrassment to the bishop, and more.

"Norman hasn't changed since I first met him. He is still out to shock. People say that I write to shock. That isn't true. I set out to tell the truth, and the *truth* shocks. Norman was just trying to shock with filthy language tonight. It was appalling."

I started to defend Norman, but he would have none of it.

"I met Norman in 1948, whenever he published his first book." It was *The Naked and the Dead.* "It was at a very large and crowded party. I don't remember where," he continued, "but I was with Frank [Merlo]. I had had an eye operation, and I was having trouble with my eyes. And Norman came up to us, to Frank and me at this crowded party and said, 'I'm Norman Mailer. Why the fuck didn't you greet me. Who the hell do you think you are!' I was stunned, I had never met the man in my life, I couldn't see in any event, even if I did know who he was. Norman was very angry and I think quite drunk and he said something about going outside and settling things! Then Frank said, 'I do the fighting for Mr. Williams!' And Norman walked away. Frank was a very tough Sicilian."

Years later, when I asked Mailer about the incident, he said that Tennessee had exaggerated it.

I told Tennessee at Joe Allen's that Norman had mellowed and that I was certain he had not intended to insult him tonight or any other time.

Tennessee narrowed his eyes, and glared at me. "He frightens me because he's not stable. I get very nervous around him because I never know when Norman's temper will explode and he'll start hitting people. I don't believe he likes homosexuals. I think he is the kind of man who beats them up. He has this thing about Hemingway, and he thinks he is the new Hemingway, and Hemingway was a closet homosexual!" Tennessee declared.

That was one of his favorite theories, that Hemingway was latently homosexual and his terrible mistreatment of F. Scott Fitzgerald was based on sexual longing for Fitzgerald that he could not admit; that was why Hemingway struck the macho pose and wrote the way he did and finally killed himself, because he could not finally truly become what he was fated to be: a homosexual. His last New York play, *Clothes for a Summer Hotel*, would be about the relationship between Hemingway and Fitzgerald and in it he would attempt to give dramatic life to his theory.

The conversation shifted when Snowdon, who was wearing a flier's jumpsuit, asked Tennessee what religion he was, since he must be very devout to become so upset over Mailer's little play.

"I was born a Catholic, really," Tennessee replied. "I'm a Catholic by nature. My grandfather was an English Catholic [Anglican], very, very high church. He was higher church than the Pope!" He laughed. "He loved dressing up in vestments, and I think he secretly envied Mary [Cardinal] Spellman because her drag was so much more flamboyant than anything the Episcopalians could come up with. However, my conversion to the Catholic Church was rather a joke because it occurred while I was taking Dr. Max Jacobson's miracle shots. I couldn't learn anything about the tenets of the Roman Catholic Church, which are ridiculous anyway. I just loved the beauty of the ritual in the mass. But my brother, Dakin, found a Jesuit brother who was very lovely and all, and he said, 'Mr. Williams is not in a condition to learn anything. I'll give him Extreme Unction and just pronounce him a Catholic.'"

Tennessee paused, sipping his wine. He enjoyed telling tales on himself. "I was held up in the Roman Catholic Church, Mary, Star of the Sea in Key West, a rather ugly church with a very beautiful name. I've wanted to use its name as the title for a play but I have never written one that fit. In the church, people were supporting me on both sides because I was in a stupor and just about dead, and I was declared a Catholic. What do you think of that?" He cackled. "Does that make me a Catholic? No, I was whatever I was before.

"And yet my work is full of Christian symbols. Deeply, deeply Christian. But it's the image of Christ, His beauty and purity," he said quietly. "And His teachings, yes . . . but I've never subscribed to the idea that life as we know it, what we're living now, is resumed after our death. No. I think we're absorbed back into what, what do they call it? The eternal flux? The eternal *shit*, that's what I was thinking!"

Shevelove asked him if he had ever tried to study the teachings of the church after he was baptized.

Tennessee laughed. "Well, after I got out of the loony bin where Dakin had put me, I was invited by the Black Pope to come to Rome and visit him. Do you know who the Black Pope is? He is the head of the Jesuits and they say even the Pope is afraid of him. I flew to Rome with Gigi (his black Boston bulldog) and we arrived at the Vatican. The Black Pope lives in this rather severe stone building at the end of an immense courtyard. Gigi and I started walking toward the staircase at the far end of the courtyard, at the bottom of which stood the Black Pope in his cassock. Before I made it halfway across the courtyard Gigi broke from her leash and went tearing across the cobblestones, barking furiously! She ran up to the Black Pope and started chewing on his cassock while the poor man tried to kick her off as gently as possible, trying to maintain his dignity. I walked up to the Black Pope. I picked up my dog, and turned on my heel and left without a backward glance!"

"Why did you leave without meeting the Black Pope?"

"Why? Because Gigi was always a far better judge of character than me!"

Tennessee was leaving New York. He called me early one morning from the Plaza Hotel, his voice very hoarse and tired, and asked me to stop by for lunch that afternoon and then take him to the airport.

"I'm going to sleep now. Uh, some hustler is coming to sit in the other room while I sleep. I don't want to be alone, baby, you know?"

He often would call an escort service and have a male hooker sent over, not for sex but just to keep him company. He always thought he would die in his sleep, alone, so he never wanted to be alone when he took his pill and closed his eyes.

Shortly after eleven, I arrived at the hotel. Tennessee's door was answered by an athletic-looking, dark-haired young man wearing a bath towel. He was about nineteen, and looked Italian.

"Hi!" he exclaimed. One word, and I knew I was dealing with a dumbo.

"How's Tennessee?" I asked, walking into the sitting room of the suite.

"Tennessee?" The kid went completely blank.

"The man sleeping in the other room?"

He grinned. "Oh, *him*. He's sleeping. I looked in when I got here. He was sleeping."

I nodded. "Good. He had a bad night."

"Sure. Listen, man. I need cab fare."

I looked the young man over. "Why don't you get dressed?" He was naked except for the bath towel.

The question caught him unprepared. He thought over a reply for a very long time. "I'm doing exercises."

He began doing deep knee bends, dropping his towel, grinning idiotically at me as he bobbed up and down.

"No, stop that! This isn't a gym, for Christ's sake! We've got to get out of here. Tennessee has to catch a plane for New Orleans."

The youth stood up, staring at me in a way that seemed smug, a bit sultry, a hint of the knowing false innocence of a Caravaggio. He was tugging, not at all absentmindedly, on his foreskin with one hand as he stared me down. "I need cab fare." Insistent now.

"I'll give you twenty bucks, okay? Now get dressed."

I wanted him out of the room fast, and I did not want him haggling with Tennessee in the bedroom over his sitter's payment. I was irritated by him, by the kind of sexual teasing I had witnessed so many times in the young men around Tennessee. I resented the exploitation the tease represented, the boring cocksureness, the attitude that everyone was makable, everyone was there to be had.

"Twenty bucks?" He sounded disappointed. He was fishing for more.

"You *ate*, didn't you? I see dirty dishes all over the goddamn table. What'd you order, steak?"

"I had eggs. They were cold."

"Sorry. But at least you were fed."

"Him?" He gestured with his thumb toward the bedroom, speaking in a whisper. "He's a sin-*g*er on the television?" Sin-*g*er, as in Long *Gi*-land.

"Yeah, sure," I said. He thought he was Tennessee Ernie Ford. I pulled twenty bucks out of my pocket and gave it to him. "You better get dressed." He stood his ground, tugging on his penis with his hand, his mouth slightly open and smiling. "You want some meat?"

For a moment I hated him, and then it passed. I shrugged. They also have to live the life.

"Get dressed, and get out."

He gave one more pull on his member and then pulled on his clothes.

After he left, I went into the bedroom to check on Tennessee. He seemed very small and strangely delicate and young huddled under the covers. Sixty years old, yet to me he seemed half that age. I pulled a blanket off the empty twin bed and threw it over him. By the side of his bed was a pile of newly published university textbooks with student editions of his plays. The room was a mess of scattered towels and clothes and paper bottles and dirty cups and records and review books and manuscript pages and unopened mail and his youthful journals.

We had gone the afternoon before to Manhattan Storage, where he had a locked bin, and on the way we had stopped by Payne Whitney Clinic at New York Hospital to visit Philip, a writer whom Tennessee would become publicly engaged to and almost marry in the years ahead. Philip had tried to commit suicide. When we got to the hospital he had checked out.

"Shouldn't we try to find him?" I suggested in the taxi.

"Philip's always attempting suicide," Tennessee remarked, "we'll have ample opportunities to visit him again soon."

(Tennessee was very good about visiting sick friends. A year or two later, when a friend of ours was in hospital, we visited him together.

He was in the hospital for an operation to remove some benign polyps from his rectum. On the way to the hospital Tennessee stopped in Times Square and bought a pair of jockey shorts for him. On the back he had printed: CLOSED FOR REPAIRS. Our friend was nothing if not promiscuous.

Tennessee gave him the shorts, and he responded by telling us this story:

"The morning of the operation a black male nurse came into my room to shave my ass. I told him I didn't want my ass shaved. I don't have any hair on my butt. The nurse said, 'Roll over! Every man has got hair on his ass!' So I rolled over, and the black nurse took a look at my butt, and said, 'You're right, son. Well, I guess grass don't grow on a busy street!' ")

At Manhattan Storage was a large bin full of plastic palm trees, wicker furniture and battered filing cabinets filled with old manuscripts, everything covered in a layer of soot. Tennessee went through the drawers, pulling out manuscripts; the ones he didn't want he threw to the floor. Finally he found what he wanted, two-dozen notebooks in which he had kept a journal from the time he was a boy until 1940.

That night, after dinner, we picked up *Screw* magazine and went back to the Plaza and called one of the hustlers who advertised in the magazine's pages. After sex, we lay on the bed, the three of us, drinking, while Tennessee read for hours from his journals, howling with laughter. When he would finish one he would toss it to the floor and begin another. It was beautiful to listen to, the writings of a young, romantic, and unhappy boy who wanted to be a poet, who hated his mother and father and detested the city of St. Louis where he was forced to live in a miserable household on a seedy street in a dark apartment. Throughout the journals run the anguish and modest hopes of that lonesome child, his daydreams of escape.

The next day, in his room, the notebooks were scattered about. I poured myself a vodka. I leaned against the wall between the two windows overlooking Central Park and watched the smoke from my cigarette curl in the hard winter sunlight. I could hear Tennessee's labored breathing. I felt great love for him. I thought of him as a kind of warrior in the dark heat of battle, and I was sentimental enough in the warmth of the room and alcohol to think that Tennessee did everyone, especially writers, great honor by his struggle and survival. And I envied him, not his fame or his money, which held little interest for me, but his tenacious grip on truth, on the essentials of survival. While in many areas he was self-indulgent and undisciplined, in his writing he was sure and true. He had come into playwriting almost by accident. But once come into it, into writing, he never let go. Nothing ever bent him away from his art.

I woke Tennessee up by kissing him.

After he dressed, I helped him pack. He asked me if I wanted the college textbooks with his plays inside. He very proudly showed me the books, opening them to their indexes, reading out the names of his plays. "They study me in universities all over America," he told me, "they do, baby. I don't think you knew that."

I told him I had studied his plays at Columbia.

"There, too?" He smiled, pleased. "You see, I am not finished yet. The critics can attack me but a whole new generation . . . ?" He shrugged.

When the bags were packed I checked the room. He had left behind his youthful journals. He said he didn't want them. I put them in his suitcase anyway.

We went to the bar downstairs for lunch. I had to borrow a hideous black tie to be admitted.

Tennessee wore dark sunglasses to cover his eyes, which he said were bothered by the pollution in the air.

At lunch we spoke about Carson McCullers.

"She was the best American writer," he said. "We used to sit at the same table, I on one side, and Carson on the other, and work together. She was the only writer I ever knew I could work with in the same room."

"Carson McCullers and Jane Bowles were my best friends as writers. I think if poor Carson had not suffered this very early stroke when she'd barely turned thirty, she would have been the very greatest American writer. She had recurrent illnesses, of course, each diminishing her power. It was a tragic thing to watch. It went on for years.

"I met her in Nantucket. I'd written her a fan letter about *Member of the Wedding*. I thought it was so lovely. I

knew cousins of hers. And at my invitation, she came to
the island to be my guest. Such an enchanting person!
This was the last year before she had a stroke, the year
Carson lived at 31 Pine Street in Nantucket with Pancho
and me."

Pancho had been a lover of his at the time.

"One summer Carson was a writer-in-residence at
McDowell Colony, I believe, one of those sanitariumlike
places in the middle of nowhere that writers are forced to
retreat to in packs," he continued. "Katherine Anne Porter was also there at the same time, and Carson fell madly
in love with her. Now when Carson was in love there was
no stopping her. She pestered Miss Porter with love letters, made unscheduled visits at all hours to her cottage.
Finally, she lay down in front of Miss Porter's front door
and refused to move. She lay there for nearly two days and
Miss Porter would come and go, stepping over her body
the way you step over dogshit. Carson finally gave up. It
was one of her few defeats in love."

In his *Memoirs*, Tennessee later wrote of Carson Mc-
Cullers.

"Carson and her husband Reeves have come into
Paris from their 'Ancien Presbytère' in the country. They
are staying in the same hotel as Frank and I, the Pont
Royal. It is the evening of the Paris premiere of a Magnani
film, and, having received a summons to attend it, I'm
getting into my tux when the phone rings. Carson is on
the wire, greatly agitated.

" 'Oh, Tenn, darling, we've had to move from the fifth
floor to the second because Reeves is threatening to jump
out the window. Please come at once and try to dissuade
him.'

"This was a summons even more urgent than Anna's, so I rushed to their room.

" 'What's this about suicide, Reeves? You can't be serious about it!'

" 'Yes, completely.'

" 'But why?'

" 'I've discovered that I am homosexual.'

"Not foreseeing, of course, that he was really going to kill himself a year or two later, I burst out laughing.

" 'Reeves, the last thing I'd do is jump out a window because I'm homosexual, not unless I was forced to be otherwise.'

"Both the McCullers were amused by this, and Reeves's suicidal threat was put aside for a time.

"I arrived late for the Magnani premiere. Her eyes were daggers as I slunk into her box.

"At the Ancien Presbytère, to which the McCullers returned, there was a cherry tree from which Reeves kept suggesting to Carson that they should hang themselves.

"He even had two ropes for the purpose. But Carson was not intrigued by this proposition.

"One of her relentless illnesses forced her to return to Paris for medical treatment.

"Reeves drove her in, but on the way he produced two ropes and again exhorted her to hang herself with him.

"She pretended to acquiesce, but she persuaded him to stop at a roadside tavern and get them a bottle of wine to fortify themselves for the act.

"Soon as he entered the tavern, Carson clambered out of the car and hitchhiked a ride to the American Hospital in a suburb of Paris.

"She never saw poor Reeves alive again. He killed

himself, some months later, with a bottle of barbiturates and booze."

At the Plaza bar, I asked Tennessee about Carson's last days.

"The last days were horrific. She was paralyzed with a muscle disease. Finally, she could only use one finger. She sat at her typewriter every day and wrote and everytime she hit a key she felt pain. But she wrote until she could not write anymore. Carson was heroic. Miss Rose loved her more, I think, than any of my other friends. Miss Rose called her 'C.' I don't know why.

"A few weeks before Carson died she came to New York by ambulance and took a suite here, at the Plaza. She invited all her friends to come by and say good-bye to her. She couldn't move by then.

"When she died, her lover, a black lady, lived in Nyack where I used to take Miss Rose to see Carson. Carson and I have the same lawyer, and I'm as frightened of her as was Carson. Floria Lasky.

"When Carson died, her body was placed in a sealed casket at the funeral home in Nyack. There was a viewing the day before the funeral. The casket was covered with a blanket of roses, and that night her lover's son came into the funeral parlor. In a rage he tore off the blanket of roses and tried to topple the casket to the floor, but he was restrained. You see, he had been jealous all those years that his mother had lived with Carson.

"My other great writer friend was Jane Bowles. I first met her in Acapulco in the summer of 1940, after I had broken up with Kip. I took a trip to Mexico on one of these share-the-expense plan tours. I went down with a Mexican boy who'd married an American hooker, you know? He met her at the World's Fair. The poor girl was terrified. She was a sweet girl, but she was a hooker and he didn't know it. And she'd come to my room at night and tell me they were having terrible problems sexually. I think he was gay, you know, because all the *other* men in the car were. That's a pretty good indication!" Tennessee laughed. "She said she wasn't getting any sex, and she thought I'd provide her with some.

"I said, 'I'm afraid, honey, it's not quite what I do anymore because, frankly, I'm homosexual.'

" 'Oh, that's all right,' she said, 'I know female hygiene is a lot more complicated!' God, I thought that was a funny answer!

"Apparently, their marriage worked out somehow. I left some of my gear in the trunk of the car, and several years later, after I'd become known, after *The Glass Menagerie,* she shipped it all back to me with a very lovely note.

"It was that summer in Mexico when I met Jane Bowles. I knew she was there with Paul. Poor Paul was always sick. He couldn't eat anything in Mexico. But there's very little in Mexico you *can* eat, at least not in those days. They were such a charmingly odd couple, I loved them both. Jane produced such a small body of work, but it was tremendous work. And Paul's work? I guess it's about as good as anything now."

In February, the Russian poet Yevtushenko arrived in New York to begin his American tour. Neither Tennessee nor I had ever met him, although we had enormous respect for him, which was prompted largely by the courage he displayed in the poem "Babi Yar," and in his criticism of the Warsaw Pact invasion of Czechoslovakia.

The week he arrived I met him at a party given in his

honor by Mr. and Mrs. H. J. Heinz. Their duplex apartment overlooked the East River. It was a large affair, many people from the arts invited, and yet curiously there were no representatives from Russian émigré groups, and except for myself, only one other writer. Perhaps that was not so odd, not so odd anyway as the connection between the Soviet poet and the Heinz family, certainly a premier dynasty among American economic royalists. Mrs. Heinz, called "Drue," was editor of the literary review *Antaeus*, which published pieces by Tennessee, and the Heinz family had given the city of Pittsburgh the concert hall where "Yevtushenko and Friends," his road show, was to be staged.

Warren Beatty and I rode the elevator to the Heinz apartment in the company of Yevtushenko and his "translator." The presence of the "translator" bothered me. I have seen enough visiting Russian cultural heroes to spot the KGB or the CIA in their omnipresent companions. I may be wrong about his "translator"; however, I have never seen Yevtushenko in New York without one on his heels, which increasingly struck me as ominous, since he spoke perfect English. In fact, it was only when the occasion suited him, usually at public readings and television interviews, that he fell into a thick, guttural, nearly unintelligible Russian-accented English. But that was part of the act.

Yevtushenko was dressed in a sweater and baggy trousers. He was a tall man, lanky, rather all-American farm boy in appearance as if he had just come in on the Greyhound from the Great Plains; his hair was light in color and cut Marine-short; his skin was very pale and rather pasty in texture. At the party he was melodramatic, loquacious, overbearing, intense, conceited, possessing enormous stamina and acute cleverness. People told me with amazement that he made do on very little sleep, drank heavily all night long, and rose early for long days of television appearances, poetry readings, interviews, and walking tours, only to finish the evening with more booze. A truly Siberian endurance. Around him I felt like a *Pravda* caricature of the dissipated, effete Westerner.

I asked Yevtushenko how it was that he was free to travel and speak out when so many of his fellow Soviet writers were confined in labor camps or "psychiatric" wards?

He replied by accusing me of having been produced in the same "anti-Soviet factory" as all the other anti-Communist critics.

"You Americans. It is so simple for you. You do not understand us. You know little about survival. I am the greatest poet in Russia! It is a difficult thing for the government to put *me* in jail. I am too *cunning.*" He tapped his head with his finger. He was sounding like a boastful Cassius Clay. In Moscow, he continued by way of illustration, he was stopped by a policeman for drunken driving. Instead of arresting him, the policeman implored him to drive home more carefully for the "little poet" was too precious to the Russian people to risk his life.

"But what about the imprisoned writers? What about the Jews?"

He squinted and then rested his hand on my arm. I was wearing a red SDS button with the words "Smash Imperialism" and a clenched fist imprinted on it. He fingered the button. "Smash imperialism, you see?" It was so simple. "That is Vietnam, my friend."

He never answered the question.

Later that night Warren Beatty said to him, "I think you're the greatest poet in Russia."

Yevtushenko was sitting at a round table eating. He looked up, visibly offended. "No, *du monde!* I am also the greatest living Russian actor! They want me to give a prize as the greatest actor. But the government says No, please, Zhenya, you cannot also have that! That is too much for us to give you. A prize for the greatest poet, yes, Zhenya. But as an actor, too? That would give you too much power, the people love you already too much!"

Zhenya was nothing if not modest.

One more note about the Heinz party. When Yevtushenko walked into the Heinz apartment, Drue informed him that they had imported Russian vodka on ice if he cared for some.

"Vodka!" he exclaimed, shocked. "*Champagne!* French! *Brut! Très brut!*" He seemed accustomed to giving orders. That was the commissar in him, I thought.

I called Tennessee the next day at the Hotel Élysée. He was in town for the production of his play *Small Craft Warnings*, and I knew he admired Yevtushenko and wanted to meet the poet, so I gave him a full, somewhat negative report.

"Do you think he can help me get my money out?" he asked, referring to the millions of rubles his work had earned in the Soviet Union but which he was prevented from taking out of the country by Soviet law. Off and on over the years he talked of going to Russia—the government had invited him to come as an official guest many times—but he always hesitated at the last moment because he really hated Russian totalitarianism as much as he hated the cold Russian winters, and he also felt, accurately, that his trip there would be misinterpreted, espe-

131

cially by Jews, as an endorsement of the Soviet Government. And, finally, Truman Capote had filled his head with horror stories about his time in Russia as a writer for *The New Yorker.* Nevertheless, Tennessee enjoyed musing about going there and using his rubles to buy dozens of sable coats, which he legally could do, and bringing them back to the States to make a killing reselling them.

When he learned I had met Yevtushenko, he hit on the idea that the poet could use Tennessee's money to buy the stuff and bring it home to Tennessee when he next visited America. It was obvious Tennessee didn't know the Russian.

"He will be sympathetic to another artist's financial requirements," he confidently assured me. "We poets stick together!"

So Tennessee got in contact with Yevtushenko and gave him free tickets to see *Small Craft Warnings* at the Truck and Warehouse Theatre in the East Village.

In his novel *Moise and the World of Reason,* Tennessee would write about this period in New York. One of the characters, the Big Lot, is me.

The next day, Sunday, Yevtushenko came to Tennessee's rooms, the Victorian Suite at the Élysée, to have lunch. He was about an hour late, something that angered Tennessee, and he was accompanied by a very fat, silent man whom he introduced as his interpreter, which seemed suspicious because, as I have said, the poet spoke impeccable English.

As soon as he walked into the door he launched into an attack on Tennessee's play.

"You put only about thirty percent of your talent into it, and that's not just my opinion but that of people seated around me," Yevtushenko declared.

In his *Memoirs,* Tennessee says he was distressed but kept his composure.

"I'm very happy to know," Tennessee replied, "that I still have so much of my talent left!"

Yevtushenko went on and on disparaging Tennessee's work, not an exercise he ever appreciated listening to from anybody.

Finally they went off to the Oak Room of the Plaza Hotel for lunch, and as they entered, Yevtushenko announced that he was a connoisseur of wines, a statement that set off the early warning system in Tennessee's billfold. He immediately proved he was a connoisseur, Tennessee recalled, by summoning the wine steward with imperious rudeness and ordering two bottles of Château Lafite-Rothschild at about eighty dollars a bottle, and a bottle of Margaux. Then he ordered an enormous bowl of beluga caviar, which ain't cheap, and the best pâté and steaks for himself and his husky interpreter.

Tennessee, horrified by the display of conspicuous consumption at his expense, called him a "capitalist pig!" and said, "Being a homosexual, I am very concerned over your [Russia's] treatment of my kind in your country."

"Absolute nonsense," Yevtushenko countered, "in Russia we have no homosexual problem!"

Tennessee gagged. "Oh, is that so! How about, say, Diaghilev, Nijinsky, or some of the other artists who have left the Soviet Union to avoid imprisonment for being one of my kind?"

"We have absolutely no homosexual problem!"

They drank more wine.

Tennessee brought up the subject of his Russian royalties. He was one of the two or three most popular American writers in the Soviet Union. The Communists liked to believe that his plays literally depicted the lives of everyday Americans debauched by the capitalist system.

Yevtushenko enviously told him that he was a millionaire in Russia and that he should come over and settle in the Fatherland and live like a king.

Tennessee declined.

When the bill came it was so large that it required three pages to itemize the costs. Tennessee was not at all amused.

A few days later, we attended the performance of "Yevtushenko and Friends" at Madison Square Garden's Felt Forum. The poet had urged Tennessee to attend and at the last moment he decided to brave it. It was a mistake.

It was one of the most appalling evenings in the theatre I have experienced, and I have been to a lot of bombs. Tennessee was equally bored because he slept soundly through much of it.

Most of the reading of the Russian's work was done either by Yevtushenko himself in his heaviest Russian accent, with his arms flailing the air, his voice rising and falling like a bear in heat, his eyes rolling heavenward, or by an English actor named, improbably enough, Barry Boys. Only Mr. Boys could outwail, outrumble, outweep Yevtushenko in the histrionics competition.

We left when the audience, punished beyond endurance, started to boo loudly.

Outside the theatre Tennessee was delighted he had come, and that the show had been such a complete embarrassment.

"And he thought *my* play was bad!" he said smugly.

I asked him what he thought of Soviet art after seeing the real thing in action?

"Soviet art? It is a contradiction in terms!"

Ten years later in Chicago, Tennessee thought back on his encounter with the "great" Russian poet and was still steaming about being stuck with the lunch bill.

"What's happened to him?" he wondered. "Is he still in favor with the Soviets? I remember when he was last in the States he asked me to have lunch with him. He ordered bottles of Château Lafite-Rothschild. And the bill was so tremendous it occupied three pages! I was stuck with it, of course. I told him he was a fucking capitalist pig!

"He was accompanied by this very fat gourmand of a translator who didn't translate anything," he recalled in anger. "And the alleged translator didn't understand a damn thing except how to eat and drink like a rich capitalist!

"I've heard a lot of people speak against Yevtushenko. I don't know how far he can be trusted, but he's charming in his way. If you can *afford* it!"

One last incident that I think illustrates the character of Yevtushenko as Tennessee and I came to understand it during his visit to New York.

Yevtushenko was dying to meet President Nixon, which says a lot right there. But it was no easy task. How was he to arrange it? By chance he learned that Senator and Mrs. Jacob Javits were giving a party for Henry Kissinger. Warren Beatty was among the invited. (Beatty was already on Yevtushenko's program as one of the "Friends," although Warren had the good sense not to appear at the Felt Forum.) Yevtushenko tried contacting Warren, and then he called Peter Glenville. Glenville reached Marion Javits and arranged an invitation.

When Yevtushenko entered the senator's Park Avenue apartment he stopped and glanced around the room and then announced in a loud voice, "There are too many god-damn Jews in here!" His remark was heard by at least six witnesses. No one rebuked him.

At dinner he sat himself beside Henry Kissinger and begged him for an invitation to the White House. The great Russian Communist removed his wristwatch and presented it to Kissinger, saying, "I give it with my deepest respect and love." Kissinger accepted it happily.

He got his White House visit.

Several weeks after the end of his American tour we were having dinner with one of the women closely involved in his visit to this country. "He is a clever man," she said, knowing him well. "He is tough and clever. And he despises us. He knew he could make an anti-Semitic remark at the Javitses' and get away with it. He knew he could go around the country attacking America and refuse to accept criticism of Russian oppression and the rest. His own stinking role in Russia. I guess it is because he senses we're weak. Good old American masochists. Oh, Christ, I bet the bastard's having a bloody good laugh on all of us. He'll go back to Russia and tell his cronies what bloody fools the Americans are, what saps. He comes over here and everyone lines up to kiss his Russian backside. It is too disgusting."

I spent an evening at the house of Joe Dallesandro, one of Warhol's superstars. Joe and Paul Morrissey shared the house, and with them I watched a replay of a show about Andy Warhol I had hosted for public television.

After the show the telephone rang and it was Tennessee asking us to meet him at Max's Kansas City bar, which was uptown from the East Village, where Joe lived. He was very insistent that I drag Joe Dallesandro along, since he was more than a little sexually intrigued by Joe.

Joe was nothing if not physically beautiful, with a handsome Italian face, a well-proportioned, muscular body, well endowed. He more than a little resembled the late Frank Merlo, and perhaps that was the real basis of Tennessee's pining for him. Joe came from a working-class Italian family in New Jersey, like Frank Merlo, and he was, if not well educated, certainly street smart. Before Warhol discovered him in the wilds of New Jersey, he had made some blue loops and done some soft-core porn. And yet there was to him, uncorrupted, a gentleness and sweetness of disposition that was utterly beguiling. When he wasn't making movies for Warhol (*Trash, Lonesome Cowboys*) or running errands, you could find him at the Factory, sweeping up the place, taking out the garbage, doing menial chores. He was like a member of Andy's household, and Warhol's relationship with him was like that of an indulgent father with a slightly delinquent son. Of the Warhol superstars, Joe lasted the longest and ended up having a credible, if unprofitable, film career.

Over the years Joe maintained Tennessee's affection and interest, and for a while he tried to interest movie producers in casting Joe in the title role of *One Arm*. It is, I believe, the only completed film script of his that has never been produced, probably because no Hollywood studio is willing to take a chance on a movie about a down-at-heels male prostitute who ends on Death Row. The story on which the script is based, was written after the success of *The Glass Menagerie*, when he fled to Mexico to escape the foul smell of success and lived in Mexico City, where he was happy for a time.

He wanted Paul Morrissey, who had directed Warhol's movies, to direct *One Arm*.

In 1975, Tennessee flew on the same plane with Dallesandro, Warhol, Rex Reed, Sylvia Miles, Maria St. Just, and others to the Venice Film Festival, where he was to be a judge of the competition. He stayed at the Hotel Excelsior on the Lido. He was nervous about the coming production of his play, *Out Cry (The Two Character Play)*, in New York, and its director, Peter Glenville, had told him that one of its stars, Genevieve Bujold, (the other was Michael York) had given a terrible reading and another actress would have to be found. Since Tennessee thought his entire career rested on the success of *Out Cry* in New York, as he would always view every Broadway production of his work, he was moving into panic, and so, naturally, he took it in mind to flee Venice as soon as possible and go with a traveling companion to Sicily and find that small farm with its goats and geese and live out what remained of his "leftover life."

One problem: he was temporarily between traveling companions, and if Sicily and the farm and goats and geese were to be realized, someone would have to materialize fast.

Depressed, he slept all afternoon in his suite at the Excelsior, the waters of the Adriatic gently slapping below his balcony windows. He swam at the Lido, wading far out before the water was deep enough. And then that evening he had drinks with Michael York and his wife Pat, of whom Tennessee was not very fond but "whom I'm always kind to, baby, because the poor creature had most of her stomach removed, elective surgery, I believe. She's afraid that Michael will leave her for someone thinner!" Tennessee joked.

Tennessee was doing his damnedest to ingratiate himself with Michael because he desperately wanted the British actor to star in *Out Cry*. The negotiations were still going on between York's agent and the play's producer, David Merrick, and Tennessee was afraid that one false move and all would be lost. His career hung on the play, like "a hat on a rack," and thus by extension, on York's agreeing to take the role.

They had dinner on the Gritti terrace, spaghetti con vongole, and Tennessee got mildly drunk on Frascati. Then they went on to the Lido to see York's new film, *Cabaret*.

They ended at the bar at the Excelsior, the Yorks and Marisa Berenson, and others, among them a producer whom Tennessee asked if he had any money. When the producer replied no, Tennessee said, "Then I'm not talking to you!"

Later Joe Dallesandro walked into the bar, and Tennessee's light lit up. *My traveling companion!*

He scurried over to Dallesandro and began talking of the beauty of Sicily, the goats and geese and that small farm with its siren call to him, and Dallesandro listened uncomprehendingly.

"I took his silence to be acquiescence," Tennessee told me. "I told him about how poor my health was, that I hadn't much time left before death knocked on my door. No, death never *knocks!* Death walks through the door, whether you want it to or not. I told Joe that I couldn't be alone and could he do a dying man a favor and come to my rooms in ten minutes to be with me until I slept. I only wanted the comfort of his presence, I said.

"Well, I rushed upstairs," he continued, laughing. "I quickly showered, brushed my teeth, I must have gargled an entire bottle of Listerine! And then I waited and waited in the dim light, a three-quarter moon above the balcony. There was a knock at my door. I threw it open. I was only dressed in a silk dressing gown. 'Joe!' I cried, as dramatically as I could, 'Joe! Hold me! I'm dying!' I fell backward in a swoon on the bed."

"What happened then," I asked him, "did he hold you?"

"Hold me? He came over and took my *hand*. I said, '*Hold me!*' and threw apart my arms. He held on to my hand, and said, 'I *am* holding you.'"

And that was that.

In New York, Joe, Paul, and I walked uptown to meet Tennessee in the backroom of Max's Kansas City bar. And someone at our table made a remark about Jim Morrison of the Doors dying in France, dying in a bathtub of a heart attack brought on by booze, or by booze and barbiturates, lying naked in the tepid water, dead in the house where he had gone to write.

The last time I saw him when he was not performing on stage was at the Bitter End coffeehouse in the Village. He was dressed in corduroy trousers, no underwear, a maroon wool shirt, and boots. He stood in the back next to me, and in the light from the stage where pop singer John Sebastian was performing, I could make out his long neck under the uplifted chin (*"I am the Lizard King!"*). But the handsome fallen angel's face was bloated, and sagged with fatigue under his high cheekbones, over his chin line; his eyes were puffed and bloodshot and narrowed (it was always his wide eyes that betrayed the tough-guy, street-boy pose, that gave the lie to his public image), and his belly hung over his belt like the belly of any other worn-out mick barfly. He was aging fast. Nearly my age, a few years on me, and I could see my future in Morrison, blurred, out of shape, the muscle tone gone in the swill of booze.

At Max's Kansas City we talked with Paul Morrissey, who had been with Jim Morrison on several occasions.

"What was he like at the end?"

"He was bewildered."

"Is that all?"

"He didn't know what he wanted. He went to Europe to be alone. It was too late then. He should have left three years before that."

Tennessee talked about death, and he suddenly seemed very sad, as if he had lost a friend, although Morrison wasn't a friend. He had only met him once, with me, at the Village Gate bar late at night. Morrison was there alone, quite drunk, and I brought him over to our table. Tennessee didn't know who he was. They talked of California, and how much they loved the sun.

At Max's, Tennessee asked, "What was he like?"

One of the boys at our table, thinking the question meant, What was he like in bed? answered, "Just another mick cock."

It made me angry that someone would speak of him like that. I told the kid to fuck off.

"Baby," Tennessee said, trying to calm me, "don't be concerned. Death is awful. But it's so *common.*"

Then Tennessee ordered another round of drinks. And started singing.

PART·TWO

There is the world dimensional for those untwisted by the love of things irreconcilable. . .

—HART CRANE

WHEN TENNESSEE WILLIAMS was seventeen, the year he had his breakdown in Europe, his first published story appeared in *Weird Tales*, a dime pulp. It began: "Hushed were the streets of many-peopled Thebes."

Then he won his first writing prize, twenty-five dollars, from *Smart Set* magazine: third place for an essay on the burning question "Can a Good Wife Be a Good Sport?"

He would later write more than fifty plays, among them *A Streetcar Named Desire; The Glass Menagerie; Summer and Smoke; The Eccentricities of a Nightingale; The Rose Tattoo; Camino Real; Cat on a Hot Tin Roof; Orpheus Descending; Suddenly Last Summer; Sweet Bird of Youth; Period of Adjustment; The Milk Train Doesn't Stop Here Anymore; The Night of the Iguana; Small Craft Warnings; Out Cry; This Property Is Condemned; Clothes for a Summer Hotel;* and his last, *A House Not Meant to Stand.*

He wrote screenplays, *Baby Doll* being the most successful.

A book of poetry, *In the Winter of Cities.*

Four collections of short stories, his memoirs, and two novels, *The Roman Spring of Mrs. Stone,* and *Moise and the World of Reason.*

He said, "I've always been blocked as a writer, but I love writing so much I always break through the block."

He won numerous awards, among them two Pulitzer prizes. He was honored by Kennedy Center for his lifetime achievement in the arts, was a fellow of the American Academy and Institute of Arts and Letters, and was given the Medal of Freedom by the President of the United States, the highest civilian honor the nation can bestow.

And when he died, he thought he was, like his father, a failure.

In July 1939, Tennessee was out of funds and reluctantly living in St. Louis. Then Louise Sillcox, the executive secretary of the Dramatists Guild, phoned him and said that he had received a grant of one thousand dollars from the Rockefellers to be paid to him in ten monthly installments. Once again, Miss Edwina nearly passed out in disbelief. Tennessee became something of a local celebrity, giving interviews to the St. Louis *Globe-Democrat* and the *Post-Dispatch*, the first of thousands of such interviews he would grant before his public life ended.

He borrowed bus fare from "Grand" and arrived in New York unshaven, tired, unbathed, and happy. He immediately walked to Audrey Wood's office to collect his first installment from the Rockefellers, found himself a small room at the West Side YMCA, where he could swim everyday. He soon took Theresa Helburn and John Gassner's seminar in playwriting at the New School in the Village. He worked desperately on a play, *Battle of Angels*, and got free passes or bought cheap tickets to every production on Broadway he could see.

February 1940, through the aid of Helburn and Gassner, both connected with the Theatre Guild, and with the help of Audrey Wood, *Battle of Angels* was optioned by the Theatre Guild, then the most prestigious producing organization in the American theatre. He was deliriously happy.

"The Sweet Bird of Happiness had just dropped another princely fortune on my head, and I hoped for more droppings in the future!"

The princely sum was one hundred dollars for the option.

While he continued to swim and write furiously, it was during this time in New York that he finally and irrevocably acknowledged his homosexuality. He began to cruise the bars in Times Square and the Village in search of sailors, who were plentiful then in New York. He would cruise with Donald Windham, nineteen, a boy from Atlanta, Georgia, who wanted to be a writer.

"I enjoyed cruising, more for Donald Windham's company, than for the pickups that were made," he told me. "After all, pickups are just pickups. But Windham was a delightful friend to be with. I always realized that he had a streak of bitchery in him. And that's why my letters to him had a great deal of malicious humor in them. I knew he liked that. And since I was writing to a person who enjoyed that sort of thing I tried to amuse him with those things. Of course, I didn't know he was *collecting* my letters! And I didn't know I was signing away the copyright."

In 1977, Donald Windham published *Tennessee Williams' Letters to Donald Windham: 1940–1965.* With coaxing from Truman Capote and Tennessee I wrote an essay for *London Magazine* reviewing the letters. The piece was critical of Donald Windham, and he responded with a lawsuit that was later settled out of court.

"I'm happy the letters were published because they're

beautiful, I think. I'm very *un*happy that he may have shut down *London Magazine* with that lawsuit," Tennessee said.

"There used to be a place in Times Square called the Crossroads Tavern, right near a place called Diamond Jim Brady's. The place was closing down, and on this occasion these big drunk sailors came and picked us up. We didn't pick *them* up. I wasn't attracted to them. I didn't want to, and I felt really uneasy about the situation. But Windham was always attracted to rough sailor types.

"As it happened, Windham was staying at the Claridge Hotel, which doesn't exist now, in the Times Square area. He had been living with a painter, Paul Cadmus. He was occupying a room with Paul Cadmus, and it was through Paul Cadmus that he met Sandy Campbell."

Sandy Campbell became and remained Windham's friend and companion.

"It had been inconvenient for Cadmus to have Donald Windham at his place one night, and so he'd gotten him a room at the Claridge. And Donald had taken the two sailors and me into Claridge's.

"I got more and more suspicious because in the lobby the sailors said, 'We'll go up the elevator, and you wait ten minutes, and we'll meet you in the corridor . . .' Or something like that. It seemed suspicious, but I was a little high, and so was Donald.

"We got up to the room, and it was really a bestial occurrence. I hated every minute of it. Finally, after they ripped the phones out of the wall, they stood me against the wall with a switchblade knife while they beat Windham, knocking a tooth out, blackening both his eyes, beating him almost to death. I kept saying, 'Oh, don't do that, don't hit him anymore! He's *tubercular!*'

"Then they said, 'Now it's your turn!' So they stood

poor, bloody Windham against the wall while they beat me nearly to death. I had a concussion from the beating. Next thing I knew I was at the emergency Red Cross station at the YMCA where I lived."

In the version of the story that Truman Capote told me, which he said was the way Tennessee used to tell it, the sailors, after beating the two young men up, tied them in chairs, robbed them, and left them sitting there after they left the hotel.

"They sat there for two days!" Truman recalled. "Finally a hotel maid discovered them and released them. When I asked Donald what it was like, he said it hadn't been all *that* bad because he and Tennessee had had wonderful literary discussions! But Tennessee said he was outraged because after they were freed the hotel charged them double occupancy for two days!"

Tennessee continued to cruise, something he loved to do all his life. Bars were about his favorite places on earth, and in every city he had particular watering holes that he frequented. In London, for example, he loved the bar at the Savoy, and Joe Allen's, Annabel's and Tramps. And he used to taxi up to Hampstead Heath to drink at King William's Pub, where the boys were. In Chicago it was the Pump Room, and in New York the Monkey Bar, Joe Allen's, the bar at the Sherry-Netherland and the Four Seasons. And for boys, the Haymarket, Cowboys and Cowgirls, and later Rounds, a saloon off Third Avenue that attracted an uptown clientele—well-dressed young men, often models, who were up for grabs and up for sale.

In July 1972, I was going to New Orleans to speak at a writers conference, and the day I left I had lunch with Tennessee. We were both hung over from my birthday party the night before. I asked him to give me the names of some bars in the French Quarter. "Good drinking bars, none of this fag stuff. A bar that seems straight where there are boys."

"Defeats in Exile," he mumbled into his wine, answering my question. "That's a good bar. It's open all night on Bourbon Street."

Open all night. Bingo! "Lovely name," I said, the romantic in me breaking forth in the redundant pity of that name, *both* the defeated and the exiled. "But what does it mean? Where does the name come from, Defeats in Exile?"

Tennessee glanced at me, shaking his head. "No, no, baby. Not *De*feats . . . it's *La*fitte in Exile. The pirate, you know? The pirate Lafitte. It has a fountain by the door with a flame burning in the center of it. Fire *and* water, baby."

"Yes. Blood and sperm." I quoted Rimbaud, playing to Tennessee's Verlaine.

"Uhh, it's a good bar, you know. The sailor bars are gone. That's where I used to drink. Now, when I'm in the Quarter, I drink at home. The Quarter, you know, is all gone down."

He did drink at home, but he also drank at LaFitte in Exile, with me.

I said that he came out as a homosexual in New York in 1939–40, but his first gay experience was in New Orleans in 1938. Before that he had had an abortive but deep love for a roommate during his sophomore year in college. Other than that he had had no homosexual encounters beyond "the sort of thing you get from going to movies and somebody gropes you, you know?"

In a 1981 interview in *Puritan* magazine, Tennessee recalled those years.

"Well, in New Orleans, in those days, they [gays] were pretty outrageous. In fact, one of my best friends carried with him a little cut-glass bottle containing smelling salts, liquid smelling salts, and whenever a woman passed him on the street—this was just camp, of course—he would open the bottle and appear to be fainting, and he would shriek *'poisson, poisson!'* ('fish'). Well, some queens who camp like that are really very funny. He made me howl with laughter. But after I went to New York and observed how people could be homosexual but not publicly noticeable, I remember coming back to New Orleans and telling them they'd have much more fun if they didn't behave that way.

"I tell you, there is a great deal of homosexuality in the South because Southern boys are usually very overattached to their mothers, or rather, the mothers are overattached to their sons. And that is conducive to homosexuality, I'm sure."

Tennessee came out on New Year's Eve 1938, in New Orleans. He had gone to a party given by heterosexual friends in an apartment overlooking Royal Street in the French Quarter. He stood with several friends on the gallery, as balconies are called in that city, and below him in another apartment a gay New Year's Eve party was going on. At midnight, when the fireworks went off and the church bells rang, he looked down and noticed a young man, a paratrooper, looking up at him.

"He grinned and he beckoned me down. Well, I couldn't shimmy down the pole on the railing, but I went down the back steps and knocked at the back door, and he opened it, and he said, 'You look so pale. Don't you want a sunlamp treatment?' Well, I thought he meant just my face, but he told me to take off everything. I got under this sunlamp; first thing I knew he was blocking me, you know. That was my first homosexual experience. It was very beautiful, and I wanted to continue the adventure. But he was going back—it was during the war years—he was going back to camp in the next day or two so I didn't see him again until many years later."

In the 1950s, when the paratrooper came to New York with his wife and children and waited outside a theatre to introduce them to Tennessee Williams, neither he nor the paratrooper, in that brief encounter, referred to the night in New Orleans long before.

"I still wanted him and I still remembered his body in the light of the sunlamp. But what could I do? He was with his wife and children, and I am not a home-breaker."

In the spring of 1940, while continuing to work on *Battle of Angels*, which the Theatre Guild now seemed certain to produce, he went up into the Adirondacks, to Lake George. Because it was too cold to swim, he spent his time hiking around the mountains.

In June, after briefly returning to New York, he went to Provincetown on Cape Cod, his first visit there. He rented a room and a bike, and claimed to be shocked by the open homosexuality of the resort's gay denizens. It could not have been too much of a shock because he bragged in letters that he was "fucking every night."

It was there that he met Kip, the first great male love of his life.

He first saw Kip on Captain Jack's Wharf, making clam chowder.

"He was wearing dungarees, skin-tight," Tennessee wrote, "and my good eye was hooked like a fish."

The iris of Tennessee's left eye had been clouded by a cataract.

"Kip was into modern dancing. And when he turned from the stove . . . I might have thought I was looking at the young Nijinsky. He had slightly slanted lettuce-green eyes, high cheekbones, and a lovely mouth. But I will never forget the first look I had at him, standing with his back to me at the two-burner stove, the wide and powerful shoulders and the callipygian ass such as I had never seen before!"

Two days later Kip invited him to move into his two-story shack on the wharf that Kip shared with a friend.

"The bedroom was a small loft with a great window that held in it all one half of the night sky.

"No light was turned on or off as Kip removed his clothes. Dimly he stood there naked with his back to me.

"After that, we slept together each night on the double bed up there, and so incontinent was my desire for the boy that I would wake him repeatedly during the night for more lovemaking. You see, I had no sense in those days of how passion can wear out even a passive partner."

In Kip's loft Tennessee wrote his only blank-verse play, *The Purification,* in which he tried to come to terms with a brother-sister relationship, an idea that had seized him and would lead him to create *The Glass Menagerie.*

One afternoon Kip rode Tennessee into downtown Provincetown on the handlebars of his bicycle and told him he had met a girl he loved who had warned him that he was turning homosexual, and Kip didn't believe he really was homosexual, not deep down, and so he didn't want to sleep with Tennessee anymore.

Tennessee never forgot Kip, never ceased being grateful that someone as beautiful as he, who could have had anyone he wanted, for a brief summer season had loved him and given him happiness. He carried snapshots of Kip with him until he lost them somewhere in the sixties. And he kept a photograph of Kip by his bedside wherever he went until finally that was taken in 1979 when Tennessee's house was broken into and ransacked in Key West. For some unknown reason the photograph that sat on his nightstand by his bed disappeared.

In 1981, when Tennessee was seventy, we sat together drinking in the Monkey Bar in New York and he talked about Kip, whom he still missed.

"Kip was very honest, and I loved him, and I think he loved me," he began, speaking quietly, not looking me in the eye. "He was a draft-dodger from Canada. He had a passion to be a dancer, and he knew he couldn't if he went into the war. It'd be too late, he felt, when it was over, for him to study dancing. You see, he was a boy of twenty-one or twenty-two when the war happened.

"I've written a play called *Something Cloudy, Something Clear* about Kip. The setting is very important in this play. It involves a bleached, unfurnished beach shack in which the writer, who represents me, but is called August, is working on a portable typewriter supported by an old crate. He sleeps on a mattress on the floor. Alongside that set is the floor of another beach-house shack that's been blown away in a hurricane. This floor, however, forms a platform on which Kip used to dance, practicing dancing to my Victrola. The subtitle of the play is *The Silver Victrola.*

"I prefer the title *Something Cloudy, Something Clear* because it refers to my eyes. My left eye was cloudy then because it was developing a cataract. But my right eye was clear. It was like two sides of my nature. The side that was obsessively homosexual, compulsively interested in sexuality. And the side that in those days was gentle and understanding and contemplative. So it's a pertinent title.

"Now this play is written from the vantage point of 1979, about a boy I loved who is now dead. The author (August) knows it's 1979. He knows Kip is dead, and that the girl Kip dances with is dead. I've invented the girl. Occasionally during the play the author onstage will make references that puzzle the boy, Kip, and the girl. But the author is the only one who realizes that it's really forty years later, and the boy and girl are dead, and he survives, still he survives. It happened in the summer of 1940, and it's a very lyrical play, probably the most lyrical play that I've done in a very long while.

"I would like Henry Fonda to play the role of August. He is an actor who possesses that quiet under which deep sorrow stirs.

"Kip died at the age of twenty-six. It was just after I completed my professionally abortive connection with MGM. The phone rang one day and a hysterical lady said, 'Kip has ten days to live.' A year before I had been told that Kip had been successfully operated on for a benign brain tumor.

"He was at the Polyclinic Hospital near Times Square. You know how love bursts back into your heart when you hear of the loved one's dying.

"As I entered Kip's room he was being spoon-fed by a nurse: a dessert of sugary apricots. He had never looked more beautiful, although the sugary syrup dripped from his mouth. His wife was there, too. They were calmly discussing taking a trip to the West Coast in a train compartment. Kip's mind seemed as clear as his Slavic green eyes.

"He asked me to sit in the corner so he could see me because with brain tumors the line of sight is affected. I sat there, wanting to leap up from my corner and embrace him, but I didn't.

"We spoke for a while. Then I rose and reached for his hand and he couldn't find mine. I had to find his.

"After Kip died his brother sent me, from Canada, snapshots of Kip posing for a sculpture and they remained in my wallet some twenty years. They disappeared mysteriously in the sixties. Well, Kip lives on in my leftover heart."

In the summer of 1940, when Kip broke with him, ending their sexual relationship, Tennessee went into panic and, typically, fled to New York and then to Mexico, the trip during which he met Jane and Paul Bowles and Leonard Bernstein, and rode around in a car full of gays with a female hooker, and learned to follow when he danced.

When he was down to his last dime, he desperately contacted his mother and the Theatre Guild and they sent him money to go home to St. Louis, where his father had bought the family its first house at 53 Arundel Place in the St. Louis suburb of Clayton.

On his return journey he read in the newspapers that Miriam Hopkins was considering the role of Myra in *Battle of Angels*.

In November, learning that Miss Hopkins, then a major Hollywood star, had signed to do his play and that Margaret Webster was slated to direct, Tennessee returned to New York for rehearsals. The play was to open in Boston, finishing its rehearsals there. It was to play there for two weeks, then have another tryout run in Washington, D.C., and finally open in New York.

Battle of Angels is about a sexually driven young writer who wears a snakeskin jacket and drives women wild with desire. He is fleeing from a rape charge, a fugitive on the lam, and he comes into a small Southern town and, in the very first scene, meets the community's richest girl, who seduces him. Later he gets a job as a salesman in a general store where he fits women with shoes (what else?) while he flirts with them. Finally he seduces the lonely wife of the old and dying owner of the store. She becomes pregnant, and in the last scene our hero is killed with a blowtorch. Later Tennessee was to rewrite *Battle of Angels* into *Orpheus Descending*, a heartrendingly beautiful play that in turn would become the movie *The Fugitive Kind*, starring Anna Magnani and Marlon Brando, one of his most moving films.

The night before New Year's Eve *Battle* opened in Boston, and it was a disaster. The audience was shocked by the open sexuality, and shocked by the scene where an artist paints the young writer as Christ. Finally, at the end of the play, when the blowtorch scene occurs, the theatre filled with smoke as the smoke pots malfunctioned, sending the audience fleeing to the exits.

As Tennessee and Audrey Wood walked across Boston Common to the Ritz Carlton Hotel there were several loud bangs, and Tennessee, knowing catastrophe when he saw it, said, "They're shooting at us!" thinking that audience and critics had taken up arms.

The play caused an immediate scandal in Boston, the critics denouncing it and the official city censor demanding the deletion of the painting of the writer-as-Christ and the watering down of the sexual tone of the work.

When the director informed him that the Theatre Guild was caving in before the censors and closing the play, Tennessee exclaimed, "But you can't do that! Why, I put my heart in this play!"

After a moment's pause, the director admonished, "You must not wear your heart on your sleeve for daws to peck at."

Tennessee fled again, this time to Key West.

"I chose Key West after my first professionally produced play opened in Boston in December 1940 and then closed after a two-week run with Miriam Hopkins, who was brilliant in it. The censors descended upon it and they cut so much that it was no longer worth continuing. So the Theatre Guild, who produced it, and I agreed to just close it in Boston because it didn't make sense anymore. Well, they gave me two hundred dollars [actually, it was one hundred dollars] and they said, 'Go someplace and rewrite it.' I wasn't about to clean it up, because I didn't think it was dirty. I thought it was erotic and passionate, you know. These things are not dirty to me at all.

"But I went down to Key West because I love swimming. It was January, and I had to go someplace where I could swim in the winter so I came down here because it was the southernmost point, and I was immediately enchanted by the place. It was so much more primitive in those early days and I was taken under the wing of an Episcopal clergyman's widow [Mrs. Cora Black, mother of Marion Vacarro]. She had the most beautiful house in Key West.

"It was solid mahogany, there were galleries around both floors, and she had a little shack in back. I spent the first night there in one of her regular rooms and I said, 'I can't afford these prices, Mrs. Black, so as much as I love the place, I'll find cheaper quarters.' She said, 'Look at that little shack back there. I think I could fix it up for you,' and she gave it to me for seven-fifty, seven dollars, fifty cents a week. And there were wonderful people here at the time. The poet Elizabeth Bishop, and Grant Wood, Arnold Blanch, the painter, and his mistress, Doris Lee." He fell in love with Key West, and returned again and again.

In December 1946, he drove with his grandfather Dakin in a white Pontiac down the Gulf Coast from New Orleans to Key West. They took rooms on the top floor of the Conch Hotel, at eight stories still the tallest structure on the island. There he finished the final version of *A Streetcar Named Desire.*

In the fall of 1949 *Streetcar* was bought by the movies for a half a million dollars. *Menagerie* was already sold to the studios. Elia Kazan agreed to direct, and Vivien Leigh and Marlon Brando, then unknown outside the New York theatre, were signed for the leads.

In October 1949, using part of the money from the movie rights to his plays he paid seven thousand dollars for a small frame conch house at 1431 Duncan Street in Key West. The house, like most of the older houses in Key West, had been brought over by barge from the Bahamas at the turn of the century, there being no suitable wood for building houses on the island. It had, like all conch houses, two rooms downstairs, and one up, one small bathroom, and a tiny kitchen. This small, humble place was to be Tennessee's home for the rest of his life.

During the winter of 1972, I first went to Key West to stay with Tennessee. From that day on, until his death, his house in Key West was my second home. Or perhaps my first, because I felt safer there, more loved, more alive than I did anywhere else. When he was there.

Since 1949 he had made many changes to the property. He had added a back bedroom for himself, and then bought the property adjoining his on Duncan Street, demolished a small shack there, and built himself a very deep, very large swimming pool. Then he knocked through part of his living-room wall, put in sliding glass doors, and built a small roofed patio outside. On the other side of the patio he had a studio built, and next to it a small guest house. Finally, in 1969, he had his tiny Pullman kitchen torn out and a large new kitchen built, one that had a stained-glass window and a cathedral ceiling. The entire compound was surrounded by a seven-foot-high white wooden fence. Around the pool he planted many coconut palms and other trees and foliage, which were lighted at night by colored spotlights.

The coconut palms were tall and stately, but they were hell during storms. The coconuts would fall and fill the pool; every few months some less than artful dodger got clunked on the head by one of the unguided missiles. Worse was when a hurricane hit the island, or a fierce gale. Then the coconuts became nature's howitzer shells, and if you were struck by one it could kill you. I went through two hurricanes with him, sitting in the house behind the closed wooden shutters, the glass doors taped with strips of masking tape, the palms firing a heavy barrage of nuts against the walls and tin roof. It never worried Tennessee one whit, but it scared the hell out of me.

At the front of the house was a small, lovely porch.

There used to be four cushioned wicker chairs there, made in the Bahamas, but in the seventies they were stolen, along with a lot of other things. It didn't matter, because we couldn't sit on the front porch anyway because of the tourists.

It was a common occurrence to hear tourists pounding at the front door at all hours demanding to be given a tour of the house or, at the very least, Tennessee's autograph. One morning I was leaving the house and discovered a French tour group, about a hundred people, lined in serried ranks on the porch and tiny front lawn while in front of them a photographer was taking their picture.

But many of the intrusions weren't as benign. I frequently called the police because strangers were standing outside the fence urinating on the lawn while they gave us the finger. Often groups of boys, usually teenagers, drove by the house shouting, "Get out of town, cocksuckers!" This sort of cruel and unwanted attention dramatically increased in the late seventies, when antihomosexual hysteria, fueled by born-again preachers, swept the island. Then Tennessee's house became an object of derision.

In 1979, late one night, unknown assailants fired shotguns at the house.

That same year, Frank Fontis, Tennessee's caretaker, was murdered by shotgun fire at point-blank range.

That year the house was ransacked twice.

That year Tennessee and I were assaulted on Duval Street in downtown Key West.

That year, for the first time, Tennessee fled Key West because he was frightened.

If you faced the house, to the left, in a rose garden, was a small white gazebo with its own ceiling fan. The fan didn't work, and in 1979 somebody stole the rosebushes. And that was it for the rose garden.

When you entered the house you stood in a tiny hall; before you were the stairs to the second floor. To your right was the downstairs guest bedroom, a small space with a double bed, a four-drawer bureau, and a closet. This was the room where Tennessee's boyfriend at any given moment would stay because it shared the bathroom with his bedroom and thus there could be, and was, movement between the two bedrooms without anyone being the wiser.

The living room was to the left, with windows looking out on the front lawn and the side garden, and french doors opening onto the patio and swimming pool.

On the wall at the front of the room was a portrait of Tennessee, in oils, done by a French painter who found himself in Key West in the 1960s and asked to paint the playwright. It was a strange picture, very unsettling; Tennessee, his face distorted by pain, his eyes anguished, stared out at the room in agony. "It is a true likeness of my soul then," he explained, when I asked if we could take it off the wall and shut it up in a closet. "It was painted during the dark years, when I was on drugs."

Tennessee was often painted by artists who would show up uninvited and ask if he would sit for them. He usually obliged because he was a painter himself—his paintings sold for between fifteen hundred and four thousand dollars, depending on their size—and was constantly searching for new models.

Many writers I know are painters. Kurt Vonnegut paints clownlike faces. Mailer does pen or pencil portraits.

Truman Capote used to make small, Joseph Cornell-like boxes with little scenes inside them.

Tennessee was very serious about his painting. He painted all the time in Key West, and when he finally got his own apartment in New York, he started painting there too. He always painted in pastel oils on standard cardboard canvases he bought at the art shop. He thought he painted realistically, that what he painted actually looked like he painted it. Many of his paintings told stories, but they always contained a human figure, oddly disproportioned and distorted, something in the manner of El Greco. I don't mean to compare his amateur work to that of the great Spanish master—I simply mean that his figures were strangely astigmatic. Perhaps, like El Greco, Tennessee's work was almost surreal because his eyesight was so lousy.

By the late seventies he discovered that he could sell his paintings faster than he could sell his writing, and he began churning them out like sausages, thinking he might have stumbled on a second, lucrative career.

There were other art works in the living room picked up here and there around the world: an enormous picture made up entirely of autumn leaves; a painting of roses by Henry Faulkner; and a few photographs.

The living room was small, as were all the rooms. In one corner was a large television in a walnut console. There was a wicker sofa, its pillows covered in yellow cotton, and a wicker glass-topped coffee table, with two wicker armchairs on the other side, facing each other.

The small bookshelf contained few of Tennessee's books. In fact, there were only four or five of his own books in the house. When I asked him why, he said, "I wrote it. I don't have to read it."

The real reason is that books of his were usually stolen by visitors.

The living room was carpeted in straw matting. The draperies were royal blue, the walls painted cream.

At the end of the room was a wrought-iron glass-topped dining table and six wrought-iron chairs. Against the back wall was a breakfront with a few martini and highball glasses, none matching the others, some books and photographs. In its lower shelves were several hundred phonograph records, none later than the 1950s. And there was a stereo record player that was usually on the blink.

To the right, next to his bedroom door, was a small desk, with telephone, notepaper, and pencils. On it was his favorite photograph of his favorite poet, Hart Crane.

With the exception of the living room, all the floors in the house had linoleum tile.

Tennessee's bedroom was large in comparison with the others. It was painted white. He had a king-size bed that sort of sank in the middle. To the left was a bookshelf stuffed with books, and on either side of the bed were two nightstands on which he spilled his pills. Against one wall was a bureau of drawers. On it was a lamp and a large bowl in which he dumped his pocket change. He always knew exactly how much change had accumulated in this non-interest-bearing account, and he would count it every few days and if there was more than a dollar in quarters missing, God help us.

His closet had a lock on it because, in addition to his clothing, he hid booze, pills, and his porno picture books there.

Opposite his bed was the altar. He could see it when he went to sleep and when he awoke. It was a folding card table with a pale pink tablecloth. On it was a curious assembly of objects: a Madonna and child over which he had placed a lavender veil; a brown ceramic Hindu god, perhaps Vishnu; a vigil candle; and a photograph of Miss Rose. He sometimes prayed here, when he was frightened or lonely, and he was very particular about the placement of the objects on the table, as if in the spatial relationship among them magic lived.

The back wall of his room was a sliding glass door that opened onto a tiny garden, a portable fountain that didn't work anymore, and the doghouse.

If you entered the kitchen, for which he paid forty thousand dollars in 1969, about ten times what it was worth then, and went through the sliding glass doors, you came out onto the covered patio. It contained six canvas director's chairs; a small, round marble table on a white wrought-iron stand; three wicker armchairs. When I first came down it also had a large parrot, a really vicious creature, that spent its days inside a large bird cage that hung from the aluminum roof. Later Tennessee gave the parrot to Leoncia McGee, his housekeeper since 1949, and Robert Carroll built a bird cage, about five feet by five feet, in which lived an assortment of budgies.

There were always a few cats about the place, a bulldog, and lots of chameleons.

At the foot of the pool were two small structures, the guest house, with no electricity or plumbing but with two bunk beds, and Tennessee's studio.

Inside the studio, which was about ten feet by fifteen, was a long writing table, really a door-size piece of wood with legs. On it was his Royal portable typewriter. There was a cot, whose sheets were rarely changed, filing cabinets, a few posters of his plays, a large photograph of

Frank Merlo, and one of himself. There was a bath with shower. Since Tennessee didn't like people snooping about his studio, which was always kept locked, the place was filthy, with manuscript pages all over the floors, empty wine bottles, discarded books and letters. It was a hell of a mess, but since the only natural light came from a ceiling skylight, itself dimmed with soot (the window was kept securely shuttered) you didn't actually notice how dirty the walls and floors were. He really didn't give a damn.

My bedroom was upstairs. A tiny space, painted white, with a single bed, and a wicker writing table and chair. There was a small bureau next to the bed used as a nightstand, and a half closet. Over the years I stored many things at the house—clothes, manuscripts, cameras, a typewriter, and so on. I felt at home. There was a landing at the top of the stairs, and opposite my room was a large bath and toilet, only the water pressure was so weak it took about an hour to fill the tub.

The first time I stayed in that room I was working on a novel that would take me almost ten years to write, although I didn't know it then. I used to read pages of it to Tennessee as I wrote it, wanting his criticism and advice. He was a terrific critic of writing because he had an instinctive sense of the natural structure of a work, like an architect. And of course he was a genius at plot and character and the poetics of language, with an absolutely perfect ear for speech.

"No," he would say, "people don't talk that way."

When I would protest that it was verbatim dialogue, thinking I had him, he would say, "Baby, don't write how people talk. Write how we *think* they talk. It is what we think we hear, not what they actually say, that sounds true."

After he had read a few chapters of my novel, he said, "Do you have a title for the book?"

I said no.

"Well, what's the novel about?"

I answered that it was about all the people we knew.

"A novel about *everybody* we know?" He rolled his eyes. He thought a moment. "Call it 'Perverted Feelings, Mutilated Souls!' "

I called it *Beau Monde*. His title was better.

Tennessee loved telling stories. One afternoon in Key West we were watching television. He often did that in the afternoon; after he had worked in the morning and then had lunch, in that period before he napped he watched television to wind down. He would turn the set on, pull one of the wicker armchairs around closer to the set, and watch whatever happened to be on, a soap or game show, whatever.

Key West had cable television then; it was the only way you could receive a picture, and the system was owned by two old Baptist ladies who had very decided views on what was proper entertainment on their video system. As a result, often during the middle of a movie, either out of boredom or censorship, they'd switch channels and instead of the movie you were enjoying you found yourself watching some TV evangelist Bible thumping or an old "I Love Lucy" rerun.

On this particular afternoon we were watching the matinee movie coming from Miami. It was *Boom!*, the film made from Tennessee's play *The Milk Train Doesn't Stop Here Anymore.*

He wrote *Milk Train* in Key West in 1962 during a very difficult time in his life. He had come down to the island after the opening of *The Night of the Iguana*, a hit, but he was exhausted after months of rewrites and, more critically, having to deal with Bette Davis, *Iguana's* star, who was an immensely difficult personality to contend with. She fought with the director, with other actors, with Tennessee.

Moreover, he had broken with the greatest love of his life, Frank Merlo, and he knew it was downhill from now on. He was very lonely.

He did the first draft of the play in 1962, and then rewrote it again and again over the next year, devoting two years of his life to the drama. The play concerns the aged Sissy Goforth, the all-powerful empress of her own island, which is joined to Italy by a goat path. One day, along that path, comes a poet and sculptor, Chris Flanders, a gigolo. He is also an agent of death, having appeared on the scene at the deaths of a number of other rich old women. There is also an ancient marchesa, the Witch of Capri. Tennessee referred to the play as "a sophisticated fairy tale." It is a play about power, about sex and death. Much of the writing is glorious.

The world premiere of *Milk Train* was mounted by Gian-Carlo Menotti at Spoleto. Hermione Baddeley played Sissy Goforth. It was a great success. Tennessee then rewrote it. It opened briefly in New York, but there was a newspaper strike and so Roger Stevens, the producer, closed it.

In November 1963, *Milk Train* opened again on Broadway, this time starring Tallulah Bankhead and Tab

Hunter. Tallulah and Tab Hunter, to put it mildly, did not get along. And she was drinking too much. Tennessee thought that the liquor and pills Goforth kept on stage as props were real.

I was at the theatre opening night, and it was one of the strangest premieres I have ever attended. Tallulah looked like absolute hell, and she was so weak she couldn't project her voice beyond the first few rows. She kept improvising lines because she couldn't remember the ones in the script, and the lines she did remember she shot out in a maddeningly fast stream, trying to get to the end as quickly as possible. I understood about every fifth word. On top of that, she and Hunter constantly tried to upstage one another, but Tallulah, being an old pro, won on points. The audience was impatient and impolite, laughing at the wrong places, the crowd largely Tallulah's gang of camp followers. I remember in one scene, where Tab Hunter, distraught, pulls his hands through his hair, some old queen in the audience shouted out, "Mary! She's going *bald!*"

Milk Train closed in New York after five performances, and Tennessee returned to Key West only to find that his house had been opened to the paying public as a tourist attraction. He hid out in his studio.

He could never seem to let go of *Milk Train*. It was turned into the movie *Boom!* starring Elizabeth Taylor and Richard Burton, with Noel Coward, of all people, playing the role of the Witch of Capri. *Boom!* is without question one of the landmarks of Hollywood miscasting.

At the end of his life Tennessee was again working on *Milk Train* with an eye toward turning it into a musical. He even had discussions with the composer Sammy Cahn about writing the music. Luckily, it was stillborn.

In Key West we were watching *Boom!* on the tube, and Tennessee was almost glowing with pleasure as he watched this box-office turkey flicker across the little screen. During the first commercial break he told me how proud he was of both the play and the movie, considering them his definitive statement on imperialism. The whole play, he explained, was an anti-imperialist, antifascist parable. To this day I still do not understand his explanation. The critics, he reasoned, mauled the play, in its various incarnations, and the movie because the ruling class lay awake at night terrified by the subversive power of *Milk Train*.

During each commercial break, the local announcer on the Miami station appeared and, between selling tires and termite protection, he offered prizes to the viewers who called in and correctly named which actor played what, where the movie was set, who directed, and so forth.

Halfway through the movie, as Tennessee and I sat there engrossed in this anti-imperialist masterpiece, he cackling from time to time, there was another commercial break and the announcer rather sheepishly came before the camera and said, "I want to apologize to our viewers for showing *Boom!* I had never seen it before, and I had no idea it was this bad." He giggled. Tennessee winced. "Please don't call the station to complain. Don't call. All the lines are busy. But if you can sit through this dog, tomorrow we will be showing a really, really terrific movie . . ." And he named some ghastly John Wayne war epic.

Tennessee was outraged. "Those goddamn bastards! How dare he say that about my movie! It's the greatest movie ever made, the best performance Miss Taylor and Mr. Burton ever gave!" He wandered around the living room shouting obscenities, raining down anathema on the TV station, the station owners, the critics, damn the whole ungrateful world.

Finally, still piqued, he went to the telephone and called Miami, only to discover that the station's phone lines were tied up. "This is Tennessee Williams, and this is an emergency!" he shouted. They put him through.

The station manager wouldn't take his call, so he irately told the operator that he was not about to stand for being publicly insulted in his own house by a bunch of yahoos, that the station would be hearing from his lawyers and the manager could go fuck himself! He hung up, and went back to watching his movie, but it had kicked the pleasure out of him.

That night we got drunk, too drunk to cook, and went off to the Queen's Room for dinner. The Queen's Room is a pretentious, overpriced restaurant in a motel on the water in Key West. Its decor is more appropriate to a San Juan whorehouse than a dining room, and it possesses a staff that is insufferably obsequious in the most insincere way possible. But Tennessee liked the joint because there was never anybody else there but us, since it was not the kind of establishment that has repeat business. And Miss Rose liked it because it reminded her of Buckingham Palace.

Tallulah Bankhead was in his heart that night, and over dinner and after dinner over drinks he talked about her. He loved her, and he never fully understood why she wouldn't speak to him anymore in the last years of her life.

"I know Tallulah was upset because I didn't cast her

in *Boom!* She had really originated the role on Broadway because there were no newspapers being published when Hermione [Baddeley] did it in New York. That may have been a blessing in disguise!" He laughed. "Tallulah worked as hard as she could, but she was beyond carrying a Broadway play by then. She worked hard when she wasn't drunk, which means she did not work much.

"We used to play bridge together. She was the best bridge player in the world. It was because of her that I began to take rooms in the Hotel Élysée, where she always stayed while in New York.

"Shortly before she died, I don't remember the year, she was performing at some hotel in Miami Beach with a bunch of muscle men. She had become a parody of herself, baby, but I suppose she needed the money. Miss Bankhead," he continued, "learned that *Boom!* was playing in Key West. She had never seen the film, although she was furious she had not been cast as Goforth in it. She hired a car and was driven from Miami to Key West, went to the movie, and then was driven to my house. She knocked on the front door. When I opened it and saw her standing there in a long mink coat, I shouted, 'Tallu, baby! Come in!' She didn't move. She just stood there glaring at me like a mongoose at a snake. And then she said in her gravelly voice, loudly enough to wake the dead, 'Mr. Williams, I have come to tell you that I have just seen that *dreadful* movie they made out of your *terrible* play!' " Tennessee laughed. "And that was the last time I ever saw her."

He said that when she was doing *Milk Train* with Tab Hunter she was continually being asked at parties if Hunter was gay.

"Well, she finally got fed up with the question, and one night some old queen asked her again if Tab was queer. Tallulah looked him squarely in the eye, and replied, 'How would *I* know, darling? He never sucked *my* cock!' "

Tennessee met Tallulah Bankhead in the forties, after *The Glass Menagerie* but before *A Streetcar Named Desire*. He had always admired her immensely, not only her talent, but her wit and outrageousness, her honesty, and her refusal to give a good goddamn. Once, listing the six "great men" of the theatre he had been privileged to know, he numbered her among them. He had wanted to cast Tallulah as Blanche in the original production of *Streetcar*. Irene Selznick had vetoed it. He had also wanted her to star in *Boom!*, contrary to what she believed. Jack Warner had vetoed that because he was afraid of her drinking, explaining, "Errol Flynn is a drunk. One is enough!"

In 1953 a new production of *Streetcar* was to be done in New York at the City Center, Herbert Machiz directing. Tallulah was living then in a beautiful townhouse on East Sixty-second Street, and Tennessee asked her to play Blanche. She accepted with delight.

The rehearsals were held in Miami, where the play was to have its pre-Broadway tryouts at the Coconut Grove Theatre. Within the first days of rehearsals, Tallulah and Tennessee were exasperated with each other, arguing over interpretation of the role, each trying to one-up the other on the basis of a more authentic Southern background. And Tallulah was Southern to the tips of her false eyelashes, being the daughter of one of the most distinguished and powerful of all Southern families, a true American patrician. And that very fact drove Tennessee to distraction because he thought she was playing Blanche as a real aristocrat rather than as Southern white trash with illusions of aristocracy.

He gave her an expensive black leather handbag from Mark Cross. She flung it at him, shouting, "A lady *always* travels in brown. But I suppose it's impossible for you to understand what a lady is!"

On opening night in Miami she gave a beautiful performance. By then she had become a camp figure, and the audience howled with laughter throughout the play, and Tallulah, who manfully did her best, was helpless before their hilarity. It shattered her.

When she asked Tennessee if she was his best Blanche, he looked away and finally said, "No, baby. You were the worst." And she agreed.

Tennessee went to New York to take in her performance at City Center, and again the play was destroyed by her gay camp followers who howled and laughed and shouted out cracks throughout the performance. He wept for her.

In the Queen's Room in Key West he said he had never heard a woman swear as much as Tallulah, nor met anyone who was funnier or more brazen.

"She was staying at the Élysée with her last husband, a young actor she had recently married. A group of us were over playing bridge, and everyone was complaining that her husband was stupid, untalented as an actor, and that she could do a lot better in the state of matrimony, you know. Well, Tallulah took offense, and told us to come into the bedroom where this gentleman was sleeping. She stood at the side of the bed. She was furious. '*Why* did I marry him, darlings?' She ripped the covers off his naked body, and pointed at his big cock. '*That's* why I married him!'"

He talked about Louis B. Mayer building a high wooden fence around her bungalow at the Garden of Allah hotel in Los Angeles because she refused to stop douching with a garden hose on the front lawn; about the young woman reporter who came to interview her for *McCall's* magazine. When the girl arrived at the Élysée, Tallulah opened the door, completely naked, fell to her knees, put her head under the terrified girl's dress, and then stood up and informed her, "Darling, with a mouth like that you ought to take up singing!"

Tennessee went on talking about her, missing her. He spoke of her kindness to Leoncia McGee, her generosity, the waste of her talent burnt out by pills and booze. She chain-smoked, and when the doctors told her she would have to give up cigarettes, leave New York, and move to the desert or her emphysema would kill her, she said, "I would rather die, darling." And she did.

"She had an awful time with men. Always falling in love," Tennessee said. "I don't believe she really liked sex very much. What she loved was being adored, and since gay men adored her more than anyone she surrounded herself with them, flattered them by her attentions. I loved her very much. I think she was one of only two or three actresses I really loved."

Tennessee loved bulldogs, particularly Gigi, a miniature Boston bulldog with the most poignant eyes. The one exception in breed was Satan, an enormous black Belgian shepherd, a dog Frank Merlo loved. Alas, Satan was a one-man dog, and his man was Frank. During the tryouts of *The Night of the Iguana* in Detroit, Frank, at Tennessee's request, came up from Florida with Satan in tow. One morning, while Frank was in the bathroom, Satan attacked Tennessee, who was lying in bed. He bit into his ankles, cutting him to the bone. He might have killed him if Frank hadn't pulled him off him. Satan was put to sleep. And it was back to bulldogs.

Of them all, Gigi was his favorite. He lived eighteen years, feeble and nearly blind at the end, barely able to walk to his water dish, his hair falling out in clumps, gasping and wheezing through the day like a fire bellows, but Tennessee loved him. I learned the depth of that love when I first flew to Los Angeles with Tennessee, who had studio meetings. We were to have dinner that night with George Cukor, a friend of both of us.

When we arrived by limousine at Kennedy, Tennessee gave me the tickets, two first class, one tourist, and wandered off to the bar with Gigi while I checked us in.

When we boarded the plane, I carrying Gigi's traveling case, the little dog gasping inside, Tennessee took his seat in first class.

I inquired where was Gigi to go, was I to strap her case to a seat in tourist?

He glanced up at me, truly surprised. *"Tourist?* Gigi sits next to *me. You* are in tourist."

He missed dinner that night at Cukor's, claiming that Gigi was too ill to attend. So I went alone, and it was not pleasant. Alan Searle, W. Somerset Maugham's old lover, was a guest, along with some semiretarded youth Alan had flown in from Chicago for the occasion. And Christopher Isherwood and his companion, Don Bachardy, completed the group. Isherwood and I got into a heated argument over gay rights, and he called me a cowardly sonofabitch, as I remember, and said, "Get out of my house at once! I order you to leave!" And Cukor had to remind him that the house was *his.*

When I returned to the hotel I was very much upset

about the contretemps with Isherwood. I told Tennessee what had happened.

He said, "Oh, baby, Chris is getting mighty old. You have to forgive him his snits.

"You know, I met him in the forties in California. At the time he was into Vedanta, an Eastern religious thing. He was living in a monastery. They had periods of silence and meditation, you know. The night I met him, through a letter from Lincoln Kirstein, I arrived during one of these silent periods. The monk who opened the door handed me a pencil and paper to write what my business was and who I'd come to see. I wrote 'Christopher Isherwood,' and they regarded me with considerable suspicion from that point on.

"In this big room in the monastery, everyone was sitting in . . . what do they call it? The lotus position? Including Christopher. All strictly observing the vow of silence. I didn't dig the scene.

"I suddenly made some reference out loud about Krishna. I didn't know who the hell he was, I was only trying to break the silence. Christopher got up and wrote on a piece of paper, 'I'll call you tomorrow.' He was very polite, and he took me to the door.

"He's a superb writer, and I haven't a clue why he went through this period in a monastery. I think it was a period of unhappiness in his life. I think his love affair with Bill Caskie was breaking up, and he had not yet found Don Bachardy. He was intensely lonely. So he went into this monastery that had this vow of silence and poverty.

"I found Chris terribly attractive, not so much in the sexual way, but as a person. Charismatic. Brilliant. And one of the greatest gentlemen I've known. So, being attracted to him, I declared myself.

"Then I found out that another one of the vows they took in this place was sexual abstinence! Christopher said to me, 'Tennessee, it's perfectly all right if I submit *passively* to oral intercourse, but I cannot perform it. I'd be breaking the vow!' I howled with laughter, and so did he. Then we cemented our friendship."

Tennessee blamed a traveling companion, a young man I'll call David, for Gigi's death. David had been a lover of mine, and had become an occasional companion of Tennessee's after we were no longer an item, as they say in the columns.

When I first met Tennessee, David was my boyfriend, and one night Tennessee came down to his apartment on Waverly Place in the Village to have dinner with us. David was a handsome kid from California. I met him at a party in New York. I was taken with David immediately. We had a few drinks together, and he told me that he was an artist and was having great difficulty getting work. At the time I was contributing editor to *Evergreen Review*, a literary magazine. "If you call me," I told him, "I will try to throw you some work." He called, and we became friends, and one thing led to another, or rather to bed.

At dinner Tennessee was stoned on some drug, looked absolutely deathly, proceeded to get drunk, and finally passed out on the kitchen table, an inadvertent unconsciousness that frightened and appalled David. It took a good while until he was willing to see Tennessee again.

When I met David he was the lover of a movie star, although I didn't know it then, and the three of us lived through a kind of French farce with me hiding in the kitchen when the star arrived—I didn't know who he was, because David wouldn't let me out of the kitchen until his "business meeting" was over—and vice versa. David, who was very clever when it came to sex and money, had both the star and me paying his rent, each without the other's knowledge. The scam worked until I ran into the star at a party, and he said, "This is becoming a joke. David is playing both sides against the middle."

The star later took David with him to France for the filming of a movie. When David came back to the States I found in his apartment a number of sexual photographs that had been taken in France of him with the star in sado-masochistic poses. I had loved David, and I was deeply angered by what I saw. I no longer liked the star much after that.

Anyway, Tennessee got to know David through me, and when I wasn't in New York and Tennessee was—this was during the Vietnam years—David would stay with him at his hotel. They had casual sex together, and that didn't bother me until I began to sense that Tennessee was moving in a little too strongly. I got jealous, not a feeling I especially like.

In May 1973, Tennessee was staying at the Hotel Élysée, and David and I went to see him. It was a Friday, a lovely, sunny spring day in New York. I was to leave that afternoon for Washington to participate in the May Day demonstrations against the war, protests that would paralyze the city and result in thirteen thousand arrests, my own among them. I didn't want to leave David behind with Tennessee.

The three of us went to a bar for a good-bye drink. Tennessee was very mournful and tried very hard to convince me not to leave for Washington, saying that I was certain to be a casualty of the fascist Nixon.

"You'll never come back alive, baby. You're on the hit list of those to be eliminated." But he protested too much, like Br'er Rabbit. He was talking a lot of rubbish. "And when you are martyred, who'll take care of me? You know I can't be alone, baby. Not with my bad heart."

David, rather too quickly, volunteered to stay with him, bad heart and all.

I told Tennessee that this was between the two of us, and David should butt out.

David moved a few feet away from us, and I reiterated to Tennessee something he knew only too well, that David was my lover and I didn't think it was sporting of him to try and take him away from me.

"Baby, I can't be alone!" he wailed.

I was angry. "Do you know the Bible, Tenn?"

"Of course I know the Bible. My grandfather was an Episcopal cleric!"

"Do you know the books of Samuel?"

He said yes, he knew them well.

I then pointed at him and shouted, "THOU ART THE MAN!" I thought I did it rather well.

His eyes filled with tears, and I turned on my heel and walked out, feeling as self-righteous as a Klansman burning a really good cross.

The phrase, of course, comes from the story of King David sending Bathsheba's husband to the front lines with secret instructions that he be placed where he was certain to be slain, because King David lusted after Bathsheba, and was determined that she be his, even though he already had God knows how many wives and concubines. When the old prophet Samuel got wind of this grievous treachery, he went to King David, and said, "Mighty King, there has been a grave injustice. A man with many sheep has killed a poor man with only one sheep and stolen that sheep."

David's ire rose, and he demanded of the prophet the name of the man so that he could have him killed. The Prophet Samuel pointed an accusatory finger at the king and said, "Thou art the man!"

Back to Gigi. Years later David, Tennessee, and Gigi flew to San Francisco for an opening night. David was to take care of Gigi, but he, being the promiscuous tart he has always been, had tricks coming in and out of his room at all hours. The dog tended to get in the way during the rush hour in sexual traffic. David locked the poor beast in a large closet. Shortly after their return East, Gigi gave up the ghost, and Tennessee was distraught. He concluded those hours of confinement in a dark closet had done the dog in.

When Tennessee returned to New York he called me up. I was living at the Dakota then. It was very late at night, and I was impossibly drunk. Another close friend of mine had bitten the dust, making sixteen who had died of drug overdoses, suicide, disease, or accident in three years.

When the phone rang I had been sitting alone drinking vodka for hours and feeling sorry for myself and trying to figure out how I could get a hold of some Seconal at two in the morning.

"How are you, baby?" Tennessee asked, his voice very tired.

It was the wrong question to ask. I poured out my story, mourned my dead friends, complained my rent was due and I didn't have any money, couldn't get to sleep without a pill and my apartment was as pill-free as the Sahara. I went on and on.

About fifteen minutes into my whine, Tennessee

started to cry. His sobs turned into wails. I became alarmed, despite the fact that I was quite pleased that my tragic litany had moved him so forcefully to tears. I started to backtrack, explaining that, well, I was not all *that* close to my departed friend, I was sure I could get up the rent money somewhere, the New York *Times* owed me a check (the *Times* seemingly *always* owed me a check), I was positive I'd pass out soon and the pill would be irrelevant.

"But you don't understand," he explained through his tears, "I'm not crying for you. My *dog* died!"

Dogs. His last dog was a huge bulldog he named Cornelius, out of spite for his father. This dog was the most godawful creature ever inflicted on man. The animal stank to high heaven, had foul breath that would kill any living thing within five feet of his mouth—we once poured Listerine into his water dish thinking that might be a solution. It didn't work. I then suggested we try oven cleaner. Tennessee balked at that. We stayed with the mouthwash, but it only made Cornelius fart more. That dog had enough gas in him to light the state of New Jersey.

We could never housebreak him, and did we try! That dog had his nose rubbed in shit more times than Nixon. And he shat his weight in dung every day. Every day I was picking up dog shit off the living-room carpet, which was made of woven straw so you could never completely get the crap out. I poured Lysol on the spots, used airsprays, perfume, finally sprayed the entire carpet with Final Net hairspray thinking that would act as a sealant and prevent Cornelius's valentines from seeping into the material. Nothing worked. One day I spread newspapers over the entire living-room floor. Tennessee made me take them up because he was spending hours a day at the dining table, hidden behind fifteen thousand frontispiece galley pages of a special Franklin Mint edition of his plays, and he had to sign each and every page to get the fifteen thousand bucks payment. He claimed the newspapers distracted him, that he was suffering from horrible cramps in his hands, and if he looked down at the floor a headline would catch his eye and he would forget how to sign his own name.

But Cornelius's world view was not confined to the living room. He perceived the entire world as one big toilet. Outside, the patio and the walks along the pool became minefields of shit. That dog's bowels were a hazard to human life and limb, and a lethal danger to drunks, which pretty much defines the members of the household, for if we did nothing else in that house, we drank.

Push was very quickly coming to shove. We had on our hands an animal that farted more than a cook in a beanery, dribbled saliva constantly, snored with a constancy and volume that sounded like the London Blitz, produced enough manure in a month to supply the farms of Iowa for a year, and farted with such noise, with such frequency, with such odor as to make the place a firetrap simply on the basis of the amount of methane gas he was pouring into the rooms. Something had to be done.

As usual, when confronted with a crisis, especially a domestic one, Tennessee pretended it didn't exist. First Leoncia, the black housekeeper who was Tennessee's age, nearly blind and could barely walk, refused to clean up the shit and finally balked at setting foot in the patio—which meant she stopped cleaning his studio, something she conscientiously did when she could get inside. She

feared breaking her already enfeebled legs by a slide in
Cornelius's daily production. "I wasn't put on this earth
to clean up doggy-doo, Mr. Tom. You don't want no
manure in you livin' room then you's goin' have to do
somethin' about it yourself!"

It then fell to me to clean up after the beast. I lasted a
week, shovel in hand, and then refused to do it anymore.

"The dog's got to go," I told Tennessee.

"But he is a fine specimen. I paid six hundred dollars
for him. Purebred."

"You got robbed."

"Baby, he's got a bloodline longer and bluer than the
Queen of England. A purebred, the aristocrat of the ca-
nine kingdom!" he declared, with excessive pride.

"Yeah. Purebred what? He's a shit machine, and you
know it."

"A shit machine?" Tennessee feigned outrage, something he was very good at doing. "Why, he's just a puppy,
a child. He'll learn to control his bodily functions. It took
Gigi some time to learn."

Tennessee was not about to admit that he had been
taken by whichever dog dealer saddled him with this mentally defective creature. He once bought a "Bulava" wristwatch from a street peddler in New York for fifty dollars,
not noticing that the long hand covered up an "a" where
the "u" should have been. When I pointed out to him that
the thing was a piece of junk, he replied that I had holes in
my head. Didn't I know that the watch was all the more
valuable because it was extremely rare, given the misprint
in the manufacture? He asserted it was more valuable than
a British Black Guinea stamp. But he never wore the
damn thing again.

"Learn?" I shouted. "He's nearly a year old and that

dog doesn't even know his own name! He eats Topaz's food! (Topaz was the cat.) He tries to eat tin cans, the tires on bikes. Yesterday he ate Richard's reading glasses. For Christ's sake, Tenn, he eats the plants!"

Tennessee was unmoved. I went on.

"He is the dumbest animal God ever made, and you know it." Tennessee was beginning to look glum. He hated Cornelius as much as I did, only he was too god-damn stubborn to admit it. "He's so dumb he doesn't even know he's a *dog!* He thinks he's a *cat!*" Which was true, because he was around Topaz all the time and had picked up her habits, like trying to get into the bird cage and eat the budgies, and sleeping in a cardboard box, and messing Topaz's litter box. The dog was a nightmare.

I gave Tennessee an ultimatum. I was not going to break my back shoveling up piles of dog shit anymore, and if the dog wasn't gone in a week, *I* would leave.

Well, days passed, and the manure piled up until the house smelled like a dog run, and the patio—where we normally ate—was a doggy outhouse, the humans having fled inside. On the fourth day of my strike we sat eating lunch outside. It had rained the night before, and that morning Tennessee was beaming with satisfaction, con-vinced the heavy rains had washed away our problem. They hadn't. We ate lunch, not tasting a thing because everything tasted like doggy-doo, and Cornelius ambled about the patio in his hopeless way, farting from time to time so we wouldn't forget he was there, trying to crawl onto our laps or break into the outdoor bird cage. Then he did something that so appalled and astonished us that we sat there speechless and wide-eyed in sheer amazement.

To put it bluntly, he ate his own droppings.

Tennessee and I looked at each other, and then we laughed for a long time.

"Baby, he is a zoological wonder! The one-can dog! You feed him once and then he makes his own supply for the rest of his life. Why, he is an evolutionary mutant. I can make a fortune putting Cornelius out to stud."

As the deadline on my ultimatum was fast approaching, Tennessee decided to get rid of Cornelius, but he had to do it in such a way that he would not have to admit that he had been wrong about the dumbest dog in America.

This was his plan. When we would leave the compound by the back, where the carport was, Tennessee would sneak into the front garden and unlatch the door. When we came home, Cornelius would be gone, having wandered out the gate in search of birds and other cat food.

This happened three times, and three times Tennessee raised a hue and cry, moaning and carrying on about how much he loved the monster, how inconsolable he was. Then he would get on the telephone and call the local radio station and offer a hundred dollars reward for the return of his dog. A day or two later some greedy neighbor would show up at our door with the retardee in hand, and, after pocketing the money, make some remark about how bad the beast smelled and a hundred dollars was hardly going to cover the cost of new carpets in his Ford.

Each escape brought less hue and cry, and each return of the prodigal home a progressively smaller reward. By the third time, Cornelius's redeemable value had plummeted to ten bucks. Finally, Tennessee didn't even bother calling the station to raise the general alarm. And three more times that dog left home, and three more times some damn fool brought him back.

The last time the door was opened and a grinning neighbor stood there returning Cornelius to us, Tennessee turned to me, and said, "Well, I guess he'll be with us always, like malaria and the clap."

In 1979, Frank Fontis, the caretaker of Tennessee's property in Key West, was murdered. It was an especially vicious killing. He was shot at point-blank range late at night in the living quarters of a railroad museum he operated as a tourist trap on the island.

Fontis was a well liked, middle-aged queen with no known enemies in the Keys. He was a gardener by trade. Swishy, a bit of a camp, he took great pride in working for Tennessee and being his friend. About six feet tall, he was fat, with a round face, a jovial disposition, and, as far as I knew, clean of drugs. Like Tennessee, he was at times hypochondriacal and loudly self-dramatic. He was also unusually generous, particularly if you were young, pretty, and male. That may be the reason why he got into such deadly trouble.

When Tennessee or I were not using the house and it was empty, Fontis stayed there. Often he gave parties, and I know from others that he let homeless youths, pickups, stay there, too.

In the winter Key West is invaded by young drifters without funds who turn to drug dealing, petty theft, and prostitution to make do. They sleep in battered campers parked along public beaches or in cheap rooming houses; they lounge at night along Duval Street, displaying a mixture of sullen sexual availability and thinly disguised threat, much like hustlers everywhere. They are hungry, desperate, on to the game, with eyes open to the easy mark. Fontis was just the right sort of pushover to hit, being fat, trusting, defenseless, and homosexual.

So one night that January he was discovered naked and bloodied on the floor by the front door of the tourist trap he owned. Scattered near and over his body were several hundred dollars in bills, as if someone had tossed them into the air in glee after blowing his life away.

On the telephone table by his bed was found a single piece of paper. On it was written: "My best friend Miss Lillian Carter." Next to her name was her unlisted phone number in Plains, Georgia. It was the only phone number in Fontis's possession.

Even stranger was the fact that early that morning, persons unknown broke into Tennessee's house and ransacked the place.

Tennessee was in New York at the time, staying in the apartment he kept at the Manhattan Plaza, a high-rise development on West Forty-second Street where only people in the arts were allowed to live. Most of the apartments in the two towers were federally subsidized. His was not. He was working on *Clothes for a Summer Hotel* with José Quintero, who would direct the play on Broadway.

The morning after Fontis's murder, Tennessee called me and asked me to come to the apartment. When I arrived he was agitated, somewhat despondent, and anxious because he could get no word on the events in Key West. Together we phoned various friends on the island, trying to get a line on the murder and the condition of Tennessee's house and property. When we didn't have much luck, Tennessee asked me to fly to Key West and stay in his house until he could join me there several days later. I agreed.

He seemed very forlorn and at a loss. That had so often been my perception of him since we first met—the sense of unadmitted sadness, an arresting loneliness that is articulated only in his work. And physical vulnerability. When you were Tennessee's friend, it was easy to forget the greatness of his literary achievement, and see only someone in need of friendship and concern. Tennessee quite unintentionally elicited from those around him a desire to protect him. But from what?

Much of my perception was influenced by the environment in which I normally found him. Hotel rooms littered with clothes, pills, manuscripts, unopened mail. Or rented apartments where even the furniture was leased. He seemed at home nowhere, except possibly Key West. And yet his curiosity, his sexual or rather *affective* needs were such that he ventured where it wasn't safe to be. I don't simply mean the young men we met or the various dives and bars he accompanied me to. I mean his compulsion to travel, to stay in flight like some land bird lost over the vast sea, whether alone or with a companion, all over the world in search of a place and someone with whom he could be content. Safe. In 1981 he told me that he had given up sex. All he wanted, he said, was someone to caress on occasion. Not much to ask, but since the death of Frank Merlo in 1962 that longing to find someone to love and caress had been largely unfulfilled.

"As long as Frank was well, I was happy. He had a gift for creating a life and, when he ceased to be alive, I couldn't create a life for myself."

So I went to Key West unexpectedly, at his request. I was happy to go because it is a splendid place for a writer to work. There are few distractions, unless you find honky-tonk bars and artsy-fartsy shops or the Conch

Train Tour your ticket. Even the beaches are small and poor, the surf dead, the restaurants mediocre at best, the sex ungenerous and often diseased. But what Key West has, or had, was quiet, and the finest weather and fishing in the United States.

But now the quiet was broken, and the island found itself in the midst of a crime wave, though a small one, to be sure, as crime waves go in America. This one was primarily due to two unrelated factors: drug smuggling and antihomosexual bigotry.

The smuggling attracted to the island a lot of dangerous thugs, and it corrupted some of the police. By the time I arrived that winter, out of Key West's normal contingent of twenty-seven cops, only eleven were left, the others having quit or been indicted.

Also, a local Baptist pastor, a Reverend Wright, had started a campaign to rid the island of gays, not an easy proposition, since they constituted a large percentage of the population.

The "conchs," as longtime residents of Key West are called, were feeling pressed by the growing influx of well-to-do gays and rich Europeans, largely Italian and British, who had set in motion a process of gentrification that had raised property values and taxes even while it brought in the big spenders. The character of the island was changing. There were now chi-chi boutiques, restaurants with cutesy names and menus in French, and ugly time-sharing hotels springing up. The merchants loved it, but the bulk of the God-fearing conchs were left out of the growing prosperity. These people, fishermen and people employed in the tourist industry or by the Navy at low wages, hated the newcomers, resented their fancy ways, and feared being driven off the island by rising taxes and property speculation by developers. It was a real Us against Them atmosphere; all it took was someone to light the fuse, and that someone was a Baptist preacher, who else?

Key West has always had a gay colony, mainly because a third of the island is a naval base. Where there is "seafood" (that was how Tennessee referred to sailors) you will find men to eat it. According to the Kinsey study on homosexuality in the military, the Navy has by far the highest percentage of active homosexuals among its personnel, far higher than any other service. So it is reasonable that where the U.S. Navy docks, gays will gather.

Anyway, this preacher had taken out a full page ad in the Key West *Citizen* calling, in Jesus's name, for vigilante squads to drive the sodomites from the blessed isle. Not unexpectedly, a certain element of the populace responded with brutal enthusiasm. Males, gay or straight, were assaulted on the streets by gangs of youths swinging lead pipes and bicycle chains; gay-oriented businesses were attacked; a German tourist on his honeymoon was mistaken for a gay and beaten and killed in broad daylight on Duval Street; people leaving the Monster, a gay disco, were assaulted; two homosexuals sitting by the pool at the Pier House Hotel were stabbed at dusk, for no apparent reason; the body of a gay youth was found floating by the Mobile pier, stabbed to death. The atmosphere was decidedly nasty, the future risky.

I stayed at Tennessee's house, spending the first few hours pulling the house together again. Someone had torn the place apart searching for something, I didn't know what.

The night after I arrived, a gang of youths in cars came by the house, throwing beer cans against the windows, setting off firecrackers, and shouting anti-gay obscenities. I called the cops. They never showed. I wondered if Tennessee had sent in his annual contribution to the policeman's fund. If you didn't, the cops had a tendency not to show up when you called. Sometimes they didn't answer the phone at all. At lunchtime, noon until two, they never did.

I was used to it, but it still bothered me, although it never seemed to bother Tennessee, this ritual of anonymous public insult. The first winter I stayed with him, I had opened the door in the morning to retrieve the mail and saw three construction workers leaning against the picket fence bordering the front lawn. They were peeing on the yard. When they saw me they shouted, "Hey, pussy, you want some dick?" and gave me the finger as I retreated into the house. When I complained to Tennessee, he replied, "Baby, it's probably good for the plants." And went swimming.

Several days after I arrived Tennessee and José Quintero flew down. I told Tennessee my fears about our remaining on the island. He wasn't the least bit frightened. He never was.

I said I thought the police were hopeless, and probably corrupt to boot.

He looked disappointedly at me. "You think the police are corrupt now?" he asked. "You should have seen them when I arrived here in the forties. Then they found a body at the bottom of the bay wearing cement shoes. After they dragged the body from the water, the sheriff looked at the dead man, then he looked at the cement shoes the dead man was wearing, and promptly declared it a suicide!" Tennessee howled with laughter.

A few nights later the two of us were walking down Duval Street, Key West's main drag in every sense of the term. We had had dinner with Quintero at the Queen's Room, and gone on to the Monster with him, and left him there. We then went to a piano bar where we sang along with a black singer who did whatever songs Tennessee requested.

It was a warm, lovely night, and we were in a good mood, high but not drunk. We sang Southern hymns as we ambled along.

After strolling a few blocks along Duval, we spotted five young men sitting on one of the concrete planters on the sidewalk. We approached them. Tennessee explained that we were itinerant choristers trying to earn an honest buck and would they care to hear a refrain of a hymn? Not waiting for an answer, we burst loudly into a rendition of "I Come to the Garden Alone." I thought we sang pretty good.

As we were singing, the five men surrounded us, and it was soon apparent they didn't appreciate the music and in fact were up to no good.

I spotted a knife in the hand of the leader of the thugs, a tall, burly fellow in a thickly knitted, gray turtleneck sweater.

"Let's get the fuck out of here!" I said to Tennessee.

He was not about to run.

He glared up at the bear of a man confronting him, looked about at the others, and said, "I have a very good memory. I will remember your faces tomorrow. So get out of the way!"

They didn't move. Then the big man swung his leg, trying to kick Tennessee in the face. He missed because I pulled Tennessee back.

"Let's go, Tenn!" I pleaded, grabbing his arm.

He jerked his arm away, giving me a look of withering contempt for my cowardice. And then he turned his attention to the chief bruiser.

"My name is Tennessee Williams!" he declared, "and I am not in the habit of retreat!"

Whereupon they hit *me!*

After knocking me to the ground, they slugged Tennessee, picked him up, threw him on top of me, and gave me some swift kicks in the side for good measure. They fled down the street, and it was over.

Later, when I asked him if he had any idea who the bastards were who jumped us, he said, "Baby, they were probably New York drama critics!"

The next day I was able to identify two of the boys from the police mug book. One was the son of a Key West cop. None of the group was ever arrested for their attack on us. Months later, when I went to the sheriff's office to inquire why nothing had been done, I was told that they were really good boys and I didn't want to screw up the lives of young people, did I?

I told Tennessee I wanted to file a federal civil rights suit against the Reverend Mr. Wright because his newspaper ads and his public pronouncements had incited violence against us and other gays. And I wanted to file suit against the city to force the police to make the arrests.

He looked at me woefully and shook his head.

"Do you want to come back to Key West again?" he asked. "More to the point, baby, do you want to leave the island in one piece?"

I said yes.

"Well, then. Don't forget those cement shoes."

That afternoon, Tennessee, frightened, fled to Los Angeles.

There is a postscript to this story.

The summer of 1981, when I visited Miss Lillian Carter in Plains, we talked about Frank Fontis. She was the first person to be notified of his murder. When her phone number was discovered by his bed, the police called the Secret Service, who contacted her to determine the nature of her relationship with the murdered man.

She had met Fontis only once, when she was in Key West with several women friends the year before his death. They stopped him on the street to ask directions, and he recognized the President's mother and invited them to see Tennessee's house. After giving them a tour, he took them to lunch. She never saw him again.

And this: after his death I learned that Fontis had given a large Christmas party at Tennessee's house, inviting about a hundred people, some of them old friends of Tennessee's. Most of the crowd were addicts and dealers. It was a very sinister affair, and Tennessee's friends left early. For weeks Fontis had gone around Key West throwing money around like there was no tomorrow, which, it turned out, for him there wasn't. One night he drunkenly gave a hustler a thousand dollars, and bragged about it the next day.

Apparently Fontis had gotten involved with cocaine smugglers, providing a safe house for their stash. And one day they came for the coke and old Frank couldn't produce it. So they killed him. They tore Tennessee's house apart twice trying to find out if he had hidden the contraband there.

The more I thought about it, the more I came to believe that the reason the police did not come when they were called, and why they did not come when Tennessee's alarm system was activated, something I did several times to see if they would appear, was not because Tennessee hadn't paid in his annual donation to the policemen's fund. No, it was because they were working hand-in-hand with the coke smugglers, or they *were* those very smugglers, and so ignored alarms and calls, assuming it was friends of theirs at work in our house who would not want to be inconvenienced by an official visit.

After Fontis died, the police obtained a court order to open his safe deposit box at the bank, and his home safe. Inside was a collection of material stolen from Tennessee —play scripts, notebooks, signed editions. From time to time Tennessee used to complain about missing manuscripts, first editions of his work and other things that disappeared with disconcerting regularity. He had never suspected Fontis, and the discovery that his friend had been a thief hurt him very much.

CHAPTER · SIX

A Streetcar Named Desire brought two people into Tennessee's life: Marlon Brando, who would attain stardom in the role of Stanley Kowalski; and Frank Merlo, who was destined to play a different role, that of his lover and companion; he was the man who held Tennessee together until he himself fell apart.

In the spring of 1947, after doing everything he could to persuade Irene Selznick and Audrey Wood to engage Elia (Gadg) Kazan as the director of *Streetcar*, Tennessee left New York for Cape Cod, relieved because Kazan had agreed to undertake the production. However, Kazan was convinced to undertake the play, not by the persuasive powers of Selznick or Wood, but by his wife, Molly Day Thacher Kazan, an old pal of Tennessee's since 1939, when he had won the award from the Group Theatre, for whom she worked. Kazan had been Tennessee's sole choice for director ever since he saw his production of Arthur Miller's *All My Sons*, an experience that left him in awe.

Kazan, who was born in Turkey, emigrated to the United States as a child. After he graduated from Yale, he entered the theatre, becoming the most important director of his day. He had an uncanny feel for the American vernacular, and an instinctive sympathy for and understanding of the private sorrows, hidden fears, and unspoken longings of his adopted nation. I do not know whether that was because he was born abroad and thus later was in but never part of America, perceiving its people from a distance, with informed disengagement, as Tennessee believed; or whether it was simply that he was a man exceptionally gifted with the ability to interpret and bring to life the words and visions of other men.

"He was the greatest director I ever knew," Tennessee said. "The only one I could completely trust. We often disagreed on cuts and rewrites, but I would do them because he was usually right.

"In the fifties, during the witch-hunts, when he testified, you know, before the [House Un-American Activities] Committee, they say he named names. Well, I guess after that many of his friends turned their backs on him. Lillian [Hellman] was out to lynch Gadg. She never forgave him, but Lillian always had a skin thinner than ice in August. She never forgave *anybody*. I always thought she knew more than she let on about the Communist Party. She never did say whether Dash [Hammett] had been a member. I think he was, and that's why she made this huge smokescreen to cover up the fact. Even after the poor man died.

"I always thought Gadg had his reasons [for testifying]. He was very devoted to his family. I think he believed that if he didn't cooperate, the Government would attack his family, deport them, jail them, you know. That was when Nixon and his fascists were in the saddle and people were blacklisted and couldn't get work and some disappeared off the face of the earth. Only God can read the heart of a man, and only God can finally know and judge his heart. What I knew of Gadg's heart I trusted, and I loved."

From *Streetcar* on, almost every play he wrote he tried

to get Kazan to direct. Every other director was always Tennessee's second choice.

In 1947, he went to Cape Cod with Santo, his boyfriend at the time, a young man given to jealous fits. Santo had rather too much of a love of booze, and Tennessee was quickly tiring of his violent outbursts. They had met the year before in New Orleans, where Tennessee had written the first draft of *Camino Real,* and had just begun *Streetcar.*

They took a small bungalow on the beach between North Truro and Provincetown. It was actually one large room, with two double-decker bunk beds and a bathroom. Soon Margo Jones and her friend Joanna Albus came to visit. Jones was interested in producing and directing Tennessee's *Summer and Smoke.* Known as the "Texas Tornado," she was a pivotal force in regional American theatre, specifically in Houston and Dallas, where she ran the amateur groups that comprised the theatrical culture in those cities. She was a tough, outspoken, bitchy, formidable woman, dead certain of the rightness of her opinions, and perhaps because of that she was a major reason why American theatre finally took root west of the Hudson River.

Margo Jones and Joanna Albus were the first people Tennessee read *Streetcar* to; this was in 1946 in New Orleans, when they came to visit him while he was staying there briefly with his grandfather Dakin. He read to them from an uncompleted first draft of the play.

"I think they were shocked by it. And so was I," he wrote. "Blanche seemed too far out. You might say out of sight."

Jones was supportive of the play but urged him to rewrite it and to soften Blanche's hysteria. He listened, and ignored her.

Because the ocean was too cold to swim in off the Cape, Tennessee and Santo accepted Irene Selznick's invitation to visit her in Los Angeles until the water warmed. Tennessee, by now a minor celebrity, was given a cottage in Malibu to stay in, another of Irene's generosities, and through her he met many of the stars of the day, for the first time on a somewhat equal footing: Ethel Barrymore, Cary Grant, Rex Harrison, Clark Gable, and John Garfield, whom Tennessee thought should be cast as Stanley.

It was also then that he became friends with the director George Cukor, attending an all-male dinner party at his sprawling Beverly Hills mansion. Tennessee was staggered by the art in Cukor's house, by the sheer immensity of the place, and by the fact that Cukor not only knew Katharine Hepburn, but was a close friend of Greta Garbo's. He excitedly spoke to Cukor about *Streetcar*, and the possibility of Garbo's playing Blanche.

It was through George Cukor that he first met Garbo, the meeting a disappointment because both he and the actress were too shy to make conversation. Tennessee was terrified of her. Later, what he remembered was her beauty and the way she drank vodka straight. Nothing came of her playing Blanche. At that point in her life Garbo was not about to return to acting in order to play a distraught Southern woman moving into madness. What she most wanted to play was an androgynous role, neither sex, something like Peter Pan. What she wanted to play was Oscar Wilde's Dorian Gray, a part about as far from Blanche DuBois as you could get.

Tennessee saw Garbo five or six times in the following years.

She and Helen Hayes attended a party he gave in

Chelsea in New York before the opening of *Streetcar*. He was flabbergasted that she was there.

"There had been a terrible blizzard in New York," he told me, "and Garbo arrived all bundled up with a hat pulled down over her ears. All you could see were her eyes.

"My apartment in Chelsea was small and not very well furnished. There was hardly *any* furniture, and what little there was the Salvation Army wouldn't take!

"There was a lovely fireplace, and on this cold night I had a fire going. Garbo stayed by the fire, she didn't take off her coat or even her gloves. I spoke with her. I was very nervous. She is the only actress that always intimidates me. Whenever I have seen her, I cannot really believe she is there, you know? She is the greatest actress we have ever had, don't you think? I mean movie actress.

"As we stood by the fireplace talking, a guest of one of my guests came over to us. He held a Kodak camera in front of his face and pointed it at Garbo like a gun. Garbo went pale. She stiffened. Before I could prevent the calamity, this guest of a guest had taken her picture. It was like he shot her. She fled into the night. I think she believed I had put him up to it."

After *Streetcar* opened, Tennessee mentioned to George Cukor that he had written a movie script titled *The Pink Bedroom*, and Cukor suggested that Garbo read it.

He arranged for Tennessee to have a meeting with her in her New York apartment at the Ritz Tower on Fifty-seventh Street and Park Avenue.

Tennessee arrived at her flat terribly excited. He had had a few drinks to fortify himself on his way to her place, and once there had adopted her custom and swilled vodka straight, a drinking technique he was not used to. He got drunk, which allowed him to overcome his shyness, and proceeded to give Garbo a monologue describing his script. She listened politely, nodding, saying very little beyond, "Wonderful! Wonderful!" Her remarks emboldened him, and he began to believe he had scored the Hollywood coup of the century: Garbo would return to the movies in a film written by him!

Tennessee poured himself more vodka, and talked more about his script and who should play opposite her, and so on. Finally Garbo, having heard enough, slumped back in her chair, sighing heavily.

Did she want to play the role? he asked.

"Yes, it's wonderful," she replied. "But not for me. Give it to Joan Crawford."

Five years later Garbo came to a party given for Tennessee by Constance Collier, the character actress. At the party Tennessee went up to Garbo and gushed, "You are the only great tragedienne that the screen ever had, you've *got* to resume your career!"

Garbo exclaimed, "This room is stifling!" and ran across the room and threw open a window and stood staring out it for several minutes as if she were thinking of jumping.

Collier took Tennessee aside. "Never speak to her of acting again. She always goes into a fit at the suggestion."

I happened to be with Tennessee the last time he saw Garbo. It was in 1975 when he was in New York, playing the role of Doc in *Small Craft Warnings*. He had taken on the part because the box office had slumped and he thought people who wouldn't come to see the play would come to see him. He was right. It was also during the run of *Small Craft Warnings* that he did a stint as a local television weatherman as a way to drum up publicity for the play. It was one of the most humiliating of his public appearances. On the news he was introduced as the station's new weatherman. He stood, looking furious, beside the weather chart with its temperatures, storm fronts, and the rest. Holding a long pointer in his hand, he proceeded to read the weather forecast. However, he couldn't see the cue cards, was blinded by the studio lights, and so spent a minute or two trying to fake the weather report, banging the pointer at the chart in a futile attempt to demonstrate professional authority. Finally, he said to hell with this, and declared that he was an artist and not a performing seal! He then tried to walk off the set with as much dignity as possible only to get his feet tangled in the floor cables and nearly topple on his face, his humiliation bringing peals of laughter from the television anchor people and crew.

It was not a happy time for him.

One afternoon he decided to buy Miss Rose a mink coat. She was coming down the next day from the sanitarium to have lunch with him, and he wanted to surprise her. First we went to Bloomingdale's, where, in the fur salon, he introduced himself as Rose Williams, speaking in a falsetto voice as he tried on a number of mink coats and camped about the place outrageously.

Finding nothing suitable for Rose, we walked over to Park Avenue to get a taxi. While we stood trying to wave down a cab, a woman came rushing up to us.

"Are you Tennessee Williams?" she asked.

Tennessee grinned, delighted at being recognized by what he assumed was a fan.

"I saw your play last night," the woman continued.

"Yes?" He was still smiling.

"Yes. Tell me, how can I get a refund? I thought it was just *awful*."

Tennessee, angered and hurt, ran into the street.

We took a taxi downtown to B. Altman. Tennessee bought Rose a cloth coat. The sense of play had been knocked out of him by the woman's cruel remarks.

We left the store and walked up Fifth Avenue, and at the corner of Thirty-fifth Street I spotted Garbo, who walked hurriedly past us. I pointed her out.

We quickly followed her. She paused at Altman's steps, as if she were suddenly undecided about entering the store.

"Miss Garbo," Tennessee said, "it's Tennessee Williams."

She turned and smiled behind her dark glasses. "Oh, it's you."

He said he was acting in his own play downtown, and he would be honored if she would accept tickets and come and see him.

"How wonderful," she said. "But I can't accept. You see, I do not go out anymore."

Then she turned and hurriedly entered the store. As he watched her disappear, Tennessee commented, more to himself than to me, that she was the saddest of creatures, an artist who abandoned her art. And that was worse than death, he said, it was worse than anything, to live on without your art.

In June 1947, Tennessee and Santo returned from Los Angeles to their bungalow on Cape Cod. He continued to work on *A Streetcar Named Desire* (he had originally titled it *The Poker Night*), and here added Blanche's famous exit line to the play. He continued to worry about the casting of the leading roles, especially Kowalski and DuBois. And Santo continued to drink and throw fits. Margo Jones was still staying with them in their small house.

In the meantime the electricity had gone on the blink and the plumbing had broken down and Tennessee and his guests were having to live by candlelight and avail themselves of the ocean when the use of a toilet was required.

Kazan wired Tennessee, telling him that he was sending up to the Cape a talented young actor he thought might be perfect for Stanley, and asking that Tennessee allow him to read for the part. Two or three days later, Marlon Brando had not appeared and Tennessee gave up expecting him. Finally, after a few more days, Brando appeared without notice. There was a pretty young woman with him.

Coming into the house, Brando asked why the lights weren't on. When informed that they weren't working and nobody had a clue as to why, he went over to the fuse box and, inserting a penny, brought the electricity magically to life. Tennessee was very much impressed.

"Then, before he was famous, Brando was a gentle, lovely guy, a man of extraordinary beauty when I first met him. He was very natural and helpful. He repaired the plumbing that had gone on the whack, and he repaired the lights that had gone off. He did it without our asking him to help. He just stuck his hand down the toilet and pulled out handfuls of shit and then washed the bowl down with water and fixed something in the tank and it worked.

"He was about the best-looking man I had ever seen, he and Frank [Merlo] and Monty, for different reasons.

Their looks were very different. Brando was sexy like an animal, smoldering.

"After he repaired the plumbing and after he repaired the lights he just sat down and read the role of Stanley. I cued him. After five minutes, Margo Jones gave this Texas whoop, and said, 'Oh, this is the greatest reading I've ever heard, even in *Texas!*'

"There was no point in discovering him, it was so obvious. I never saw such raw talent in an individual, except for Laurette Taylor, whose talent was hardly raw. I knew at once that he was Stanley. And that's how he got the part."

That night in Cape Cod they had dinner together, and later they read poetry aloud. Tennessee was surprised that Brando showed no elation at having been cast in *Streetcar*. He spent the night sleeping on a blanket in the middle of the floor because there was no available bed.

"Brando was always shy with me for some reason," Tennessee later wrote, "The following morning he wanted me to walk up the beach with him, and so we did —in silence. And then we walked back—in silence."

After Brando was cast, Tennessee went out to the Coast again to see Jessica Tandy, who was playing in *Portrait of a Madonna*, one of his shorter plays. She had received critical raves. After attending a performance he immediately decided that he had found his Blanche, and cast her in the part. He left the rest of the casting to Kazan, and returned to Cape Cod.

One night he and Santo went to Provincetown to hear the jazz singer Stella Brooks, whom Tennessee adored. But his very enthusiasm for her made Santo jealous, and during the performance he shouted obscenities at her, and when Tennessee tried to shut him up, he turned on him, threw his drink at Tennessee, missed, and walked out of the bar in a rage.

Tennessee sat alone in the bar of the Atlantic House, listening to Stella Brooks. Finally, feeling lonely and depressed, he wandered out on to the frame porch to have a cigarette and take the night air. He believed then that he would never find a companion with whom he could make a life; the closest he had come was Kip, and Kip was gone. He put up with a series of lovers, lasting weeks or months, whom he indulged and supported and who, by their very dependency on him, grew frustrated and angry, until their rage broke forth in violence. He tolerated their destructiveness because he thought he could do no better. He made do. Until Frank Merlo came into his life, and then he did not have to make do anymore until Frankie died, when the old pattern reasserted itself. But by then he was weakened by drugs and booze and grief, tormented by a loneliness that never left him, and so he again put up with a series of companions who robbed, humiliated, and abused him, because they saw what he no longer could: his greatness. They hated him for being what they longed to be and could never be. And he hated himself for what he was. If one is to understand Tennessee's self-destructiveness, one has to accept the reality of his profound and hurtful self-loathing and self-contempt.

On the porch of the Atlantic House, Tennessee stood smoking. And then he noticed a young man walk out from the bar, lean against a railing, and light a cigarette. They stared at each other, Frank Merlo dressed in blue jeans and a tight white T-shirt. Frank was in his twenties, with a beautiful, muscular build; he was about Tennessee's height, with short legs and long hands. He had dark, widely placed eyes, above them long brown eyebrows that emphasized their beauty. He had a long, narrow face, with a prominent nose and a large mouth, a slightly horsey-looking face, and for that reason and one other Tennessee would come to call him "the Little Horse." In *In the Winter of Cities* there is a poem dedicated to Frank, entitled "Little Horse."

Frankie grinned at Tennessee, dropped his cigarette and crushed it out with his toe. "Let's go to the beach."

They drove in Tennessee's white Pontiac convertible out onto the dunes, and for more than an hour made love on the beach.

"After dropping Frankie off where he was staying," Tennessee wrote, "I parked the car and wandered dreamily about town. While I was wandering through the heavy fog of Provincetown, Santo took my car. He first went to the home of Stella Brooks, who he thought had enticed me to her lair. Poor Stella, she knew me too well for that. Santo gave her a clout in the eye and he left her place a shambles."

Unable to find his car, Tennessee started walking up the hill toward North Truro, his mind filled with visions of Frank. Santo came speeding along the road, heading the car straight for Tennessee, luckily missing him. Tennessee made his way home by foot.

Santo was given the boot.

After *A Streetcar Named Desire* opened in New York, in December 1947, Tennessee went to Europe, first staying in Paris and then moving south to Venice and Rome. *Streetcar* had been an unprecedented smash in New York, and Tennessee discovered that he could not tolerate the publicity. He felt he was no longer his own man; it frightened him, and he fled. In Rome he was befriended by Luchino Visconti and his young, blond Florentine lover, Franco Zeffirelli.

That winter, 1948, he took an apartment on Via Aurora in Rome. He met a street boy, whom he called Rafaello, seventeen years old. Rafaello soon moved in with him; Tennessee bought him clothes and shoes, since the boy was in tatters when they met. Occasionally he thought of Frank Merlo, but gradually those thoughts receded as his love for Rafaello grew.

"Life that winter in Rome: a golden dream, and I don't mean just Rafaello and the mimosa and the total freedom of life. Stop there: what I *do* mean is the total freedom of life and Rafaello and the mimosa, and the letto matrimoniale and the Frascati when morning work was over."

That spring, at a party in an apartment at the American Academy, he met Gore Vidal, and they became friends.

Early in the summer he left Rome and went to London for the rehearsals of *The Glass Menagerie*, which was being directed by John Gielgud and starred Helen Hayes, never one of Tennessee's favorite actresses. Sensing that the play, with Miss Hayes playing Amanda Wingfield, was doomed in London, he returned to Paris, taking a suite at the Hôtel de l'Université on the Left Bank. He spent time with Vidal, who was staying at the same hotel, and became friends with Jean Cocteau and his lover, Jean Marais.

Then he returned to New York for the Broadway production of *Summer and Smoke*, taking the *Queen Mary* on the return crossing; Truman Capote was his shipmate. He had met Truman earlier that year in Italy, and it was on the *Queen Mary* that the two young writers became friends, a friendship that lasted until Tennessee's death.

On board ship was a dipsomaniacal Episcopal bishop, and both Truman and Tennessee enjoyed telling the story of their encounter with the cleric.

Truman was slight and very blond then, with a thin face and huge blue eyes. He was also very flirtatious, with a wicked wit that had not as yet become mean. That would happen years later, when his own life started going out of control. But on the *Queen Mary* he was bitchy without being malicious.

The bishop was very fat and very drunk and very unsteady on his feet. Each day he came early to the bar, occupied a stool, and sat in wait for the appearance of Tennessee and Truman. When they finally came in, the bishop's gloom would lift, he would grin and wave at Truman, and, uninvited, stumble his way across the bar and plop himself down on the bar stool nearest to Truman.

This went on for days, the love-smitten bishop way-laying Truman on the decks, in the bars and lounges, beside the pool. Truman became increasingly angry and increasingly frustrated. No matter how broad the hints, the Episcopal pest refused to take them.

One night, the two young men were having dinner in the dining room and the bishop abruptly pulled up a chair, uninvited, and began trying to engage them in conversation. Truman tried to cut him off by telling him he was not interested in any church of any denomination, and in fact despised organized religion in all its forms and practices.

The bishop smiled agreeably.

Truman then began to stare at the bishop's massive ring of office, about the size of a pigeon's egg, as Tennessee recalled.

"You know," Truman drawled sweetly to the bishop, "I've always wanted to have a bishop's ring."

The bishop laughed indulgently. "Only a bishop can have a bishop's ring, dear child. Although a bishop's friend might be permitted to wear it from time to time in the privacy of a bishop's room."

"Oh, I don't know," Truman lisped sweetly, "I believe I might be able to find one in a pawnshop. You know, one that had been hocked by a *defrocked bishop!*"

The bishop turned beet red and made a hasty retreat. They never saw him again. Tennessee concluded that the good bishop had either hidden in his stateroom for the remainder of the voyage, fearing that Truman was about to rouse the crew against him, or the poor man had leaped overboard. It was the latter explanation that Truman favored.

"I met Truman after he had just published *Other Voices, Other Rooms,*" Tennessee recalled in 1980. "I thought he was quite cute, slim, with this marvelously witty, slightly malicious tongue. I got mad at him after a while. He said something cruel about Frankie. Frank Merlo, Jack Dunphy, who was Truman's friend, and I, we were all traveling in my Buick Roadmaster convertible. We'd gotten as far as Naples. At a waterfront restaurant in Naples Truman said something quite cruel, and I said I'm not going on to Ischia with this man. After a couple of days, Frankie talked me into it. And we went anyway.

"I never disliked Truman after that. I just realize that he has this impulse to be catty at times. I think it's because he's a little guy who has been picked on a lot, especially when he was growing up. You know, Truman makes the mistake of claiming he was born in New Orleans, and giving interviews, even points out the house he was born in. Everyone knows he was born in Huntsville, Alabama. Everyone in Huntsville claims him. They all know it, it's registered.

"Now why does he do such things? He has told people that we had an affair when we met, in 1948, that I cruised him, followed him home, and practically raped him. Well, I never had sex with Truman. He is not my type. He is too effeminate, although I know many men like that kind of homosexual. So do some women, but he was never my type. And as for raping him! It is a physical and psychological impossibility to rape little Truman. Rape implies the refusal of consent, and consent is one thing I have never known Truman to refuse!

"Why does he make up stories about himself? I think it's because the poor little man likes mystery, likes to confuse people about himself. Well, Truman's a mythologist, baby, you know that. That's a polite way of saying he does fabricate. I love him too much to say he's a liar. That's part of his profession."

In early fall, 1948, Tennessee accidentally encountered Frank Merlo in a delicatessen on Lexington Avenue late at night.

"I was living in an apartment designed by the artist Tony Smith on East Fifty-eighth Street. I went out to take the night air, and passed an open delicatessen, and I went inside to buy cigarettes. Frankie was there with a war buddy of his, who was straight. And I said, 'Why, Frank!' I was thrilled to come on him suddenly like that. I thought I would never see him again after we made love on the Cape. No, that isn't true, baby. I think I knew when we first met that we would live our lives together.

"Frank smiled, and he said, 'Hi, Tenn.'

"And I said, 'Why haven't you called me?'

"And Frankie replied, 'I read about your great success, and I didn't want to seem like I was trying to hop on the bandwagon.'"

He told Tennessee that he had seen *Streetcar* and loved it. Tennessee then invited Frank and his friend to come back to his apartment and have a late night picnic.

"He and his buddy came home with me to this lovely apartment. We ate roast beef on rye with pickles and potato salad. Frankie and I kept looking at each other, and I couldn't wait for his friend to leave, but I didn't indicate in any way that he ought to excuse himself because I was afraid that Frankie would leave with him. Presently his buddy said he was going back to New Jersey and why didn't Frankie stay the night with me? And Frankie just stayed on, giving me the happiest years of my life. The happiest, you know?"

Tennessee later wrote of their first night together "on that magical carpet of a bed back of the submarine garden" in a poem called "A Separate Poem."

Truman Capote had a different recollection of how Tennessee came to meet Frank Merlo. He claimed that he met Merlo before Tennessee did, only it was during the summer of 1948 in Greenwich Village.

"Frankie was a fixture on the gay scene in Manhattan then," Truman recalled. "He was this very butch number who had been in the military during the war, and now the war was over and every queen in New York was delirious because the town was crammed with ex-servicemen. I mean, he casually knew a lot of people in the theatre, actors and writers, people like that. In the forties New York seemed much smaller than it does now, and the gay community was very tight, very inbred, and if you met one gay you very quickly met them all. I mean, we all knew each other, and when there was a new boy in town we passed him around.

"Now I know Tennessee hadn't met him then because we had just come from Europe on the *Queen Mary* and he never once mentioned Frankie. I was sitting having lunch in a restaurant on Seventh Avenue with [an interior decorator]. And Frank Merlo walked by outside the window. And I said to my friend, 'My God! Look at *that!*'

"He laughed, and said, 'Oh, that's Frank Merlo. Practically every faggot in New York has had him!'

" 'Well, *I* haven't!' I said. So my friend went outside and grabbed Frankie and brought him back for me to meet. And after lunch we went [to my friend's] apartment in Brooklyn Heights and had sex. First I had Frank, and then my friend did.

"A few days later Frank and I were walking down Fifty-seventh Street and we ran into Tennessee by Carnegie Hall. He couldn't take his eyes off Frank. I introduced them, and Frank and I walked on. Frank didn't seem at all interested in pursuing Tennessee until I mentioned that he had a hit play on Broadway and was probably making one hell of a lot of money.

"That night Tennessee called me. He couldn't get Frank out of his mind. He kept saying, 'Oh, I love *Italians,* baby! I love Italians!' That was hardly exactly news to anybody who knew Tennessee! So I gave him Frank's telephone number in New Jersey. And that is how they met."

I have great doubts about Truman's story. One, because Tennessee emphatically denied it, and it was extremely rare for him to lie. And two, because Truman only liked Irish men. I don't know why that was. With the exception of one Jewish conductor, with whom he claims to have had a brief affair when he first arrived in New York from the South, Truman never went to bed with any man who was not Irish, the blacker the better. He did boast of sexual relationships with women, sex being limited to the oral variety. But who knows what the truth is? What I do know is that all the boyfriends of Truman's whom I have known had the map of Ireland on their faces, and most were drunks, abusive ones at that. Frank Merlo was not Truman's type.

However, I think Truman's version is of interest if for no other reason than that it shows his jealousy of Frank and Tennessee's relationship, something that brought happiness to them both, a thing that Truman always envied in others. And his unfair dismissal of Frank as a hustler on the make, only interested in Tennessee because of his fame and money.

In his *Memoirs* Tennessee wrote of an incident that occurred about two months after he and Frank became lovers.

"Frankie and I had been out late one evening and when we returned to the apartment the transom on the front door was open and from within came the voice of Truman Capote, shrill with agitation. We let ourselves in.

"In the apartment were Truman, Gore Vidal, and a

female policeman . . . It seemed that Truman and Gore, still on friendly terms at this point, had got a bit drunk together and had climbed in through the transom of the apartment to wait for me and Frankie.

"The [policewoman] had been passing along by patrol-car as they were climbing through the transom. She pursued them into the pad and she was now in the process of searching the premises for suspected narcotics and she was holding Gore and Truman for breaking and entering.

"She had located some Seconals in the bedroom and she was making a big deal of it."

At that time, Tennessee only used barbiturates occasionally, and then only to get to sleep. That would change.

"Frankie and I managed to calm her down enough to prevent the arrest of Truman and Gore. Having only turned up a few Seconals in the way of dope, she stepped angrily out."

In December 1948, Frankie, Paul Bowles, and Tennessee took their first trip together, booking passage for Gibraltar on the Italian liner *Vulcania*. In the years to come, Tennessee would remember it as Frank's and his true honeymoon, the happiest voyage he ever made.

They had a first-class stateroom. Tennessee would wake early and write. Frank slept late and soundly, a habit he maintained until his health collapsed. Tennessee was working on *The Rose Tattoo*. *Summer and Smoke*, produced by Margo Jones at the Music Box Theatre on Broadway, was still doing good business. Things had never seemed to go so well in his life as they did on this journey across the Atlantic. He was now a famous man and, by any reasonable measure, a wealthy one. He was being touted accurately in the press as the greatest American playwright since Eugene O'Neill. He had Frankie, and for the first time in his life Tennessee felt secure in love. He looked to the future with great optimism—his letters from this period are filled with humor and joy, as if he had suddenly, quite inadvertently, turned a corner to discover that the world was beautiful. Happy to be alive, he drank very little and stopped using drugs. Frankie disapproved of them.

Frank Merlo had taken over his life, and I mean that in the best way. Frank made certain Tennessee ate properly, got enough sleep, and he created the atmosphere that enabled Tennessee to do the finest work of his career. In many ways, Frank was like a wife and mother to Tennessee. I don't intend that in any sexual sense, I mean in the duties those roles traditionally entailed. He nurtured him, loved him, worried about him, protected, praised, and comforted him, and kept him from harm. And Tennessee responded with a love and sexual ardor that he described, somewhat ashamedly, as "inordinate." Simply put, he could not get enough of Frank.

In Gibraltar, they were met by Jane Bowles, and went with her and Paul the next day to Tangier by ferry, Tennessee beside himself with the delight of showing the world to Frankie.

After a few days in Tangier they drove by car toward Fez, stopping at the border of Spanish Morocco to clear customs. As they waited in the customs shed, Tennessee noticed that the brakes on their car had given way and that it was rolling backward toward a deep ravine. Frank ran out and stopped the car moments before it almost rolled over the edge, a singular display of courage that deeply impressed Tennessee.

In Fez they stayed at the Hotel Jamais, once the palace of the sultan, where they took the largest suite in the place. Tennessee was sparing no expense where Frankie was concerned.

It was in Fez that Tennessee received a cable informing him that *Summer and Smoke* was about to close in New York. It sent him into a deep depression, one that he could not break, all his fears of failure returning with a vengeance; the terror that *Menagerie* and *Streetcar* had been a fluke, an accident, and now fate, having let him taste success, was having a laugh by snatching it away. And Frankie, would he stay with him if the hard times returned? Truman had put doubts in his mind about Frank's motives, and now Tennessee tortured himself with fears of being abandoned, and with those fears came jealousy, unreasoning, without cause. He began to suspect that Frankie was having an affair with Paul Bowles; his jealousy was fed by Frank's kindness to waiters or attendants, by his smiles to strangers.

They drove to Casablanca, nearly quarreling in the car, and took a ship to Marseilles, the journey unpleasant, Frank responding to Tennessee's suspiciousness and depression by sulking.

In January 1950, Tennessee and Frankie settled in Rome. Once more things seemed to be going well for them. Producer Cheryl Crawford was set to produce *The Rose Tattoo* in New York, and Tennessee was again filled with optimism. Eli Wallach was cast as Mangiacavallo, Don Murray as the young sailor, and Maureen Stapleton as Serafina. Tennessee insisted on Maureen's getting the part, despite the director's and producer's belief that she was too young for the role.

"*The Rose Tattoo* was my love-play to the world. It was permeated with the happy young love for Frankie, and I dedicated the book to him, saying: 'To Frankie in Return for Sicily.' "

He also signed over to Frank half his royalties from the play.

Irene Selznick was the first producer to be offered *The Rose Tattoo*. She turned it down, and as a result, Tennessee's friendship with her began to cool.

In April, Tennessee and Frank were still happily living on the Via Aurora in Rome. It was there that he wrote the short story he would later turn into *The Roman Spring of Mrs. Stone*.

In May Frank and he traveled to England to visit Sir Laurence Olivier and Vivien Leigh. They spent the night at their country house in Sussex. The Oliviers wanted to co-star in the West End production of *Streetcar*. Upon meeting Vivien, Tennessee felt at once that he had found his greatest Blanche.

When they returned to Rome, the weather was hot and very uncomfortable, the city overrun with tourists. Tennessee couldn't write, badly wanting to move on, but he stuck it out for several more months because Frankie was so happy there.

In September they returned to the United States, stopping a few days in New York before flying on to Los Angeles, a city Tennessee hated more than any other in the world.

"I always feel like a whore there. I don't appreciate works of art being referred to as a 'property,' like a play of mine was a piece of undeveloped land in the Hollywood Hills. It is a city where everyone and everything is assumed to be up for sale. Everyone is thought to have a price. Well, some things cannot be priced!"

Tennessee used to moan every time he had to go to Los Angeles on business. Like William Faulkner, he viewed it as a place where one held one's nose and got as much money as one could in as short a time as possible, and then grabbed the red-eye out.

"The only culture in L.A. is in a carton of yogurt!"

Warner Brothers had bought the rights to *The Glass Menagerie*. Tennessee and Frank went to the studio to have lunch with Jack Warner in the commissary. When they arrived, Warner stood up, and said, "Well, well! At last, here you are! Welcome to Warner Brothers!" And shook the hand of Frank Merlo, thinking he was Tennessee.

Tennessee started to laugh, and Warner, now utterly confused, said to Frank, "And what do you do, young man?"

Frank looked him straight in the eye, and replied, "I sleep with Tennessee Williams."

They stayed in Los Angeles until the film was cast. Tennessee wanted Bette Davis to play Amanda Wingfield, but she wasn't available. Gertrude Lawrence was cast in her place, a ghastly misjudgment. Kirk Douglas was given the role of the Gentleman Caller, and Jane Wyman played Laura.

"Jane Wyman was in the movie of *The Glass Menagerie*. What else is there to say? She married Ronald Reagan. The no-nose girl married to the no-brain man!"

During the fifties, as his fame grew, Tennessee became very sensitive to slights against Frankie, insisting that he always be included whenever Tennessee was invited anywhere. It didn't always work out that way.

Tennessee was angered when Irene Selznick invited him to her socially prestigious dinners in her Hotel Pierre apartment and would add, "Oh, and ask Frankie to drop in afterward, if he likes."

"Tell her to go fuck herself," was Frank's usual response.

Or Tennessee would raise hell when they checked into a suite in a fancy hotel and there would be two single beds rather than one king-size. He would threaten to leave and never return unless they were moved to a suite with a proper bed or a proper bed was delivered to the suite they were in at once.

When the Royal Orleans in New Orleans refused to allow them to share a room with only one bed, Tennessee created a scene in the lobby.

"But it simply isn't done, Mr. Williams," the night manager tried to assure him. "We never allow two men to sleep in the same bed. Why would two men want to sleep in a bed together?"

"So they can *fuck!*" Tennessee said, before he and Frank marched out. He never stayed at the hotel again, until it was sold to new owners and the policy was changed.

By the middle fifties, Tennessee had become overly dependent on Frank Merlo, and as his dependency waxed, Frank more and more withheld sex, sensing that he was smothering under the weight of Tennessee's demands and needs, in part sexual, but primarily emotional. He began to have affairs on the side with other men. Tennessee knew about them—Frank never hid anything from him—and pretended not to be bothered. Inside he was in torment. By the summer of 1955 he required stimulants to write, commencing an addiction to amphetamines. He could not concentrate otherwise, distracted by worry over his career and his fear of losing Frank.

In 1959, *Orpheus Descending*, his reworking of *The Battle of Angels*, his first play in New York, was a massive failure. It was directed by Harold Clurman and starred Maureen Stapleton and Cliff Robertson, but even with talent like that it could not be redeemed. It was mercilessly savaged by the New York critics, the first time Tennessee had really felt how deep and cutting were the fangs of the daily critics. He was to suffer their bite many times again before he was through.

He fell apart, shattered, and was referred to a psychiatrist, one Dr. Lawrence Kubie, who strongly suggested that the solution to his problems was to throw Frank Merlo into the street. It was like asking Tennessee to hang himself. Frank had become his life.

While still emotionally in pain, he went through the rehearsals and opening night of *Suddenly Last Summer*, which he managed by washing down barbiturates with glasses of vodka.

He was in panic opening night, fearing another failure following on the heels of *Orpheus Descending*.

He was taken back to his apartment by Frankie, who tried to calm his hysteria. They watched the television reviews, the first notices to appear on any opening night in New York. They were dreadful. Tennessee was in despair. Then Frank went out and got the early editions of the New York *Times* and the *Herald Tribune*. The play got raves.

By January 1960, Frank Merlo's health began to fail. He was increasingly irritable and fatigued, and disinclined to have sexual relations with Tennessee. At first, Tennessee, who was in Key Biscayne, working on a production of the first draft of *The Night of the Iguana* at a nearby theatre in Coconut Grove, assumed the change in Frank was due to drug use. But after a few weeks the symptoms could not be ignored, and Frank went into the hospital in New York for examination. When the two-week run of *Iguana* was over, Tennessee returned to Key West, where Frank joined him.

Things didn't improve. Tennessee was drinking heavily, in part because he sensed that things would never be the same again between him and Frank, and Frank, for his part, knew he was sick but didn't know how badly or with what. What he did know was that he was tired all the time, sleeping excessively; he was depressed, moody, very much unlike himself. He was also losing weight. Increasingly paranoid, largely as a result of his use of amphetamines, Tennessee attributed Frank's general condition to love-sickness—he was obviously suffering from unrequited love for some boy he had met and resultantly was not eating, was depressed. Crediting illness to betrayal, Tennessee set about, perhaps unconsciously, to punish his companion. He had two or three sexual affairs with young men in the house in Key West in full view of Frank.

Once again Frank went to New York for a physical checkup and this time was hospitalized for more than a week. His absence upset Tennessee, who, as usual, saw the hospitalization as a ploy on Frank's part to engage in this fictitious affair with a boy in New York.

Tennessee reacted by having an affair with a young painter from Tangier, whom he had met a year or two before. Tennessee invited him to come down to Key West. One night, in a moment of deliberate provocation, Tennessee invited one of Frank's best friends to dinner, along with several other people. They dined on the patio, and before the meal was finished, Tennessee and the young painter from Tangier slipped into the house and began making love on the living-room sofa, in full view of their guests.

Frank's friend, shocked, with good reason, called him at the hospital in New York informing him what was going on in his absence. Unwisely, Frank checked himself out and took the first plane back to Key West, arriving without warning, planning to confront Tennessee with his infidelity. Years before they had agreed to allow each other outside sexual contacts on condition that they didn't take place in "their own bed," a reasonable understanding. Only now Tennessee had deliberately violated that understanding, doing it in such a way that Frank was bound to find out and was obliged to act. I am convinced that by this point in time Tennessee had decided, whether consciously or not, to end the relationship with Frank Merlo, and his engagement with the Tangier painter was the occasion through which he would do it.

The question is why. Until the end of his life, and in much of his writing, Tennessee declared repeatedly his love for Frank Merlo, that no one in his life had ever owned his heart to the degree that Frankie did. Especially in his letters he writes of his longing for Frank, his passion and commitment; and, after Frank's death, Tennessee's sorrow and grief and, yes, guilt were unremitting. That said, it is undeniable that it was Tennessee who ended the relationship. The reason, I think, was his paranoid belief that Frank had ceased to love him. Certainly Frank was increasingly sexually disengaged from Tennessee, and the few times sex occurred anymore between them it was the result of Tennessee's importunings and threats. And that wounded his pride. Like many insecure people, Tennessee had an outsized sensitivity to slights. He took offense quicker than anyone. And if you couple that with his sense of physical self-loathing, then Frank's sexual rejection of him became intolerable to his sense of self. Frank had to go.

The next night, when Frank returned to Key West, he refused to eat. He wouldn't talk. Instead he sat in a corner of the living room, looking small and ill, his eyes staring sadly at Tennessee and the young painter, feeling like a stranger in his own home. Then he lost control, exploding in anger, throwing himself at the young painter, grabbing him by the throat, trying to strangle him.

Tennessee called the police and had Frank removed from the house.

The next day, Frank came home. Tennessee did not exchange a word. Frank simply watched in silence as he packed up his manuscripts and carried them to the car. When Tennessee and the young painter entered the car, Frank sat on the front porch with Leoncia, the housekeeper. As the motor started, Frank ran down the steps to the car.

"Are you going to leave me without shaking hands? After fourteen years together?"

They shook hands, Tennessee saying nothing.

Tennessee and the painter drove to Coconut Grove, checking into a seedy motel. After a few days the painter left for San Francisco, Tennessee went on to New York, and it was over.

In the spring of 1962, Frank came to New York and checked into the Hotel Dover. He badly wanted to see Tennessee, who was afraid of being alone with him, fearing violence. Tennessee told him that he would see him, but only on condition that Audrey Wood be present, concluding that Frank would not cause a disturbance in the presence of that formidable lady.

The meeting took place in his apartment on Sixty-fifth Street, Tennessee nervous and shy, Frank hurt, lonely, baffled by Tennessee's coolness, and more than a little frightened because he knew he was very ill. Audrey handled things in her usual calm, businesslike manner, keeping the conversation on matters financial. Frank yearned to talk to Tennessee about things of the heart, desperately needing an explanation why he had been so abruptly, indeed brutally abandoned. What had he done?

They never talked of that. Tennessee merely confirmed that Frank would continue to own ten percent of *Camino Real, Cat on a Hot Tin Roof,* and *The Rose Tattoo,* and he would still receive a "salary," actually an allowance, of one hundred and fifty dollars a week as long as he lived. Tennessee also had signed over two houses in Key West to him, and assured him that he would never have to worry about money. But that was not Frank's worry. Frank was alone, for the first time in fourteen years, and he was dying, something Tennessee didn't know, and he wanted to come home. He wanted to be with Tennessee.

Frank, who came from a large, working-class Italian family in New Jersey, always had a radically different view of what their companionship should be. Very domestic, he wanted a life where they lived, more or less, in one place, kept regular hours, had decent, pleasant friends, gave cocktail or dinner parties that ended at reasonable hours, went to bed on time. In other words, Frank tried for fourteen years to housebreak Tennessee into the kind of middle-class domestic life that Frank craved, a type of existence utterly foreign to the man Tennessee was.

Ironically, Tennessee finally was more like his hated father than anyone else, at least in the way he lived—an itinerant soul, (his phrase "the fugitive heart" applies again), who couldn't stay in one place for very long. Like his father, he spent much of his life in hotels, living out of suitcases and dining on room service, liked booze and wild parties, opened up his life to street boys and hustlers with whom he had fleeting affairs. He could not settle down; he required drama, *self*-drama, a continuous commotion and social disturbance. Tennessee did not like to be alone, didn't like quiet, and he wasn't happy unless every few days he could start reading the riot act. He bored quickly, needing almost constant distraction. There was no way, once sex had moved from center stage, that he could live the kind of middle-class domestic life Frankie wanted. It was an arrangement beyond his capacity to endure. From one point of view that is most regrettable, because if he had allowed Frank, or whoever, to care for him and protect him and to break his bad habits, drugs especially, Tennessee most likely would have lived much longer. But would it have stifled his creative genius? I think yes. He required the constant exercising of his emotions, taking them to the breaking point and then coming back and writing what he had experienced. His anger or his joy, his laughter or his sorrow seemed always larger than life, exaggerated because they were never held back. He had no inhibitions on his feelings; he simply let them fly or burst forth with astonishing force until he was exhausted. It was, I believe, in those periods of emotional exhaustion, like dwelling in the calm eye of a hurricane, that he created his work. In other words, his creativity depended upon the very emotional instability that would undo him in the end, an instability that he instinctively knew was crucial to his work. And admitting that he loved Frank Merlo more than anyone else, save his sister Miss Rose, he loved his work more. He could, and did, survive Frank, however badly. What he could not survive was the death of creation.

When the meeting with Audrey Wood ended, Tennessee asked Frank to leave the apartment with her. Frank was reluctant to go, but did.

Ten minutes after he left, he called Tennessee from a pay phone at the corner and asked if he could come back to the apartment to talk, explaining that it was impossible to declare his true feelings in Audrey's presence. Tennessee, afraid that he might break his resolve and invite Frank back into his life if he were alone in private with him, insisted that they meet in a public place. He suggested a bar.

Years later Tennessee would explain that he didn't allow Frank in the apartment because he worried that Frank might physically assault him. He had no basis for that, since Frank had never attacked him beyond throwing a meat loaf and a bowl of vegetables in his direction a few years before. It was another rationalization he clung to after Frank's death, when it was painfully clear that lost from his life was an affection that was irreplaceable, and that he had been a cad to boot.

At the bar, their conversation was awkward, Frank demanding explanation, Tennessee complaining about how much work he had to do, that he needed to be alone to do it, but admitting that he might have acted badly to Frank.

"Frank, I want my goodness back," he said, not knowing what he meant.

Frank returned alone to Key West, staying in the second-floor bedroom at Tennessee's house, believing that any day Tennessee would come home to him.

In the meantime, Tennessee had met a young poet and flown off with him to Tangier, renting a cottage near the beach.

In the fall, Frank had lunch with several friends at an outdoor cafe in Key West. He was terribly thin. During the meal he felt ill and bent over the table and blood poured out of his nose and throat. He was rushed to the hospital, X-rayed, and informed he might have lung cancer.

He was flown to New York to undergo surgery for cancer at Memorial Hospital.

Tennessee returned to New York from Tangier and, upon being told by Marion Vacarro that Frank was to be operated on for a lung tumor, he was seized by remorse.

He visited Frank in his room at Memorial before surgery and was surprised to find him fatalistic and calm. It was as if emotionally he were already half dead.

The operation was a failure; the tumor was too near Frank's heart to be removed.

Tennessee and Frank were told he had only six months to live. Tennessee burst into tears.

He visited Frank in the recovery room each day, Frank too sick and weak to be able to say more than a word or two.

After he was released, Frank went alone to Key West,

refusing to stay in Tennessee's house. Instead he took a small cottage nearby and waited stoically to die.

There is some dispute about whether Tennessee ever visited Frank in the hospital, but rather turned his back on him. I don't believe that to be true. It was several days after Tennessee returned to New York from Tangier before he even knew that Frank was hospitalized and that he might have lung cancer. Capote told me that Frank, who didn't have much money, was first put in a cancer ward with a dozen or more other patients. "It was a charnel house," Capote said. "I mean, you can't believe the noise, the screams. All these dying people in terrible agony, most of them old, looking like cadavers, screaming in pain! My God, it was a nightmare. And there was poor little Frank, who weighed practically nothing. He didn't have a private nurse. He didn't have a television set. All he could do was lie there listening to people scream and watching them carry the corpses out of the ward.

"I was stunned. I mean, I hate hospitals anyway but I had never seen anything as bad as this. Poor Frank was very depressed, and I think he had given up. Who wouldn't? I couldn't believe that Tennessee would allow Frank to die like this.

"Well, I called him at his apartment. He had already heard that Frankie was in hospital, but he had no idea how bad the place was. I sure let him know. I said, 'Tennessee, you have got to get him a private room and private nurses, and you have got to go see him. You can't let him die like this!' I don't think Tennessee wanted to do anything. I mean, I think he wanted to pretend he didn't know about it, like it wasn't happening. He was pretty drugged up then, and I don't think he could make himself face what was happening to Frankie.

TOP LEFT: The Miss Rose altar opposite the foot of Tennessee's bed in Key West. It was a very special shrine that he created himself, from time to time adding small religious objects, dried roses, pictures of his sister, and small shells found on the beach. Their meaning was obscure to me, but in some way, known only to him, they touched God. It was here that he prayed when he was frightened. TOP RIGHT: Tennessee and I, drunk at his house in Key West, late night in the early seventies. ABOVE LEFT: Tennessee at home in Key West. He is wearing his gold Chinese "imperial" robe, and a woman's wig. It is late, and we are drunk, and are about to make the rounds of bars in Key West with Tennessee playing the role of his sister, Rose, and me playing Tennessee.

The chair was a handmade wicker piece from the Bahamas. Tennessee owned two of them, claimed they were priceless, and wouldn't let anyone sit on them. When visitors, not knowing the house rules, continued to seat themselves in these priceless antiques, Tennessee went out and bought two enormous Raggedy Ann dolls. He plopped them in the chairs, tied them in place, and thereafter the chairs went unused. ABOVE RIGHT: Candy Darling and me embracing in the back room of Max's Kansas City Bar in New York, April 1970. Candy, who was a man who dressed otherwise, was one of Andy Warhol's stable of Underground Superstars. Occasionally Candy was Tennessee's date, and she starred in the original New York production of *Small Craft Warnings*. *Credit: Dotson Rader*

TOP LEFT: Tennessee speaking at the Cathedral of St. John the Divine, December 6, 1971. The occasion is the Remember the War peace rally, protesting American involvement in Vietnam. It was the first time Tennessee publicly spoke out against the war, and it marked the apex of his involvement with the American Left. *Credit: Nancy Crampton.* TOP RIGHT: Tennessee and Norman Mailer at the Cathedral of St. John the Divine in Manhattan, December 6, 1971. The picture was taken moments before both Norman and Tennessee addressed a huge antiwar rally inside the cathedral. Later in the evening an excerpt from Norman's play *Why Are We in Vietnam?* was performed before the altar. Its language sent Tennessee out into the night in a rage. *Credit: Pictorial Parade, Inc.* ABOVE LEFT: Tennessee and Geraldine Page backstage in her dressing room at the Cort Theatre in New York. It is opening night of *Clothes for a Summer Hotel,* his last Broadway play. It is his birthday, and his fortieth anniversary as a playwright. *Credit: UPI/Bettmann Archive* ABOVE RIGHT: Tennessee and Richard Zoerink in Richard's apartment in New York, February 1974. Richard threw a party for Tennessee, who arrived with Robert. It was the first time any of Tennessee's friends met Robert, the young man who would become his companion and live with him longer than any other aside from Frank Merlo. *Credit: Dotson Rader*

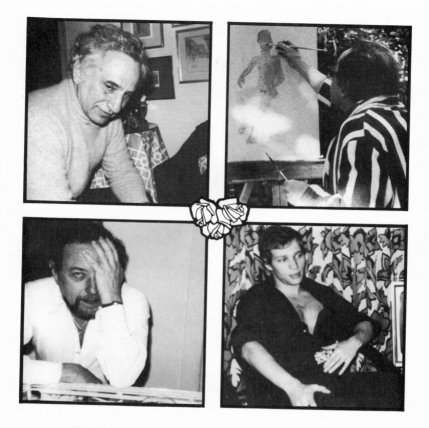

TOP LEFT: Elia Kazan in my apartment in New York, May 3, 1972. For the last few years Tennessee had believed that Kazan didn't like him anymore because he wouldn't direct his new plays. Kazan, however, was devoting himself to writing novels, having effectively left the theatre. I invited Kazan to come to my apartment to have chili, and I asked Tennessee to come too, but I didn't tell him who would be there. I thought it might scare him away. At dinner, the two men were delighted to be with each other again, and Tennessee's fears of having lost Kazan's friendship passed. *Credit: Jack Weiser* TOP RIGHT: Tennessee painting in Key West in 1979. Tennessee painted most of his life, but in his last years, as his literary career declined, he devoted himself increasingly to painting. He thought if all else failed he could make a decent living selling his pictures. ABOVE LEFT: Key West, 1972. Tennessee stoned on Valium and liquor, his hand covering his bad eye. ABOVE RIGHT: This picture of Jon Uker was taken in May 1974, when he stayed with me in the French Quarter in New Orleans. Later that year I introduced him to Tennessee. Jon is an actor, and Tennessee grew fond of him. Often when Jon was short of funds, Tennessee would pay him a small salary to be his traveling companion. Jon was the last person to see Tennessee alive, being with him in his suite at the Hotel Élysée the night he died. *Credit: Dotson Rader*

November 19, 1981. Tennessee with his sister, Miss Rose, walking to the Shubert Theatre to receive the third Commonwealth Award for his contribution to the theatre. It was Rose's birthday, and on receiving the award he asked that it be dedicated to her.

Tennessee loved Miss Rose more than anyone else, and he cared for her until his death. Rose is wearing one of the many coats Tennessee bought her, this particular one purchased the day we ran into Greta Garbo at B. Altman on Fifth Avenue. *Credit: UPI/Bettmann Archive*

"Well, after I called him, and Irene [Selznick] visited Frankie, and *she* gave Tennessee hell, and others called, and then we started a fund to raise money to pay for a private room . . . I think Tennessee was shamed into doing something. He finally visited Frank, and paid all his bills. But it took him a while."

Other friends of Tennessee's claim that while he paid Frank's hospital expenses he never visited him. He was terrified of hospitals and thought cancer might be contagious.

A few weeks after Frank had rented the cottage on Baker's Lane, Tennessee returned from New York, bringing Frank their bulldog Gigi to keep him company, and making him a gift of a monkey named "Creature," whom Frank adored.

Two weeks later Tennessee asked Frank to move back into the house on Duncan Street, which he was sharing with the young poet, "Angel," with whom he had traveled to Tangier. He asked Frank if Angel could stay, Frank agreed. Tennessee and the poet shared the bedroom downstairs. Frank took his old room upstairs.

By May, the cancer had spread beyond his lungs and his decline became rapid. Then Tennessee, thinking a change of place might cheer Frank up, flew to Nantucket, taking a small beach cottage there the second week in May. Frankie flew up to join him.

"I went over to the mainland to meet him," Tennessee wrote. "It was a bitch of a night. An unseasonably cold blast of wind was sweeping across the water: we missed the regular ferry to Nantucket. I hired a small boat to take us over, Frankie and Gigi and I. The cold turned icy. Frankie held Gigi tight against him, sitting bolt upright and silent during what seemed an endless crossing."

It was quickly apparent that the Nantucket cottage wouldn't do. Frank was barely eating, his body weakening with frightful speed; he silently sat for hours staring into space, his eyes seeming unnaturally large and, to Tennessee, beautiful in a painful, unearthly way.

Frank returned to Manhattan, staying in the East Sixty-fifth Street apartment, commuting between it and Memorial Hospital. He underwent cobalt treatments, a procedure that turned his chest black with burns. The disease spread ineluctably from organ to organ, defeating him. His weight fell below a hundred pounds.

Tennessee got rid of the Nantucket cottage and returned as quickly as possible to New York to share the apartment with Frank. Tennessee slept on the living-room sofa, Frankie in the bedroom. Each night Tennessee listened to him bolt the bedroom door, a sound that haunted and pained him for the rest of his life.

"Did he, poor child, suppose that I would still be apt to follow him in there and use his skeletal body again for sexual pleasure? . . . I think it was a thing he did automatically: perhaps it was death that he thought he was locking out."

He spent sleepless nights listening to Frankie cough away his life.

Finally, it was time for Frankie to enter the hospital for the last time.

"As he dressed to go, I entered the bedroom to assist him," Tennessee wrote, "but he would accept no assistance. He threw off his robe. His body, that of a little Hercules in the past, had turned to something more like the skeleton of a sparrow."

When they arrived at Memorial, Frank was too weak to walk, and for the first time accepted a wheelchair. He was placed in a cancer ward where most of the patients had inoperable brain cancer. Tennessee begged him to go into a private room, but Frankie demurred. "It doesn't matter at all to me now, I think I like being with them."

A few days later, when Frank seemed to have stabilized, Tennessee flew to Abingdon, Virginia, for the opening of yet another version of *The Milk Train Doesn't Stop Here Anymore*. While there, he was called and told that Frank was declining fast, his condition having suddenly taken a turn for the worse. Tennessee flew back to New York and visited Frankie the following morning.

Frank was taking oxygen, and he was unaccountably restless, getting out of bed every few minutes and stumbling across the room into a chair; sitting there a moment or two and staggering back to bed.

Frank complained to Tennessee of his terrible restlessness and his unbearable fatigue. Tennessee tried to get him to lie down quietly, to try to sleep. And then thinking that his presence was keeping Frank from sleep, asked him if he should leave now.

"No, I'm used to you," Frank said, turning on his side and lying there silently.

For another hour Tennessee stayed at Frank's bedside (he had that day been moved to a private room), and finally, thinking he was asleep, left.

"No, I'm used to you," were the last words that Frank Merlo said to Tennessee Williams, five words that he could not forget, and when, even twenty years later, he would recall them, tears would come to his eyes. They were words that baffled him, their meaning escaping him. Snagged on them, caught by this mere slip of language, Tennessee was haunted by them until he finally relaxed

into the belief that they were Frank's way of saying he loved him and always would.

Frank was unlike Tennessee; he couldn't declare love at the drop of a pin the way Tennessee did. It was a reluctance to admit deep feeling very common, certainly, to American men of his generation. "I love you" was the most difficult of declarations for this Sicilian from New Jersey to make. He was never able to tell Tennessee, face to face, that he loved him. The times he said it was over long-distance telephone when Tennessee, ending the conversation, would say, "Do you love me, Frankie?" And Frank would hurriedly answer, "Sure I love you."

After leaving the hospital, Tennessee went out with some friends to a gay bar and got drunk. He sensed what was coming.

That evening a nurse entered Frank's room and gave him a shot, a painkiller. Frank sat up suddenly, gasping for breath, and then collapsed onto the pillows. Minutes later, he was gone.

Frank Merlo's entire family came to New York for his funerals at a Catholic church and later at the Frank Campbell Funeral Chapel on Madison Avenue. Tennessee attended both.

He didn't go to the cemetery for the interment. Unable to bear watching the burial, he returned to his apartment with Elia and Molly Kazan. When they left, he lay down on the bed that had been Frankie's, and he wept.

What followed were the worst years of his life.

CHAPTER · SEVEN

IN THE EARLY 1970s I went down to Key West in the winter to stay at Tennessee's; he was to join me there in ten days. It was February, and the weather was unusually hot. I was then a contributing editor to *Esquire* magazine, and I owed them two articles, which I proposed to write in Key West during the period before Tennessee joined me. But he, thinking I might be lonely without him, asked Henry Faulkner, a resort painter, to look out for me.

By "resort painter" I mean an artist who does those godawful oils of flowers and birds and other animals with enormous, baleful eyes staring out at you with a kind of cartoon pleading; the kind of painting that Wally Findley specializes in selling to the tasteless rich in Palm Beach and other resort towns. Only Faulkner didn't have a gallery; at best he was lucky to place his work with the few art dealers on the island who tried to peddle them to daytrippers from Miami.

Henry Faulkner was an old friend of Tennessee's, having known him since the war. Henry religiously spent each winter in Key West. What I did not know about him then was that he was an amateur pimp, and was amazing in his ability to procure young men, primarily sailors, at a moment's notice.

Henry was small and wiry, with a thin, wrinkled face —he was about Tennessee's age—and a decided limp that got worse as he aged, since he suffered from a disease that made his muscles progressively deteriorate. One leg was much thinner and weaker than the other, much like Tony Snowdon's polio-withered leg. Henry spent his mornings driving around Key West in his jeep. When he spotted a likely prospect, say a young sailor trying to stagger home from the bars, he would shout, "Do you want a blow job!" It was an astonishingly effective, if direct, lure. In the mornings, every morning, Henry appeared at my front door with a jeep full of young men he offered to me gratis at Tennessee's request. I turned them down. Since this was one of my first times staying with Tennessee, I was not as yet sure of the house rules, and I suspected that Tennessee would not appreciate returning to the compound to find half the Gulf fleet encamped on his property.

Then one morning good old Henry, with the regularity of the postman, showed up on our doorstep with a blond young man, about twenty-two, who had recently returned from army duty in Vietnam.

"He needs a place to stay. He is sleeping on South Beach, and he's AWOL!"

I invited the serviceman inside. Shy, seeming shell-shocked but perfectly nice, he ended up staying in the house until Tennessee returned. He was from Kentucky, of Polish descent, with a name I found unpronounceable, so I called him Kentucky.

I worked in the mornings then, and after lunch Kentucky and I lay naked, taking the sun beside the pool. It was a pleasant few days. Then Tennessee returned a day early, standard procedure for him. He never warned you when he was coming, not when there was the chance of catching you unawares doing something that might permit him to stage an emotional scene, an activity he immensely enjoyed. And that was fine, as long as you did not take it seriously.

Unexpected, Tennessee walked out on to the patio and spied the two of us sunning. I said, "Hi, Tenn. You're home early."

He ignored me, his eyes riveted by Kentucky; walking over to him, he knelt down and began caressing his penis.

"That's Tennessee," I explained, since the young man was obviously bewildered by this fully clothed, strange, and somewhat elderly gentleman touching his private parts without so much as a by-your-leave.

After a few moments Tennessee glanced over at me and said, "It's a rosebud like Frankie," meaning the boy's uncircumcised penis resembled, as it undoubtedly did, a rosebud.

Ever since hearing that remark, I have understood the references in his work to roses—a rose tattoo, for example —in a sexual sense, symbolic of the male organ. The rose as an image is increasingly prevalent in his writing after he met Frank Merlo. Now I do not want to make too much of this. Suffice it to say that the erotic content he perceived in roses came from his identification of the rose with sexuality, specifically male. But, too, there were other "roses," i.e., his sister and his maternal grandmother, the two women closest to him in his life, and it is only a guess on my part to suggest that his homosexuality may have come from a compulsion to repress feelings of sexual desire he felt as a boy toward Rose and even his grandmother. It is indisputable that he adored the rose, his sister and maternal grandmother (nonsexually), and the male (sexually).

After getting Kentucky somewhat aroused, Tennessee

took him by the hand and led him into the bedroom, where they disappeared for several hours.

(I am reminded of going to see *Citizen Kane* with Tennessee in San Francisco. It was during one afternoon when we had time to kill so we went to an art theatre to see Orson Welles's classic film. In the scene where Kane lies dying, and breathes his last, with the word "Rosebud!" Tennessee laughed.)

Things went well with Kentucky for a few days; Tennessee was smitten with the Vietnam veteran; we sat out on the patio after dinner, drinking, and Tennessee lifted his hand to the boy's face, touching his chin so that Kentucky's face turned at an angle to the light. "So much like Frankie, baby," he said in wonder.

Kentucky, who was on the lam, had no money. He hinted several times to Tennessee that he needed a few dollars; Tennessee ignored him, fearing, I think, that if he gave him money Kentucky would have the means to leave, and that he did not want him to do.

Then, one evening before we were to go off to dinner, Kentucky took me aside, telling me that he had to leave Key West and wanted enough money to take the bus home. He had not seen his family since he returned from the war, and he was homesick.

Tennessee was dressing in his bedroom. I knocked and went inside.

"He wants to leave, Tenn. He wants to go home, and he needs money to get there," I began.

Tennessee looked suspiciously at me. "Are you his agent? What is your *cut* going to be? Ten percent? Twenty?" he demanded.

"You're crazy," I said, finding his paranoia irritating. "All he needs is bus fare."

He exploded. "I don't have any money! I am surrounded by lazybones boys who think I should support them. Well, the milk train doesn't stop here anymore! I gave Frank property. I gave him the royalties from my plays and when he died he left them to his family! Wasn't *I* his family? Shouldn't he have returned them to me? Don't you think his family today should return to me what is mine? Tell Kentucky to ask Frank's family for money. They are the ones with the *loot!*"

He was furious. He marched into his bathroom and slammed the door.

I went back into the living room where Kentucky was, and I told him that Tennessee was upset and that I would get him bus fare and pocket money once he calmed down.

Kentucky shrugged. "I have to go, man. I miss my people." And he left.

Ten minutes later, when Tennessee came into the living room, where I was sitting alone, he demanded to know where Kentucky was. I told him that he had left to go hitchhike his way home. He stared at me, fiercely angry, and I could almost see the wheels turning as his brain went into overdrive to find some sinister reason why the boy had walked out.

"My watch!" he suddenly shouted.

"What about your watch?" Tennessee had an old gold Swiss wristwatch that he loved, although it was as ugly as sin.

"That child has swiped my gold watch! I knew he was a thief, one of Henry's hustlers!"

I replied that Kentucky was not the kind of kid who stole, and that Tennessee had, as he so often did, misplaced the damn thing.

While I went searching the house for his watch, Tennessee got on the phone and called the sheriff, informed him that *my* houseguest had stolen a two-thousand-dollar watch and that he wanted the boy tracked down and arrested.

I found the wristwatch in the drawer in a metal cabinet in the bathroom where Tennessee had absentmindedly put it. I came back into the living room and threw the watch at him. "There's your goddamn watch!"

His face fell. I asked him what was wrong. He said that he had just called the sheriff to make a complaint of theft against Kentucky. "Oh, baby, he is AWOL. What have I done?"

He slumped on to the sofa. I made him a drink. He was despondent and remorseful, and when he was like that all my love for him came to the fore because he seemed so helpless and alone, childlike in his sense of having done something bad. I tried to cheer him up as he waited, like a condemned prisoner, for the cops to arrive.

Around ten that night, the sheriff came to our door; beside him Kentucky stood handcuffed. They had found him hitchhiking on the highway on Shark Key, making his way north. His forehead was badly bruised.

I went and got Tennessee. When he saw Kentucky, he started to cry, explaining that it was all a mistake, the boy had not stolen the watch but that he had misplaced it. "Let me give you money," he pleaded. Kentucky shook his head no. Tennessee ran to the living-room desk, got his checkbook, and signed his name. "Take it, baby. Fill in any amount you want, whatever you need! And forgive me."

They left, and we never heard from Kentucky again, and I do not know if he made it home. I very much suspect that he was never able to cash the check, and that the police probably dropped him off at the highway, gave him a few hours to leave the Keys, and cashed the check themselves.

That night, late, I heard Tennessee crying in his bedroom.

As I said before, after Frank Merlo's death, Tennessee spent the remaining years in a search for someone to take his place, to make a life with. There were a whole series of companions, some of whom treated him badly, others whom *he* made miserable.

In 1976 he left New York to visit a friend of his, a professor in California named Oliver who he thought was dying from terminal brain cancer, an idea he found hugely amusing. The professor taught English literature at one of the Southern California colleges, and among the authors he taught was Tennessee Williams. While Tennessee was in Los Angeles the professor persuaded him to appear for free at one of his classes and speak to the students about his plays. Tennessee agreed, something that was unlike him. He despised academics and normally would not set foot on a college campus unless they were paying him big money to do so. That was one of the reasons he had acquired so few honorary degrees. He did not believe that the award of a sheepskin was compensation enough for him to endure a few hours on campus. It was not the students he objected to, it was the schoolteachers.

Two years before he died, the University of Pennsylvania voted to give him an honorary doctorate. Tennessee was out of the country at the time, and his agent rashly consented to the degree, promising that Tennessee would be there for graduation and even make a brief acceptance speech in exchange for the doctorate. When his agent informed me that Tennessee was due in May at the University of Pennsylvania's graduation, I told him he was out of his mind. "How much are they paying him?" I asked. On being told that all the school would cover was his traveling expenses, I said the agent had better call the university back and make his apologies, because there was no way on earth Tennessee was going to attend anybody's graduation without cash up front.

That wasn't simply because of greed, it was because he knew that academic critics and the critical establishment in general held his later work, certainly from 1970 on, in low esteem. He thought them wrong and suspected that their attitude was a result of their disapproval of his personal life.

"After *Time* magazine disclosed that I was homosexual, the good notices ceased in New York. The *Times* and the other New York papers, taking their orders from the [Henry] Luce empire and the sinister Gelbs, wrote me off. And soon, so did the teachers."

His animosity to the academic world was further hardened when he learned that the Columbia University Board of Trustees had voted to overrule a faculty committee and refuse to honor him with an honorary degree because William Paley, who was chairman of the board, believed to do such would be tantamount to the university's giving its seal of approval to his life-style (i.e., homosexuality).

While speaking to the college literature class in Los Angeles, Tennessee was transfixed by a young man sitting in the front row, again a blond. His name was Chris, and he lived in Topanga Canyon, where he worked as a groom and horse trainer. Tennessee quickly fell in love with him, bringing him back to New York.

They stayed together in the Hotel Élysée, in the Victorian Suite, and Tennessee was very happy for a time. He had begun writing his *Memoirs*, a book that was to become an international bestseller.

It was late fall, and Tennessee, knowing that Chris loved horses, decided to go with him to a dude ranch at Montauk at the tip of Long Island. They bought boots and outdoor gear, and rented a small cabin at the ranch. They stayed two weeks, and except for one afternoon, it rained continuously. The cabin was unheated, damp, and Tennessee caught cold. Despite this, each day he went riding with Chris along trails through the scrub pines along the sea. He hated horses, and yet the mornings found him and Chris saddling up; a few hours on the range and Tennessee returned to the cabin, barely able to walk, finally developing painful hemorrhoids. They returned to New York. Tennessee checked into the hospital to have the growths removed. I visited him there.

"It was awful, baby. Gloomy and cold. There was no electricity in our cabin and we had to get by with kerosene lamps that produced the greatest stench! After a few days I couldn't even walk. I kept telling Chris that the horses were destroying my posterior. He didn't believe me, being a true cowboy, although a *California* cowboy, which isn't quite the real thing. We didn't have a car. We were trapped in this cabin in the rain, and every time I told him we had to go somewhere for a hot meal (we were living on cold sandwiches we purchased at the [ranch's] office), he said that sandwiches were good enough for him. Finally we borrowed an old convertible, where the passenger door was broken. It was tied shut with a rope, but not tightly, because I had to sit there holding it shut to keep from being hurled onto the highway.

"We drove over to Dick Cavett's house, where I expected to be asked to share a hot meal. I wasn't."

When Tennessee was released from the hospital, he took me and Chris to Elaine's to celebrate Chris's birthday. It was a sad occasion, not because it was a birthday but because Tennessee had called Elaine the day before, ordered a cake as a surprise, purchased a gift for Chris (a garnet and gold ring), only to be told that afternoon that Chris wanted to go home to California. He missed his horses.

After dinner I went back to my apartment at the Dakota. I was awakened at about 3 A.M. Chris was calling from the Élysée, telling me he was leaving within the hour for Los Angeles. Knowing that Tennessee at that point could not be alone, I told him to wait until I got there.

Chris was sitting calmly in the living room. Near him was a backpack filled with his clothes.

He told me that Tennessee was in bad shape, that he had had a lot to drink after dinner, had shouted at him, accusing Chris of using him, not loving him, and then had taken some pills and passed out in the bedroom.

Chris was, without any question, the best-looking of Tennessee's companions; he was also honest, gentle, simple in his tastes and ambitions, and decidedly naïve, believing that Tennessee really did want to buy a ranch where Chris could keep horses, and that Tennessee would raise goats and geese and live the remainder of his life quietly with Chris and their animal menagerie. Every time some new soul fell for his goats-and-geese routine, my admiration for Tennessee's powers of persuasion went up a notch.

I told Chris that it was impossible for him to leave. It was after 3 A.M., it was pouring rain—there was a wicked storm that night—and even if he could get to the airport, which I strongly doubted, the planes weren't flying in this weather.

"I'm going to hitchhike to California," he calmly informed me.

And then it occurred to me: he didn't have a plane ticket.

"You mean he hasn't given you any money to fly home?" I asked, knowing the answer. It angered me, because Chris had been extremely good to Tennessee, had asked nothing in return, and now that he wanted to leave, Tennessee was sticking him.

"You wait here," I went into the bedroom. Tennessee was lying on the bed still dressed in suit and tie, breathing heavily. I shook him, and I shook him hard, but I could not get him to wake up. He may have been awake all along, simply playing dead because he didn't want to deal with the situation at hand.

I found his checkbook, wrote out a check for six hundred dollars made out to cash, signed Tennessee's name, and took it downstairs to the hotel desk and had it cashed. I went back upstairs, handed Chris the money, and kissed him good-bye.

It was the only time I ever forged Tennessee's name to a check, and I do not regret it.

I stayed the night with Tennessee, leaving at noon. I came back about six to have drinks with him. Later we were to go on to a party for John Cheever.

Tennessee had gotten out of bed about a half hour before I arrived; he was badly hung over, and I think a little sick at heart over Chris's departure. He was between engagements, back at square one again, and he didn't like it a bit.

We had drinks, and he read to me from his *Memoirs* manuscript, a very funny passage about a critic giving Mary Poppins the clap in New Orleans. Then he read more passages about the celebrated who had passed through his life, people who had deeply hurt him, particularly producers and actors who had made their careers and fortunes on his work and who he now admitted had badly used and then discarded him. The more he read, the unhappier he got. Finally, I suggested that he should shower and get ready to go out to the party.

He went into the bathroom and was gone an inordinate amount of time. I never heard the shower running.

I knocked, and then opened the bathroom door, to see him sitting on the toilet seat, wearing only his jockey shorts, his head in his hands, his shoulders trembling. He had been dyeing his hair, and the dark brown liquid covered his scalp and ran like blood down his neck and on to his shoulders, ran like blood over his chest. Pulling his hands away, his face wet with dye, he glanced up at me, his eyes looking wounded, "Get me a priest, baby. I want to die. Get me a priest."

I went into the living room, suddenly feeling very frightened and at a loss. I made a drink. I heard him turn on the shower, and then leave the bathroom and pad into his bedroom.

After a short while, I opened the door. He was lying under the covers, only his head visible, staring at the ceiling. On top of his chest lay a Gideon Bible. The scene startled me; he looked like a body laid out for its last rites.

I called Bishop Paul Moore, at whose cathedral Tennessee had spoken against the Vietnam War years before. The bishop was at a dinner party. He left immediately and came to the Élysée. When he arrived all I could tell him was that Tennessee wanted to die.

I do not know what was said between them in the bedroom behind closed doors, but when the bishop emerged with him they were both smiling, although I sensed the priest was disturbed by what he had heard.

That year, when Tennessee finished writing his *Memoirs,* he went down to Key West. There, Tom Congdon, who was editor on the book, went to work with him.

A few days later, when Tennessee returned to New York, I stopped by to see him, and asked him how the editing went.

"Baby," he said, "I went down to Key West with a book this big . . ." he held his hands about a foot apart, "and now I have a book *this* big!" his hands about an inch apart.

The book, over his objections, was heavily edited, the publisher's lawyers cutting huge sections of the manuscript, deletions Tennessee thought were unjustified. He had received an advance of $25,000 on signing, and another $25,000 later. He asserted that he never received the second payment or any domestic royalties or foreign rights money from his bestselling autobiography.

None of this is true however. He never had the vaguest idea how much money he made or where it went. Each month his New York accountants would send to him a large packet containing hundreds of checks for him to sign, checks to pay taxes, bills, Miss Rose's expenses, charitable donations. Tennessee was in the highest tax bracket, and resultantly he had to give tens of thousands of dollars away each year or the government took it. But he never seemed to know what checks he was signing or where the money was being donated. And he was as terrified of his accountants as he was of his lawyers and agents, and thus, while he thought he was being taken to the cleaners—he *always* believed people were taking him to the cleaners—he didn't do a thing about it. He claimed once, in explaining to me why he was not going to send his brother Dakin any more contributions to aid his senatorial campaign, that he was chronically short of cash "because my accountants, who are Jews, donate my funds to Jewish causes. They have, I believe, built at least one wing at the Jewish hospital in Long Island that they have thoughtfully named in memory of their mother!"

He didn't trust bankers, either. In Key West one afternoon, Henry Faulkner showed up at Tennessee's house bringing two midwestern couples with him. The men, both fat and middle-aged, their gray hair cut short, military style were dressed in brightly colored blazers and even brighter slacks. Their wives were wearing double-knit pantsuits and lots of cheap jewelry. Following Henry inside the house, they stood with pompous self-importance, nodding in agreement as Henry demanded to see Tennessee. I knew at once that Henry was out of cash and had found these suckers to buy his paintings. In fact he had waylaid them as they disembarked from the Conch Train, a series of open trolleys lashed together that went about Key West disturbing the peace. After numerous complaints that reached to the mayor's office, Tennessee had succeeded after years of campaigning in forcing the tour trolleys not to drive along Duncan Street announcing his house. It wasn't the noise that bothered him. What infuriated him was the Conch Train guide's spiel: "And on your left is the small house of Tennessee Williams, the famous author of *God's Little Acre* and *Tobacco Road!*"

Recently Henry Faulkner had been banned from the house, Tennessee having taken to calling him Sticky Fingers because he stole everything in sight. I was pledged to never let Henry be alone in one of the rooms, but always to stick by him closely enough to catch those quick fingers pocketing the property. Tennessee had a valid point, because whenever Henry came by and wandered off to visit the bathroom, a journey of discovery that invariably took him through every nook and cranny in the place, we discovered that towels and linen, cameras, money, even canned goods were missing. By this particular visit, we were practically out of towels and soap—shades of Miss Rose!

(After he was finally banned for good, although Tennessee granted reprieves in moments of weakness, Henry took to climbing through the living-room window when we weren't home and really making a haul.)

Tennessee was locked in his studio. I knocked and told him Henry had arrived uninvited with two Kansas bankers and their wives in tow. He told me to inform them that he was dead.

I returned to the living room to catch Henry trying to shove martini glasses into his trouser pockets. Retrieving the crystal, I informed the assembled that Mr. Williams was indisposed.

Henry laughed. The bankers were not amused, and rather heatedly informed me that they were not in the habit of being treated this way, their time being extremely valuable; that they had journeyed a great distance at considerable expense with their wives to purchase two of

Henry's flower pictures to hang in their parlors back home, the very paintings that sat in Mr. Williams's studio on loan to him from Mr. Faulkner.

Well, they were not in the studio, they were in the bedroom closet with the rest of Henry's recent production, and they were definitely not on loan, since they had been purchased by Tennessee along with the rest of Henry's stuff, very much against his better judgment.

With the bankers and their wives following him, their visages masks of offended dignity, Henry scurried through the house and out through the patio where he pounded on Tennessee's studio door, demanding that he come out and permit the paintings to be viewed.

He did, in a rage, buyers and painter following him into the living room where they stood aghast as he opened the bedroom closet and began hurling scores of Henry's paintings at them. "Take the fucking things!" he yelled.

"Your behavior is disgusting," one of the wives declared.

"How dare you use language like that in the presence of Christian ladies!" a banker said. "Who do you think you are? You are nothing but a pervert!"

That did it. Tennessee flew out of control, shouting, "Out! Out!" as he rushed to the front door, pulling it open. "Get the fuck out of this house! Moneychangers! Bloodsuckers!"

As they fled, one of the bankers declared, "You will be hearing from my lawyers in the morning!" not the most congenial thing to say, since Tennessee loathed members of the Bar only marginally less than he hated New York drama critics and ax murderers.

"God said it is far easier for a camel to get through the

eye of a needle," Tennessee responded, "than it is for a fucking *banker* to enter the gates of Heaven!"

In the last years of his life Tennessee hated writing letters, and if he absolutely had to, if a phone call wouldn't suffice, he would scribble off a quick note with a pen or pencil, whatever was at hand, having largely abandoned the typewriter for correspondence. I am not sure why that was, unless he was trying to spare the words and energy for his work. Two letters were equal, in his estimation, to the work required to write a good poem.

Tennessee, by the way, always wrote on a manual typewriter, never comfortable with an electric because the automatic keys, he explained, moved faster than his thoughts. A word processor would have completely undone him.

There is a direct connection between the instrument a writer employs and his ability to create. That relationship between instrument and hand, and hand and brain, is established early in a writer's life and after it is set becomes as hard as hell to break. Norman Mailer, for example, sits and writes in a tiny script on three-by-five filing cards, a slow process, given the speed with which a modern word processor works. Truman Capote also wrote in longhand, only he used school notebooks and yellow legal pads. Hemingway used to write, again in longhand, standing up before a tall, pulpitlike desk, much as Churchill did, although he tended to dictate to secretaries more than actually write. Tennessee was wedded to old Royal portables, the type he first used when he started to write. There is something in the tactile process of writing, the very physical act itself, that is necessary to creating. If, for instance, a writer turns from using a manual typewriter to using a very different machine, say a silent word processor, he discovers quickly that he can't write as well; the new feel and unfamiliar sound of the word processor makes him self-conscious of the act of writing, and it is self-consciousness that defeats creation. It is as if the brain unconsciously demands the feel and sounds it has become accustomed to in order to become alert to imagination.

Tennessee never saved letters and usually didn't read them unless he knew the writer very well or thought there might be a check inside the envelope. His mail used to pile up by the bagful in Key West, and from time to time he dumped the load on the dining-room table, making a futile stab at sorting through the correspondence, pulling out a letter here and there from someone he knew, and then just giving up and tossing the entire mess into the rubbish. There were exceptions. Oddly enough, if you were someone who wanted to engage in a written correspondence with him, you would have better luck if you had never met him. People he knew he phoned. Every once in a while he would happen upon a letter from an unknown writer in some godforsaken place with a host of problems defying solution, or, more typically, he might read a letter from a person asking some ridiculous question that would send his memory into overdrive. He would reply because it allowed him to remember better days.

I remember he once got a letter from some old biddy in Tennessee or Texas or someplace who was named Lanier and wanted to know if Tennessee was related to her. The day he got the letter he went into his studio and didn't come out for several hours. When he did, we sat in the living room and he read to me a twelve-page letter he had written to her about the history of the Lanier family. I was amazed. He was amused. And thus began a correspondence between him and a widowed shut-in who happened to share his middle name.

One afternoon in 1977, Henry Faulkner had shown up uninvited for lunch, pulling himself over the compound fence because we wouldn't let him in the door. Tennessee, on hearing the thud of Henry's fall onto our side of the fence, defensively retreated into his studio where he hid, drinking, behind locked doors. He was drinking a lot that year, feeling very unhappy, mainly because of Robert Carroll, whom he loved too much but could not make the love work.

I made Henry a sandwich and then hustled him off the property.

In the studio Tennessee had fallen asleep. I opened the studio door with a key, and saw him curled up on the cot. There were empty wine and vodka bottles scattered about the place, photos, half-finished paintings, paints, brushes, dirty underwear, used syringes, manuscript pages all over the place, dustballs blowing about like tumbleweeds in convention. Tennessee looked at me with half-lidded eyes, blurred from booze.

"I'll come in tomorrow and clean up your studio," I offered. "It looks like a pigsty." It did. He was offended.

With my feet, I started shoving the accumulated litter under his desk and out of the way of traffic so he wouldn't slip in the filth and break his neck. While making this temporary rubbish heap under his desk, I noticed a program on the floor from some Eugene O'Neill Festival a year or two before. I showed it to him. He took it from me, smiled, and still holding it went back to sleep.

Five or six years before, when I had first stayed with him in Key West, he had found a long letter from Eugene

O'Neill in a filing cabinet in his studio. Still in the original envelope, it was stained with wine and cigarette burns. But Tennessee read it to me, first explaining that he had received it after the opening of *The Glass Menagerie* in New York. O'Neill began his letter, the only one he ever wrote to Tennessee, with generous praise for *Menagerie* and its author. However, soon the body of the letter was darkened by O'Neill's warnings to the young playwright about the treachery of Broadway producers, the disloyalty of the audience, the egotism and callousness of reviewers, in short, the many difficulties of being a playwright in the United States, a country that seemed to have a compulsion to elevate its artists to great heights only to bring them roughly to ground. He warned him about the destructiveness that lay in wait ahead, booze and vicious women, wives who devoured the soul and spit it out (he didn't have to worry about Tennessee on that score), and he wrote at length about the terrible loneliness he felt, an isolation that Tennessee, too, would come to know, however great his gifts.

It was a very moving and a very sad letter, and I don't know what became of it. Years later, when Beverly Grunwald came to Key West to interview Tennessee for *Women's Wear Daily* (this was shortly before she died), I asked him to read the O'Neill letter to her. He couldn't find it.

What I learned from the letter, and from Tennessee's ruminations on the literary genius and personal wreckage of Eugene O'Neill, was that he considered the author of *Long Day's Journey into Night* to be his only competitor in the pantheon of American playwrights. He thought O'Neill was, after himself, the nation's greatest playwright, and he was right in that belief. Yet he was jealous of O'Neill all his life, indeed obsessed. While he never disparaged him, he firmly believed that there existed an ongoing conspiracy, directed by Leslie Gelb and his wife, both employees of the New York *Times*, to destroy his reputation in order to ensure O'Neill's place as the first-ranking of America's dramatists. Whenever he received a bad review from the *Times*, something that occurred with heartbreaking regularity once Clive Barnes had left to become drama critic for the New York *Post*, Tennessee blamed the hated Gelbs.

"Baby, they have done it again!" The unkinder the notice, the more steamed he became at the Gelbs. "You know, they think they own a monopoly on Eugene O'Neill because they wrote the definitive biography of his life, the *authorized* biography. They have made a cottage industry out of him, and they are out to protect their financial stake, and that means destroying me! They are the Keepers of the Flame, and they fight to destroy anyone's reputation whose work might reduce the intensity of that light."

For days after a bad review he muttered on ominously about the evil Gelbs using the power of the *Times* to ruin him. He may have been right.

Curiously, his admiration for the work of Eugene O'Neill never diminished, nor did his respect for the suffering of his sad life ever cease.

By 1980, when I last visited him in Key West, Tennessee's self-respect had grown so weak, his feelings of failure so unshakable, his desperation so acute that he sought even to impress me. Surely if there was one person whom he did not have to convince of his greatness, if he had one true believer by his side, it was I.

This is how he did it. He went into his studio and got the playbill from the O'Neill Festival I had found three years before. On its cover was a large, handsome sepia photograph of the playwright taken shortly before his death. Tennessee excitedly showed it to me. On it was written, with a ballpoint pen, "To Tennessee, with love, Eugene O'Neill."

He asked me to take it to the art store and have it beautifully framed.

A few days later, when I brought the framed picture home, Tennessee made quite a ceremony of housing it prominently on display on the small wicker table by the sofa, where the telephone was, in the living room. To make room for it he removed the framed photograph of Hart Crane, shoving it in a drawer.

Watching him, I felt I might cry, so unhappy was I made by this desperate act, this need of approval from the dead. I knew Tennessee had signed the picture himself, I knew his handwriting as well as my own. I knew the Festival, for which the playbill was printed, had taken place long after O'Neill had died. It saddened me to think that he thought he could fool anyone with it, and sadder still that he felt he had to try.

When I was last in his home in Key West, in July 1982, the O'Neill picture, with its framed inscription, was in the breakfront behind the dining table.

March 1981, I flew to Chicago to be with Tennessee on his seventieth birthday, a venerable age that he had never believed he would reach, convinced from his youth that he was a poet destined to die young, perhaps of consumption or some other romantic, faintly literary disorder —"romantic" in the sense that as a young artist consumption was the "artistic" disease then fashionable. (See

Camille or Thomas Mann's *The Magic Mountain).* But God had spared him, despite heart attacks, a dysfunctioning pancreas, weak lungs, semiblindness, and staggering amounts of liquor washing down a pharmacy of drugs; worse, despite defeats in love, and perceived critical failure, public contempt, and humiliation. Yet he went on.

Birthdays were important occasions for him as, for example, Christmas or Thanksgiving or other public holidays were not. He remembered his friends' birthdays, and tried to be with you as you confronted the beginning of yet another year. On his own birthdays he loved having his friends come to him, and by his seventieth his family of close friends had been reduced to a handful, many lost to death or age and illness, others having broken with him or, more typically among the famous, having drifted away, indifferent to him now because he could do little for their careers anymore. There wasn't another *Streetcar Named Desire* or *Cat on a Hot Tin Roof* left in him, and he knew it and so did they.

"I used to write symphonies. Now I write chamber music, smaller plays. Everyone expects me to write another *Streetcar.* I don't want to, even if I could."

Near the end of his life, what commercial interest there was in his work was not in his current writing or in anything done by him since the early seventies. The Hollywood studios, television networks, and Broadway were only interested in revivals of his masterpieces, a fact of life that he understood but that made him feel older and more done in than he was. For the first time since *The Glass Menagerie* magazines rejected short stories he submitted, and plays commissioned went unproduced. In 1981 he was commissioned to write an original short play for a Miami city-wide arts festival. He was paid fifteen thousand dol-

lars, submitted the play, only to have the festival or-
ganizers publicly reject it as unfit for production, substi-
tuting in its place a play by an unknown, young
playwright. As a result, he felt he had lost his usefulness
because his current work was only being done Off-Off
Broadway, if there, or in regional theatres. What he had to
say to the world today, as he entered his eighth decade, the
world was not interested in hearing.

There were exceptions, of course, none of them in the
United States. His new plays were still received seriously,
and enthusiastically, in Europe, France, England, and
Austria in particular. *Vieux Carré*, starring Sylvia Sidney,
opened on Broadway on May 10, 1976, to negative reviews
and closed almost at once. And yet, when it opened in the
West End of London a few months later, it was a hit and
ran for many months. I was there opening night, having
gone over to England with Philip Kingsley and Richard
Zoerink, very close friends of ours. Sylvia Miles starred in
London. It was a happy time for Tennessee, to see received with enthusiasm a new play that, like so many
others, had been damned in his homeland. He felt like a
prophet without honor in his own country, and I think by
then he was.

In Hollywood and on Broadway an entire new generation of actors had reached stardom, often through television, and, like most actors, they craved the creative valida-
tion that playing one of Tennessee Williams's major roles
conferred. Once they had clawed their way to fame and
money, they wanted critical respect, something you might
get from playing *Streetcar*, but could not achieve after
years of starring in "Dallas" or heading the bill at Caesar's
Palace. And Tennessee enjoyed young actors, especially
liking and admiring Michael Moriarty, Perry King, Eliza-

beth Ashley, Al Pacino, and Treat Williams. Richard Gere, he thought, potentially could be one of America's better dramatic actors, but then he was insulted by Gere and never spoke of him again.

Tennessee went to see *Bent,* a play about homosexuals sent to the Nazi concentration camps. It was directed by Robert Alan Ackerman, a young man whom Tennessee considered especially gifted and was anxious to have direct his work. In 1982 the play was running on Broadway, starring Richard Gere. After the performance, Tennessee and Maria St. Just went backstage to congratulate the actors on their performances. When Maria and he entered Gere's dressing room they found the actor lounging in a chair wearing only a pair of jockey shorts. Gere stared at them. Tennessee shyly introduced himself and Maria, and proceeded to compliment Gere on his performance. Richard Gere said nothing, simply sat there staring at Tennessee with a look of smug boredom. Maria, losing patience with what she knew was insulting behavior, told Gere that it was outrageous that he did not have the courtesy to at least stand when the nation's greatest playwright came backstage to compliment him on his acting. Gere said nothing, and Tennessee left in confusion, having once again suffered a loss of face.

Gere aside, Tennessee received an almost continuous stream of production proposals from television and movie stars wanting to "re-create" one of his classic roles. Ann-Margaret wanted to do *Streetcar* (she finally did for television, opposite Treat Williams as Stanley. Tennessee didn't live to see the broadcast.), but then, so did Sylvester Stallone. When Tennessee heard the news that Stallone was actively interested in playing Stanley Kowalski in a new film version of *Streetcar,* and that conversations among the

actor, agents, and producers were in progress, and that a
million dollars was being offered him for the rights, he
was horrified.

"Baby, there is no way that young man is going to
turn Stanley into *Rocky 5,* or is it Six? I am always in need
of liquid capital, but I would rather be reduced to being an
elevator operator in Times Square and eating at Nedick's
than allow such a travesty to occur!

"You know, most of my films were subjected to excessive censorship. Which is one of the reasons why I might
be interested in seeing *Streetcar* done again as a film by
Sidney Lumet, now that Kazan has stopped directing. But
I'd have to have a great Stanley, and the only person
they've mentioned so far is Sylvester Stallone, and so I'm
not paying much attention to this project of remaking
Streetcar until there's a suitable Stanley, and a really great
actress to play Blanche."

However, he feared, justifiably, that once he died his
heirs would go for the buck and sell him out, and that was
why he changed his will two years before his death and
left his money to Harvard and the University of the
South. While he despised academics, he thought, given
their intellectual pretensions, they were more likely to re-
sist the cheapening of his work than others. Still, he finally
could not shake the old fear and mistrust, that agents and
producers conspired behind his back to desecrate his life's
work.

In Chicago, Tennessee was staying in a gaudy suite at
the Radisson Hotel on North Michigan Avenue. It was a
huge, four-bedroom penthouse decorated in a mock 1930s
Moroccan style: fake stone walls, iron chandeliers, a massive fireplace, a staircase and balcony, all of it reminiscent
of the interior design especially popular in Hollywood

about the time, 1943, that he had been a contract writer at the film studios. For that reason he dubbed the place "The Norma Desmond Suite" after the role played by Gloria Swanson in *Sunset Boulevard*.

The oppressive 1930s opulence of the suite delighted him—the oversized chandeliers and filigreed moldings, the ratty carpets, the Art Deco furniture, and the sweeping, curved staircase, unquestionably grand enough for Miss Swanson herself. But what he liked most about his rooms was that they were just a short walk away from the hotel's swimming pool.

Swimming and writing every day had kept him alive through disease, surgery, periods of severe depression, physical attack, and the demise of those dearest to him—and nearly forty years of international acclaim, fame and rebuke, triumph and panic.

Tennessee was in town for the opening of his new play, *A House Not Meant to Stand*, the title being his one-sentence commentary on the state of the American nation. The play was being mounted at the Goodman Studio Theatre, a small house behind the Chicago Institute of Art that specialized in experimental plays and works-in-progress. Unlike the Goodman's main stage, the Studio was where new playwrights without a national reputation were allowed to test the subsidized waters. In a sense, Tennessee was back where he had started.

The play was directed by Gary Tucker, a young director for whom Tennessee had great fondness. And while Gary, who was from New Orleans, had had a relatively brief career in the theatre, he believed deeply in the quality and significance of Tennessee's current work, and that helped Tennessee believe in it himself.

A House Not Meant to Stand is set in the present-day

South, and concerns a family that is collapsing morally and psychologically, much like the house in which they live, a structure that is literally falling down around their ears. To survive with a modicum of what passes for sanity, they hold to old dreams that have become impossible and unreal, and to past injustices of the heart, pain they cannot or are unwilling to let go. It is the remembrance of hurt that keeps them alive in the present deadness around them as they confront a future that is already foreclosed.

The father, Cornelius, is a failed but unresigned political hack who can never quit campaigning, forever plotting political victories that never are actualized. The character is based to a degree on Tennessee's paternal grandfather, Thomas Lanier Williams, who happily went through the family fortune in a mindless and endless pursuit of high office. Moreover, Cornelius is a character that reflects Tennessee's brother, Dakin, who like his grandfather, has spent much of his adult life in an unsuccessful quest to be elected to something, the United States Senate and the presidency itself having in recent years been the objects of his quixotic campaigns. Cornelius in *A House Not Meant to Stand* is the only character in any of his work that is based on Dakin. It is not a flattering portrayal.

When Dakin was asked if he was angry that his brother had put him in the play, he replied generously, "No, no. He has used everybody else in the family, he might as well use me."

A House Not Meant to Stand is one of the best of Tennessee's late plays, certainly superior to *Clothes for a Summer Hotel*. Although it is bitter in places, at times meanspirited, it is suffused with poetic, gossamerlike language, both haunting and sad. A very Chekhovian work about the end of things, that moment of stasis before the final collapse, when dread is felt but unacknowledged, and passion and pain, ambition and human will no longer exist except in a fading memory, life having become an attic filled with dead objects to which memory, like cobweb, clings.

By the time Tennessee had completed the production script of this play, Dakin was his only surviving relative who was not institutionalized, his mother having died earlier in June.

Miss Edwina, physically tiny and frail, had gone to her reward at the age of ninety-five at the Bernard West Pine nursing home in St. Louis. If she had hung on for another three weeks she would have celebrated her ninety-sixth birthday.

Tennessee went home for her funeral, held in Christ Church Cathedral in St. Louis. After her burial, he was driven to Dakin's house in Collinsville, Illinois, a suburb across the river from St. Louis, where Dakin practices law and plans his political campaigns.

I once asked Tennessee what kind of law his brother specialized in?

"Specializes in? He takes what he can get, dog-bite cases!"

As I have written earlier, the two brothers had not been close since Dakin had had Tennessee committed to the nuthouse in 1969. I liked Dakin a lot and in some ways felt sorry for him—it is difficult enough growing up the runt of the litter without having a world-famous older brother whose shadow steals your sunlight. Tennessee was constantly losing his temper over one thing or another that Dakin had done, usually when he felt that his brother was raining on his parade with his publicity-seeking. Dakin loved seeing his name in print, even if it was negative, taking the lighthearted attitude that any publicity was good as long as his name was spelled correctly. If he was a political animal he was a squirrel, and bits of publicity were chestnuts he gathered and stored away against his next, inevitable foray into politics.

Dakin first ran for the Senate in 1972, and while he carried nearly one third of the state, thirty counties, and a half a million votes, he lost the Democratic primary. They loved him in Peoria, though, a city he surprisingly won.

In 1974 he challenged Adlai Stevenson, Jr., in the Democratic primary, but lost the nomination again, although he took 120,000 votes, among them Mayor Richard Daley's. The Chicago machine boss was feuding with Stevenson at the time.

Nineteen seventy-eight found Dakin at it again, running in the primary for governor of Illinois, and losing.

In 1980, he ran for President of the United States.

Dakin's campaign platform was simple and to the point: Peace and Love. And he had a certain gift for sloganeering. In 1972, in his race for the chance to challenge the incumbent, Senator Charles Percy, Dakin came up with: Make Percy Cry for Mercy!

All this was too much for Tennessee, who moaned about what an embarrassment his brother's political ambitions were to him.

"Dakin had to get ten thousand signatures to get on the ballot in Illinois. Now, baby, there was no way he was going to be able to gather those signatures in the time required. So he went into East St. Louis and met some man in a colored bar and offered him a dollar for each registered voter who would sign his nominating petition. Well, the ten thousand signatures were produced in time on the proper forms. The Board of Elections disavowed them all. It seems they were all written in the same handwriting with the same ballpoint pen, and they were in alphabetical order!"

Dakin denies the story.

In 1978, Dakin asked Tennessee to come to Chicago to endorse him in the primary for governor. This is how Tennessee remembered it: "He spent I don't know how many thousands of dollars for a big breakfast for the press in the ballroom of the Palmer House Hotel in the Loop. I had to be there at 7 A.M. to meet this great gathering of journalists. The room sat hundreds, and the food was prepared, there were scores of waiters, and only two or three members of the Fourth Estate. When one of them finally looked up from his food long enough to ask a question, it was, 'Why are you endorsing your brother for governor?' For a moment I was completely stumped! Finally I said, 'Because he's good to our mother!' "

In actual fact the press breakfast was held at Ricardo's restaurant in Chicago, and there was a good turn-out, although Tennessee did say, when asked why he was endorsing his brother, "Because he's been good to our mother," a less than ringing endorsement that was less than helpful to Dakin.

In Collinswood, after his mother's death, Tennessee talked with Dakin about her will. He was worried that Dakin, who had drawn up the will, might have arranged for Miss Edwina's 50 percent ownership of *The Glass Menagerie* to be bequeathed to his two adopted daughters, Francesca Maria and Anne Lanier Williams. He was relieved and a little astonished to discover that in the will Dakin had prepared for Miss Edwina, her rights to the play's royalties reverted to Tennessee on her death. Delighted, he reassured Dakin that, rumors to the contrary, he had not been written out of his brother's will. In fact,

Tennessee hinted, Dakin would come into a financial bonanza when he passed from the scene.

When Tennessee returned to New York after his mother's death, we had drinks together at the Monkey Bar, and he talked about her. When I asked him, naïvely, if he was heartbroken at her death, he shook his head no.

"Do you know the story about Clifton Webb and *his* mother? Well, he lived alone with his mother practically all his life. He was excessively devoted to her, and he explained to people who inquired why he remained a bachelor well into his seventies that he couldn't marry because it would kill the old lady with grief. *Shock's* more like it, because Clifton Webb didn't marry because he was as gay as the Seventh Fleet, and everybody knew it, including him.

"When his mother finally shuffled off to wherever it is one shuffles off to, Cliffy was destroyed. He couldn't stop crying, boring the pants off of everybody with his exaggerated mourning. When you saw him at a party he would burst into tears if he had forgotten that you knew his mother had dropped dead a few years before, and start to sob, telling you how much he missed her.

"Well, you know, a couple of years after she passed away he was having dinner in New York with Noel Coward and Jimmy Donohue. Jimmy was a very rich, very nice queen who was a Woolworth heiress and had had a short-lived affair with Cliffy many years ago. And then for years he was the boyfriend of the Duchess of Windsor, although it was strictly nonphysical. She gave the best blow jobs in Europe, did you know that? It's true, baby. That was her hold, if that's the word for it, over the Prince of Wales. I saw her at parties from time to time, the last was in New York after the Duke died. She was pretty gaga then. I sat next to her at dinner, and she asked me where I got the name Tennessee. I told her that I never liked the name Tom, because my father had given it to me, and I never liked my father. I also said that I wrote some pretty bad stuff under that name and when I finally thought I could write better stuff, I got rid of the name. She said, 'You Americans with your peculiar names.' By then the Duchess had forgotten that she was as American as Kleenex. She said, 'Don't you think it's wonderful that George Washington called himself George Washington? What could be a more *American* name, my dear?'

"Well, in time the Duchess and Jimmy Donohue had a falling out, I can't remember what about. The Duke got mad at him for some silly reason. He was always getting mad at people for silly reasons. So Jimmy took up with some handsome young man. Truman [Capote] ran into Jimmy and his boyfriend on Madison Avenue, and little Truman was eager to know who this beautiful creature was. Jimmy said, 'Truman, this is the boy who dances with the man who danced with the woman who danced with the Prince of Wales!'

"At the dinner in New York with Noel Coward, Cliffy started sobbing about his mother, and he wouldn't stop. Noel Coward finally had enough. Noel shook Cliffy and said, 'Darling, pull yourself together! It is not unreasonable to be orphaned at seventy!'"

Tennessee laughed. "That is how I feel about my orphanhood. At my age it is not uncommon."

I asked him how his mother was at the end.

"You know, Miss Edwina was crazy as a hoot owl when she died, not at all surprising since she was born crazy and firmly resolved to stay that way. When she could no longer take care of herself I flew out to St. Louis, and Dakin and I put her in this lovely old folks' home. It was very expensive and quite beautiful. I told her I wouldn't mind living there myself.

"Well, Mother was never one not to look a gift horse in the mouth. She constantly complained about the old folks' home. She didn't like being around old people, and she didn't like being around blacks, and like most establishments where they warehouse the old and the dying, most of the staff was black.

"Once, when she was still living at home, I came to St. Louis to see her. She informed me that the blacks were after her. They wanted to rape her in a gang assault, like General MacArthur invading Leyte! I said, 'Mother, you are pushing the outer limits of your first century, dear. I am certain the blacks have more inviting targets on which to expend their lust!' Mother was not at all convinced.

"We went out to dinner at a restaurant in the hotel, and there were black waiters and busboys. Mother had a fit, warning me in a very loud stage whisper that every one of the blacks in the restaurant had designs on her womanhood. I believe by then Mother had arrived at the conclusion she was a virgin. I once asked her, 'If that was the case, how do you explain the presence of three children?' And she said, 'God works in mysterious ways!' Miss Edwina believed that if the Virgin Mary could do the trick, why not her?

"After dinner I took Mother home. The telephone rang, and she gave me a look of sheer horror. Then she put on a brave face and marched across the room to pick up the phone. She listened a minute, and then she said in a courageous voice, 'Yes, I know who you are! And I am here! Waiting! *Unafraid!*

"Of course, Miss Edwina thought it was the blacks

calling to check if she was home so they could come by and rape her. I knew then that it was past time for Miss Edwina to be under professional care.

"The last time I talked with her at the old folks' home she started complaining again about the horse living in her room. Mother did not like roommates of any species, especially uninvited ones, and especially an imaginary horse that produced piles of manure that soiled her shoes! 'I can't step foot out of bed! And Cornelius refuses to bring me new shoes!' Mother was very angry at my father and had chosen to forget that he was as dead as the doorpost. She said, 'I must return home at once. This place is not safe for a Christian lady. The blacks are everywhere. They hide in the garbage cans so they can spy on me when I go to the toilet! This place was built *by* the blacks *for* the blacks!' "

On his seventieth birthday in Chicago, Tennessee opened up a box and discovered he had been given a literary prize by, of all people, Bulgari, the Italian jewelers, a pound ingot of solid silver that he promptly had weighed and appraised. He found the award somewhat puzzling because it was for *The Roman Spring of Mrs. Stone,* done years before. When the novel and the film first appeared in Italy the Italians were angry about his story of a Roman gigolo romancing an older woman.

In Chicago, after he opened the box containing the prize, I asked him if he thought he might soon get the Nobel Prize for Literature. It was a sensible question because Tennessee was easily among the two or three most important writers in the world.

"I'll tell you why I think I haven't gotten it," he began. "I'd heard I'd been nominated for it several times in the fifties. But then suddenly a scandal happened. This lady, I call her the Crepe de Chine Gypsy, went to Stockholm. And she lured me to Stockholm by telling me she was living in a charming little hotel near the waterfront, and that I would have my own suite with a private entrance so that I could entertain guests without her knowledge. And that I would have a fantastic time, if you know what I mean—I was at the height of my fame then—she used my name as an excuse to get all the people around that she wanted to meet but had no way of meeting. She later turned out to be a dominatrix! And one time told everyone she was pregnant. We all believed her because she blew up like a hot-air balloon, built herself a nursery. We all bought baby clothes for her, and waited expectantly for the birth, wondering who the father was. She never disclosed his name. After nine months went by she suddenly expelled the air or fluid and went back to normal size, got rid of the nursery, and never mentioned it again! *This* was the woman who was to introduce me to high society in Stockholm, many of whom influenced the Nobel committee! I should have known I was a dead duck."

Both Jerzy Kosinski and James Kirkwood confirm the accuracy of the false pregnancy, both having known the woman and Tennessee at the time.

Tennessee continued, "She gave me a huge party. Well, she had all the press there. She was like a field marshal! 'You over that way! You over there! You do not approach Mr. Williams until I give you the signal!' Barking out orders to these people who were not in the habit of taking orders. Oh, it was just terrifying. The next morning the newspapers all came out saying Mr. Williams arrived in Stockholm preceded by this very powerful press agent! And my agent in Scandinavia, Lars Schmidt, who married Ingrid Bergman, said, 'You know, you've been nominated for the Nobel Prize but now it's finished.' The scandal was so awful, the press having been abused, and they associated me with this awful woman.

"Well, after all, one doesn't *have* to get it. It'd be nice because it's a lot of money, isn't it? I could use that, if I could get it."

He thought a moment, and then he said, "Whether I ever went to Stockholm or not, I don't think I will ever get a Nobel Prize. Because I'm homosexual, and they know I am, and they never give it to writers who admit to being homosexual. I've never hidden the fact that I'm gay, and I don't give a shit whether people like it or not. I've never found it necessary to deal with it in my work. It was never a preoccupation of mine, except in my intimate, private life. In my work I've had a great affinity with the female psyche. Her personality, her emotions, what she suffers and feels. People who say I create transvestite women are full of shit. Frankly, just vicious shit. Personally, I like women more than men. They respond to me more than men do, and they always have. The people who have loved me, the ratio of women to men is about five to one, I would say.

"I know there's a right-wing backlash against homosexuals. But at the age of seventy I no longer consider it a matter of primary concern. Not that I want anything bad to happen to other homosexuals. God knows, enough has.

"I always thought homosexual writers were in a minority of writers. Nobody's yet made a correct census of the actual number of homosexuals in the population of America. And they never will be able to, because there are still too many closets, some of them rather securely locked. And it's also still dangerous to be openly homosexual."

A week after his mother's death in June 1980, Tennessee went to the White House, a place he had been to many times before, his first visit occurring while John F. Kennedy was President. By this point in his life, he didn't have much hope for any further honors, and thus he was pleased to be told he was to be given the Presidential Medal of Freedom, the nation's highest civilian award. Robert Penn Warren and Eudora Welty were also to be similarly honored at the same ceremony.

I had a small part to play, I think, in his nomination for that medal. For five or six years I had been appalled by the reviews he had received, by the pain he felt in what had become a general public disregard for him as a literary figure, one whose current work might have some relevance to present culture. Miss Lillian Carter and the President's sister, Ruth Carter Stapleton, were friends of mine, Ruth being especially close. Ruth had twice offered to take care of Tennessee at her healing center in Holovita, at Denton, Texas. She'd had remarkable success in treating addictive personalities. She had been more than helpful to me. Truman Capote was another friend whom Ruth tried to help, but by then Truman was beyond help. I don't think God himself could have done the trick. Truman wanted to die, and set about doing it slowly, and finally, sadly, succeeded.

On several occasions, the last after the disastrous opening of *Clothes for a Summer Hotel*, Tennessee's last New York play, whose closing almost drove him to suicide, I tried to get him to fly to Texas with me for treatment at

Holovita. At first he agreed, and then at the last minute balked.

"Baby, I don't need a faith healer, I need a hit play!"

From the time President Carter entered the White House I lobbied his family to award the Medal of Freedom to Tennessee. Ruth at one point asked me to write a memo for the President stating why he should receive the honor.

Shortly before the decision was made George Plimpton told me that I'd lost my marbles if I believed the President was in charge of deciding who received the Presidential Medal of Freedom. No, George told me, that decision was the province of a group of illustrious figures in the arts, one of whom, I believe, was George.

Tennessee received the honor.

And this: Tennessee was an enthusiastic supporter of Jimmy Carter, although I very much doubt if the man was aware of it. As a Southerner he took pride in Carter's electoral victory, and when Carter went down to massive defeat in 1980 before the onslaught of Ronald Reagan's landslide, Tennessee was appalled and a little frightened. He believed that Carter had been brought to his knees by an anti-Southern bias on the part of Yankees, and by the economic royalists—the political-industrial arrangement that he was convinced, I think correctly, controlled American political institutions. And by the press, not one of his favorite fraternities. And he also thought the Jews had helped to pull the rug out from under the President because of the pressure he had put on Prime Minister Begin to sign the Camp David accords.

Miss Rose accompanied him to the Carter White House to receive his award.

In Chicago I asked him about the event.

"I've been to the Carter White House before. The

first time I went there was some occasion when the film industry was being honored. At that time the Carters had not as yet adjusted themselves to entertaining. He is rather abstemious, Mr. Carter, which is the only main fault I found with him.

"We were only allowed to have one very tiny glass of what was purported to be a California chablis. I downed my glass in one swallow (it contained about a thimbleful of wine), and then tried to figure out how to get some more, not an easy thing to accomplish at the White House then. All there was was wine or fruit juice. No hard liquor. Nothing. But you could only have one glass. So I got ahold of [film producer] Sam Spiegel, who is a very portly gentleman, and I said, 'Sam, will you stand in front of the table and slip me another glass of wine surreptitiously?' So I hid behind Sam, and he snuck me several small glasses, which helped to get me through the evening.

"When I returned to the White House later to get the medal, the Carters had begun serving domestic champagne, which was at least a small step in the right direction. The White House seemed tattered, the sofa in the Red Room was frayed, and the place looked like they had been holding down expenses by cutting back on cleaning and repairs. President Carter was very tight with a dollar, and I think he considered hard liquor beyond his budgetary means. I wanted to sneak in a bottle of vodka, but I was afraid the Marines might spot the bulge in my pocket and arrest me as a suspected assassin!

"Even though he was cheap with refreshments, I did like Jimmy Carter. He was always very gracious to me, as was Mrs. Carter. I think Jimmy Carter was a great humanitarian, and his second term might have been wonderful compared to what we got [in Reagan]. I thought his human rights concern was right, and I am sorry that our government has abandoned it.

"I don't think the big-money people wanted Carter back in. He wasn't pliable enough."

I asked Tennessee if he hated the rich. He seemed surprised by the question.

"My feeling about the rich is not anger, really, but a feeling that they are emotionally restricted," he replied. "They live in a very narrow, artificial world, like the world of Gloria Vanderbilt, who can be very unpleasant, you know. Even Drue Heinz, with all that pickle money, can't escape it, although she does publish a literary magazine that's pretty good. Nobody reads it, though. People don't seem to read like they used to. They think it's hard work. Literature has taken a back seat to television, don't you think? It really has.

"We don't have a culture anymore that favors the creation of writers, or supports them very well. I mean, serious artists. I am lucky I was homosexual and so didn't have to be married and have a wife and children to support. I know many homosexuals who *are* married and put up a false front, but I was never very good at lying, even to myself. I think being single made it possible for me to practice my profession as a writer. You know what happened to poor Norman Mailer. One wife after another, and all that alimony. I've been spared all that. I give people money, yes. But I couldn't have afforded alimony, not to all those wives. I would've had to behead them! Being single made it possible for me to work.

"Why do you think our country treats its serious artists so terribly? It certainly doesn't support them financially. There is something in America that seems to resent beauty, art, and the people who create it. On Broadway,

what they want are cheap comedies and musicals and revivals. It's nearly impossible to get serious work even produced, and then it's lucky to have a run of a week. They
knocked Albee's *Lolita* down horribly. No wonder he
hates the critics so much. He has every reason to. I've
never read such cruel reviews! But I felt it was a mistake
for Albee to do adaptations. He's brilliant doing his own
original work. But even so, I think there's a way of ex-
pressing one's critical displeasures with a play without being quite so hard, quite so cruel. The critics are literally
killing writers.

"Even Lillian [Hellman] doesn't write for the theatre
anymore. And why should she? She doesn't want to get hit
in the face with shit. And her plays were always popular,
even if they weren't very good. I think her work, really, is
second-rate. She wouldn't want me to say it, but it's true.
Her plots creak. It's really stylish melodrama that appeals
to the middlebrows. It doesn't threaten anyone. And the
truth should be threatening, don't you think? I mean it
should be subversive. It should cut away the little lies we
tell each other and come to believe, like a knife.

"I saw Elizabeth Taylor at the opening of Lillian
Hellman's *The Little Foxes*, in Fort Lauderdale, and she held
that stage as if she'd always been a stage actress. But she
has a little deficiency of humor. I knew she would catch it,
I hoped she would. And she opened so well in Washington
that I think she must have caught the humor.

"I know you think Lillian Hellman is a somewhat
limited playwright. But *Hellman* doesn't think so, does
she? No! After the opening, when I saw Liz Taylor could
act on stage, there was a huge party, with great imported
champagne, the works! The director was seated next to me
at my table. He said he had to get up and call Hellman.

"I said, 'Well, tell her I want a piece of her royalties!'

"So he gave her the message, and came back to the table grinning. 'Hellman said to tell you the check is in the mail!'

"She's a funny woman, and a skillful playwright. Several of her plays are enormously skillful . . . I've heard she's dying of emphysema. Who *isn't* sick! They're all sick and dying!

"Do you know what the most difficult aspect of playwriting is?" he asked. "I'll tell you. *It's dealing with the money people.* The commercial end of it is the most appalling part. The demands for changes and rewrites don't bother me if they're made by the director, and I think they're intelligent demands. But when the money people get into the act, you're in trouble!"

Tennessee was speaking very pessimistically, an attitude of mind that was unusual for him. He seemed dismayed about American life and culture, and about the future, too. I asked him how he saw America's future.

"I think things will get worse, they usually do. I think we are headed for a nuclear holocaust sooner or later, and no one seems to care. If you don't care, maybe you deserve what you get. They say the future is the young generation. If that's true, God help us! Today's college kids aren't even noticeable now. They seem to be totally reactionary, like the rich. The ones I've met rarely seem different from their parents in attitudes and values.

"In the sixties, or even the early seventies, the kids I met seemed to be in revolt against the mores and social ideas of their parents. It may be just an illusion of mine, but it seems today that the children are frightened of deviating from their parents' way of life and thought. The Me-Me-Me Generation. Selfishness. A complete lack of interest in what's happening in the world. No interest in what's going on in El Salvador, this military junta supported by our government that rushes its troops into villages, pulls the peasants out and slaughters them! American kids don't care. In Guatemala, four hundred people a day being slaughtered, although no one mentions it much. Honduras. Don't they care, this generation? We know why Allende was assassinated, and how and why. All Latin America is in strife, and the Me-Me-Me Generation doesn't appear to care.

"The sixties were intensely alive! We were really progressing toward a workable, just society. But then Nixon came along, and everything fell back into its old routine of plutocracy. And now we have Mr. Reagan, a sleepwalker for a President! It's too much, don't you think? It's finally too much."

While Tennessee didn't care for President Reagan's policies, he did go to the Reagan White House twice, the last being on the occasion of his being honored by the Kennedy Center for the Performing Arts for his lifetime achievement. President Reagan, he reported, didn't speak to him in the receiving line.

However, a year before Tennessee died, I visited Mrs. Reagan at the White House and we had a long conversation alone in the Green Room after lunch. She asked about Tennessee, and Truman Capote, among others, and was visibly upset to learn of Tennessee's physical decline.

"Both Ronnie and I think he's our greatest living playwright, and if he [the President] hadn't been so busy making movies perhaps he might have played in one of Tennessee's dramas."

I doubted that, but I didn't tell her.

During my last day in Chicago, Tennessee and I had lunch, and then went swimming. Around four o'clock we returned to his suite, had drinks in the small library, and talked for a couple hours.

Tennessee was dressed in a loose embroidered shirt, beige slacks, and soft canvas shoes. He was tanned, having spent most of the winter in Key West. He looked ten years younger than his age. He was in an unusually happy mood, in part because the play was going well, but also because he had around him a number of close friends, among them the painter Vassilis Voglis, and Jane Smith, the actress and widow of artist Tony Smith. Also in Chicago was Dakin, with his wife and two adopted daughters, something Tennessee was not overjoyed about.

We talked about writing, a subject he rarely liked to discuss. I know very few writers who enjoy telling why and how they write, Tennessee certainly didn't; but this afternoon, with the sunlight streaming into the small room, feeling content, he was in the mood.

I asked him when he first knew that he was a writer.

"I was a born writer, I think. Yes, I think that I was. At least when I had this curious disease affecting my heart at the age of eight. I was more or less bedridden for half a year. My Mother exaggerated the cause. She said I swallowed my tonsils! Years later, when I had the *Time* cover story, and she was quoted, doctors looked it up and said, 'A medical impossibility!'

"But I do think there was a night when I nearly died, or possibly *did* die. I had a strange, mystical feeling as if I were seeing a golden light. Elizabeth Taylor had the same experience. I didn't know how common it was for people near death to be visited by a comforting light, until Elizabeth told me of her experience. It seems to beckon you, you know? But I survived that night. That was a turning point, and I gradually pulled out of it. But I was never the same physically. It changed my entire personality. I'd been an aggressive tomboy until that illness. I used to beat up all the kids on the block. I used to confiscate their marbles, snatch them up!" He laughed in recall, his memory of his childhood perhaps more vigorous than its reality.

"Then that illness came upon me," he continued, "and my personality changed. I became a shut-in. I think my mother encouraged me to be more of a shut-in than I needed to be. Anyway, I took to playing solitary games, amusing myself. I don't mean masturbation, if that's what you're thinking. I mean I began to live an intensely imaginative life. And it persisted that way. That's how I turned into a writer, I guess. By the age of twelve, I started writing."

I asked him what writers had influenced him when he was young.

"What writers influenced me as a young man? *Chekhov!*

"As a dramatist? Chekhov!

"As a story writer? Chekhov!

"D. H. Lawrence, too, for his spirit, of course, for his understanding of sexuality, of life in general. He was considered shocking once, a pornographer, do you believe that? He didn't aim to shock, he aimed to tell the truth. When I write I don't aim to shock people, and I'm surprised when I do. But I don't think that anything that occurs in life should be omitted from art, though the artist should present it in a fashion that is artistic and not ugly.

"I'm a poet. And then I put the poetry in the drama. I

put it in short stories, and I put it in the plays. Poetry's poetry. It doesn't have to be called a poem, you know."

If you started all over again, if you were young and could remake your life, would you become a writer, I wanted to know.

He laughed. "I wouldn't want to be young again and have to go through the shit all over again! But, yes, I would be a writer because that is what I am. There isn't any choice, is there? You know that. If young people are meant to be writers, they'll write. There's nothing that can stop them. It may kill them. They may not be able to stand the terrible indignities, humiliations, privations, shocks that attend the life of an American writer. They may not. Yet they may have some sense of humor about it, and manage to survive."

He paused, stood up and went to the bar and made himself another vodka martini. Then he sat down again, smiled oddly, and talked more about writing.

"When I write, everything is visual, as brilliantly as if it were on a lit stage. And I talk out the lines as I write.

"When I was in Rome, my landlady thought I was demented. She told Frank, 'Oh, Mr. Williams has lost his mind! He stalks about the room talking out loud!'

"Frank said, 'Oh, he's just writing.' She didn't understand *that*.

"In writing a play I can get started on the wrong tangent, go off somewhere and then have to make great deletions and begin over, not *all* the way over, but just back to where I went off on that particular tangent. This is particularly true of the surrealist play that I'm currently writing. I'm dedicating it to the memory of [English playwright] Joe Orton. *The Everlasting Ticket* it's called. It's about the poet laureate of Three Mile Island. I'm in the third version of *Ticket* at the moment.

"I do an enormous amount of rewriting. And when I finally let a play go, when I know it's complete and as it should be, is when I see a production of it that satisfies me. Of course, even when *I'm* satisfied with a production, the critics are not, usually. In New York especially. The critics feel I'm basically anarchistic, and dangerous as a writer. I think they feel threatened or they don't understand it and they can't admit that they don't so they do what they can to destroy it. And sometimes they succeed."

I asked Tennessee if he had a particular audience in mind when he wrote, one group or another for whom this play or that was specifically written.

"No, I don't have an audience in mind when I write," he replied. "I'm writing mainly for myself. After a long devotion to playwriting I have a good inner ear. I know pretty well how a thing is going to sound on the stage, and how it will play. I write to satisfy this inner ear and its perceptions. That's the audience I write for.

"Sometimes, though, I write for someone specifically in mind. You know, I always used to write for Kazan, although he no longer works as a director, which is a great loss to the theatre. He writes novels now that are bestsellers. Maybe he needs the money. Probably he just doesn't want to take shit from the money people and critics anymore. What made him a great director was that he had an infinite understanding of people on an incredible level.

"At one point Kazan and José Quintero were rather equal in talent. That was when Quintero began at the Circle in the Square downtown (New York) and did things like *Summer and Smoke* and *Long Day's Journey into Night.* Those early things. Then he took heavily to drink.

"He was living at a very fashionable address, the penthouse apartment at One Fifth Avenue on Washington Square Park in the Village. I remember walking with Quintero out on the terrace. I said to him, 'Why are you killing yourself like this with liquor? Because you are, you know. You're drinking much too heavily.' He always liked me very much. He was an extremely kind and sweet person. He said, 'I know. I know. It's just that all of a sudden I got all this attention, and it made me self-conscious. It scared me. I didn't know how my work was *done*. I simply worked through intuition. Then suddenly it seemed to me as if secrets of mine were being exposed.' And so he drank excessively, and now he can't drink at all.

"During *The Seven Descents of Myrtle*, as they called it, although it was actually *The Kingdom of Earth*, Quintero was drinking so heavily that Estelle Parsons said she couldn't take direction from him. David Merrick was producing, and he came to town. He said, 'I have to fire this man. He's destroying the play.' And I said, 'Mr. Merrick, if you fire poor José I'm going to withdraw the play.' So he let it come in.

"You know, in those days David Merrick was a lovely man. He's been around the bend some since, but he was so nice in those days. We both went to Washington University [St. Louis]. We were in the same drama class, I believe. In the sixties he used to come to my apartment at the Mayfair on Seventy-second Street when I wouldn't go out ever. He came over to tell me he wanted to do *Kingdom of Earth*. And I just slurred something in reply. That's how I talked in those days, baby. He said, 'It's a very funny play!' And I went *grrrowwww* . . ." Tennessee laughed. "I didn't give a shit whether he put it on or not, or whether I lived through the night. This was after Frankie died, and I was taking lots of pills, handfuls of them, I didn't even know what they were. I'd wake up and just grab a pile. People do things like that when they are feeling wretched and there seems to be no way out of misery. I got so bad that at one point Bill [Glavin], who was my companion then, tried to throw me off the balcony. He couldn't take it anymore."

I asked Tennessee how he thought up his titles. He was terrific at it, and he was generous about it, too. If a friend was writing something and got stumped for a title, Tennessee would come up with one.

"Sometimes I'll come up with a title that doesn't sound good in itself," he answered, "but it's the only title that really fits the meaning of the play. Like *A House Not Meant to Stand* isn't a beautiful title. But the house it refers to in the play is in a terrible state of disrepair, virtually leaking rainwater everywhere. That house, and therefore the title, is a metaphor for society in our times. And, of course, the critics don't like that sort of thing, nor do they dare to openly approve of it. They know who butters their bread.

"Some titles come from dialogue as I write a play, or from the setting itself. Some come from poetry I've read. When I need a title I usually reread the poetry of Hart Crane. I take a copy of Crane's work with me when I travel. A phrase will catch my eye and seem right for what I'm writing. But there's no system to it. Sometimes a line from a play will serve as a title. I often change titles a number of times until I find one that seems right.

"I've always thought the title of Tommy's [Seligson] book, *To Be Young in Babylon*, was beautiful. It's about growing up in America, and the title makes the point beautifully.

"You know, playwriting is a funny kind of art. It's both a solitary thing, and it is a group thing. Many people contribute to the writing of a play, whether you want them to or not. Performers can be enormously valuable in suggesting line changes in a play, I mean if they're intelligent performers. Geraldine Page. She's very intelligent, and she's a genius at acting. Being a genius at acting, and being intelligent aren't always the same thing. I've known more dumb actors than you'd believe. Geraldine would suggest line changes. She'd say, 'I find this line difficult to read.' I think most of her suggestions were good, although she's not a writer. So I'd make the changes to satisfy her. I often do that with actors, if they're intelligent and care about the play."

I asked Tennessee if there were any playwrights he compared himself to? He didn't like the question.

"Baby, I don't compare with Eugene O'Neill or anyone else! My work is totally in its own category. It's more esoteric than anyone else's, except Joe Orton's. And I don't compete with Joe Orton. I love him too much.

"Now O'Neill is not as good a playwright as, for instance, Albee. I don't think he's even as good as Lanford Wilson. I could give you quite a list.

"I liked O'Neill's writing. He had a great spirit, and a great sense of drama, yes. But most of all it was his spirit, his *passion*, that moved me. And when *The Iceman Cometh* opened to very bad notices, very mixed notices at best in New York, I wrote him a letter. I said, in reading your play, at first I found it too long, then I gradually realized that its length, and the ponderosity of it, are what gave it a lot of its power. I was deeply moved by it, finally.

"He wrote me a very nice reply and said he was always deeply depressed after an opening and that he appreciated my letter particularly. But that letter has disappeared like most of my letters."

I reminded him that he had read me a long letter from O'Neill years before in Key West.

He nodded his head sadly. "And that's gone, too. I wonder who takes them? I have never understood why a sane person would want to steal someone else's mail. But that's only one of a lot of things I'll never understand. What were we talking about, baby?"

I reminded him.

"Oh yes. O'Neill. He had a terrible problem with alcohol. Most writers do. American writers nearly all have problems with alcohol because there's a great deal of tension involved in writing—you know that. And it's all right up to a certain age, and then you begin to need a little nervous support that you get from drinking. Now my drinking has to be moderate. Just look at the liver spots I've got on me!"

He held out his hands for me to examine, and there were indeed a lot of spots.

"You don't suppose they make a makeup for the hands?" he asked, facetiously. "One likes to disguise one's sinful habits from other people's prying eyes!

"On opening nights in the old days, when I really could drink—I can't drink heavily now because of this pancreatitis I developed from overdrinking. Now that's a word to the wise, Dot. Anyway, when I *could* drink, on opening nights I'd either have a flask on me and keep myself drunk and stand at attention in the theatre, or else I'd dart out to the nearest bar and sit there until nearly before the curtain came down and then I'd head back into the theatre.

"Now I take opening nights much more calmly!" He

laughed, knowing I had endured a hell of a lot of opening nights with him, and they were anything but calm. "I just sit and enjoy it," he went on. "If they're giving a good performance, and they usually do on opening night, I just sit and enjoy it. After the curtain, I take the red-eye flight out of town, I have a car waiting for me with the luggage in it, the motor running, and scoot out to La Guardia or Kennedy and take the red-eye to Key West before the critics have time to raise the mob against me! The Mafia could learn a few tricks from me on how to escape in the nick of time!"

I asked him why he worked every day. I have known a lot of writers who claimed to work every day—I've even made that preposterous avowal—but Tennessee is the only writer who actually did.

"My work is *emotionally* autobiographical," he explained, "It has no relationship to the actual events of my life, but it reflects the emotional currents of my life. I try to work every day, baby, because you have no refuge but writing. None. When you're going through a period of unhappiness, a broken love affair, the death of someone you love, or some other disorder in your life, then you have no refuge but writing. However, when depression comes on of a near-clinical nature, then you're paralyzed even at work. Immediately after the death of Frank Merlo, I was paralyzed, unable to write, and it wasn't until I began taking the speed shots that I came out of it. Then I was able to work like a demon. Could you live without writing, baby? I couldn't.

"Because it's so important, if my work is interrupted I'm like a raging tiger. It angers me so. You see, I have to reach a high emotional pitch in order to work, if the scene is dramatic.

"I heard that Norman Mailer has said that a play-wright only writes in short bursts of inspiration while a novelist has to write six or seven hours a day. Bullshit! Now Norman is more involved in the novel form, and I'm more involved in the play form. In the play form I work steadily and hard. If a play grips me I'll continue to work on it until I reach a point where I can no longer decide what to do with it. Then I'll discontinue work on it."

I asked him what he was working on now.

"Now? Well, I've been busy with the production of this new play, *A House Not Meant to Stand.* The production of a play is for me an event that eclipses everything else, even turning seventy. I love the Goodman Theatre, and I'm going to work with them again. We're already making plans to move this play on to the main stage, and to do *Something Cloudy, Something Clear,* about the summer I met Kip on the Cape, though I've added other characters besides Kip and me.

"And I've got an important play, *In Masks Outrageous and Austere.* It's a line of Eleanor Wiley's, from a poem by her. It goes like this: 'In masks outrageous and austere/the years go by in single file;/Yet none has merited my fear,/and none has quite escaped my smile.'

"It happens to fit the play, which has a great deal of poetry in it and yet at the same time the situation is bizarre as hell. It's about the richest woman on earth. Babe Foxworth is her name. She doesn't know where she is. She's been abducted to Canada, on the East Coast. But they don't know where they are. A village has been constructed like a movie set to deceive them. Everything is done to confine and deceive them while her husband is being investigated. Babe is really an admirable person, besides her hypersexuality, though that can be admirable. I think it is! It's a torture to her because she's married to a gay husband who's brought along his boyfriends. I think it's an extremely funny play."

It was now dusk, and we talked for a few minutes more, and then I got up to leave, Tennessee remaining in the library. But when I got to the front door, I heard him call my name. I waited until he came to me.

"I just want to hug you good-bye, baby," he said, and did. I kissed him, and then I left.

On New Year's Eve 1979, Tennessee, Bill Loverd, who is a vice president of Random House, and a girl named Evelyn came to my apartment for drinks. Richard Zoerink and I then lived in a duplex on Gramercy Park. Tennessee looked dreadful, wearing dark sunglasses trying to hide his eyes, reddened and puffy with conjunctivitis. On seeing him, I thought he had aged a lot in the last two years. He had fallen into the habit of saying to people we knew in common, but whom I hadn't seen in a long time, "Don't be afraid of Dotson, baby. He's off drugs. He's mellowed." And so had *he*.

We men were dressed in black tie. Tennessee thought Richard looked especially nice in his black velvet overshirt and bowtie, like a French schoolboy. I had lived with Richard for six years and loved him, and he was, in many ways, closer to Tennessee than I was. I mean Richard's relationship with him was different not in degree but in kind. I think Tennessee may have looked upon us both as family, and if that is true, Richard was his youngest boy, and he dealt with him with a gentleness and indulgence I saw him show no one else. Often he would scold Richard, if he thought he was drinking too much or not writing—

he was a freelance writer—but he was always careful to praise him lavishly when he did something that made him proud. He loved to travel with Richard, and near the end of Tennessee's life, when he would call us, more often than not it was to Richard he wished to speak.

To put a finer point on it, *I* thought of Tennessee as a surrogate father, while he viewed me as a close friend. It was Richard alone whom he claimed as a son.

After drinks at our apartment, we taxied to Marta Orbach's townhouse in Chelsea for a New Year's Eve party. Marta is the ex-wife of actor Jerry Orbach, and one of the things that make her parties interesting is that there is usually present a large contingent of the Gallo family, a reputed Mafia clan from Booklyn.

At the party, in fact all evening long, Tennessee was sad. And the heavy rain didn't help. Tennessee sat in Marta's living room looking forlorn. He sat next to the oldest person present, Joey Gallo's mother. When I asked him if he didn't want to mix, he patted Mrs. Gallo's hand and said, "We old people like to stick together. I hate being old, don't you, dear? I hate it!"

After about an hour, our little party went on to Le Club, whose manager, Patrick Shields, had kindly sent a limo to collect us.

Le Club is a private club in New York. That night it was gaily decorated for the holiday, and everyone got hats and noisemakers. It was very noisy, with loud rock music blasting out of too many speakers. It was desperate; everyone was working too hard at being happy. It made me paranoid, which Tennessee already was, and I quickly shared his gloom.

Tennessee, feeling miserable, wanted to leave moments after we arrived. Finally we did, Richard and his girlfriend staying behind to dance into the new year. We walked in the heavy rain to Cowboy and Cowgirls, the best hustler bar in town. Truman Capote had introduced me to it several years before, and I in turn showed it to Tennessee.

Truman was always coming up with strange bars, and trying to get his friends to accompany him to newly discovered haunts. One was a dive called, accurately, the Toilet. It was located in a loft building near the waterfront in the Village. It sported a long bar, and at the far end of the bar was an even longer urinal where naked men lay like human deodorant cakes receiving cascades of urine, a sexual act, referred to as a "golden shower." Tennessee and I lasted about five minutes before we left in disgust. On another occasion, Truman tried to persuade Norman Mailer and me to go with him to a dinge (black) gay bar whose patrons beat up any white person who entered, Truman, for reasons unexplained, being the blessed exception. He saw this visit as a test of our manhood. We never made it. Finally, one January when Truman, Tennessee, and I celebrated Richard's birthday at Le Club, Truman tried to entice us into going to a necrophiliacs' bar on West Forty-eighth Street, a place named the Club Forty-eight. Its chief attraction, Truman claimed, was a real dead body lying naked on a steel table, the corpse rented from a funeral home. When Tennessee and I told him that the place sounded absolutely disgusting, really stomach-turning, Truman seemed confused by our objections. "Disgusting?" he said. "But they change the body *every day!*"

At Cowboys and Cowgirls, Tennessee and I sat in the back at our usual table. He was wearing a muskrat coat, and didn't take it off despite the heat inside. We ordered drinks, and when the New Year arrived, he refused to toast it. All it meant to him was that he was one year closer to the end of the line.

I tried to cheer him up, to no avail. He hated New Year's Eve, he said, because it makes you look back on life, and what you see isn't always happy.

"I now look back on periods of my life, and I think, Was that really *me?*" he commented, speaking quietly, staring down at the glass of red wine he held in his hands. "Was I doing those things? I don't feel any continuity in my life. It is as if my life were segments that are separate and do not connect. From one period to another it has all happened behind a curtain of work. And I just peek out from behind the curtain now and then and find myself on totally different terrain.

"The first period was from the age of eleven until I left the university and went into the shoe business. I was madly in love with a girl named Hazel, who was frigid. And that period in my life was marked by extreme shyness. I couldn't look at people in the face without blushing. In high school, I couldn't verbally answer questions. I could only give written answers. I couldn't produce my voice. It sounded like grunting, you know? *That* shy. I suppose it was caused by an unconscious clash in me between my sexual drives and the puritanism imposed by my mother, and the great fear my father inspired in me. He was a terrifying man. He was so unhappy that he couldn't help but be tyrannical at home. That was one period.

"The next period was happy. It was after I came out in the gay world. I didn't think of it as coming out. I thought of it as a new world, a world in which I seemed to fit for the first time, and where life was full of adventure that satisfied the libido. I felt comfortable at last. And that was a happy time, but *The Glass Menagerie* ended that period and new problems developed with success.

"From then through the sixties, because even during the sixties I was working more or less steadily, that was another period different from the rest. But at the end of the sixties I ended up in the bughouse. Finally, after [actress] Anne Meacham and I fled to Tokyo after the terrible reception of *In the Bar of a Tokyo Hotel*, I became more and more ill. I had to be assisted up stairs, baby. When I returned home alone to Key West I was *very* ill. They were building a new kitchen on my house, and the stove was in the patio. It was still operating there while the builders worked. I was stumbling around with a Silex pan, totally disoriented, trying to get in on the stove to heat water for coffee. And I just sat down on the stove!" Tennessee laughed morosely at the absurdity of it. "It was an electric stove, and I inflicted third-degree burns on my body! I think Marion Vacarro called my brother, and Dakin came down to Key West. He called Audrey Wood, and she said, 'Well, put him in the hospital.' But she didn't bother to say which one!

"Dakin, thinking I was going to die anyway, I was in such terrible condition, had me immediately converted to Roman Catholicism so I'd be saved from hell, and then he just threw me into the loony bin, right into the psychiatric ward at Barnes Hospital, which was *incredibly* awful. They suddenly snatched away every pill that I had! The injections went too. So I blacked out. It was cold turkey, baby. They tell me I had three brain concussions in the course of one long day, and a coronary. How I survived, I don't know. I think there were homicidal intentions at work there. I was in that place for three and a half months. The first month I was in the violent ward, although I was not violent. I was terrified and I crouched in a corner trying to read. The patients would have terrible fights over the one television set. Someone would put on the news, and another patient would jump up, yelling and turn on cartoons. No wonder they were violent."

He laughed loudly, his spirits seeming to revive in recalling a horror he no longer was required to endure.

I went to get us another round of drinks, and in my absence a boy named Keith slipped onto the bench where Tennessee sat. When I returned with our drinks, Keith sat snuggling against Tennessee's fur coat like a cat, Tennessee looking like a small, fat bear.

"I love fur. *Furrrr* . . ." the boy whimpered. He was stoned.

I asked him where he lived, and he replied out in Brooklyn somewhere. "I just crash there," he slurred. He had been in the city only two weeks, and came from Bellport, Long Island. He was eighteen, and looking at him I knew he would never see twenty.

Keith left the bar with us, and we piled into a taxi in the rain. It was already occupied by an angry, very drunk young man who, unaccountably, we hadn't noticed as we rushed inside the cab. He was very belligerent as we rode west. Finally, at Forty-third and Seventh Avenue he shouted to the driver, "Stop the car! Let me out. Jesus Christ, New Year's Eve and I'm in fairytown!" Keith's display of affection for Tennessee apparently unhinged him. The taxi stopped, and the fellow desperately tried to open the door, but the latch jammed, so he did the only thing possible if he were to escape homosexual contagion: he rolled down the window and climbed out.

"Baby," Tennessee remarked, "I don't think that young man was especially happy in our company." Keith burped delightedly, and slipped several tranquilizers into his mouth.

We went to Tennessee's apartment on a high floor in the Manhattan Plaza on West Forty-second Street, a place he hated. He blamed his former agent, Billy Barnes, for the fact he was housed there. He paid six hundred fifty dollars a month for that dubious privilege, signing a ten-year sublet. "Ten fucking years! You don't get ten years for manslaughter! It makes me long for an early death!" he moaned as we entered his flat.

In the apartment he pointed out the security alarms, smoke detectors, multiple locks, and other protective gadgets. "It doesn't exactly inspire your confidence in the building, baby!"

We made drinks, and Keith pulled off his clothes as he staggered about the living room, dropping them here and there. He was a tall, very skinny boy, his body almost hairless. I was beginning to suspect that he had lied about his age and was not eighteen. And being stoned, he had difficulty walking without bumping into things, or even walking at all, for that matter. By this hour, God knows how many pills later, he was almost completely incoherent, and seemed mightily pleased by the fact, giggling constantly.

He and Tennessee went into the bedroom, and an hour later, about 4 A.M., they reemerged. I was lying on the convertible sofa in the living room (all the furniture, hideous pieces, was leased). Tennessee and I tried to persuade the boy to stay the night because he was too spaced to make it through the door, and if he did, this being New Year's Eve, he wouldn't be able to get a taxi and would have to face streets filled with marauding drunks on his own.

While Tennessee and I were in the living room, Keith staggered into the kitchen for a glass of wine. We heard a crash, and rushed in to see what had happened. The boy had dropped a jug of red wine, shattering the glass; he was laughing, dancing on the puddle of wine and broken glass with his bare feet. We were horrified. He took a few steps toward Tennessee, lolling his tongue out of his mouth as if he wanted to French kiss, and then fell to the floor.

We lifted him up, and carried him into the bathroom, where we placed him, unconscious, in the bathtub. We carefully pulled pieces of glass from his feet and, not having any disinfectant, we wet a towel with vodka and pressed it against the wounds. Finally, tearing up a pillowcase, we bound up his injured feet. Then we lifted him up and carried him into Tennessee's bedroom. For a few moments we tried to decide what to do. And then the boy moaned, and opened his eyes, seeming to revive. He smiled, and asked for pills. I told him to try to sleep.

"Am I going to get paid?" he asked, still smiling.

Tennessee wrote him a check for fifty dollars and handed it to him.

"Tennessee Williams, Tennessee Williams . . ." The significance of the name sank in. The boy's eyes widened. "Tennessee Williams, will you play me one of your hit albums?" he asked. So much for literary fame.

"Fuck me," Keith said, giggling.

"You should go to sleep, kid. You're fucked out," I said.

"Use soap. Where's the K-Y? There isn't any." He sat up. He looked very young, his black hair matted with sweat, his large, soft eyes that reminded me of a deer's.

"How old are you, really?" I asked him.

He said to get his blue jeans. I did, and handed them

to him. He pulled his passport out of his pocket, showing it to us. According to it, he was indeed eighteen.

"Why are you carrying your passport?" Tennessee asked.

Keith giggled. "You never know." It was a funny, pathetic hope, carrying a passport on the chance someone might take you abroad.

He started to cry, lots of tears rolling down his face. He rubbed his eyes with his fists, like a child rubbing sleep.

Tennessee and I held him, trying to comfort him.

"I never cry," he said crying. "I miss Sally. I loved Sally. She died three years ago. Sally . . . I miss her." He passed out.

We left him in the bedroom, and Tennessee spent the night with me on the convertible sofa bed in the living room.

We slept late the next day, getting up around noon. The boy was gone. He left his shoes and socks behind. The floor of the bedroom and foyer were stained with bloody footprints, as was the hallway to the elevator.

That afternoon we had lunch at the Curtain Call, a restaurant in the Manhattan Plaza. There was a string trio playing in the empty restaurant, while outside drunks in dinner jackets and torn shirts staggered through the wet streets.

Tennessee was very worried about Keith, but there was nothing to be done. He said, "That boy doesn't have six months to live. Poor child, he has caught the contagion of death, and doesn't know he's dying."

I asked him if he was afraid of death.

"Everyone's afraid of it, but I'm no more than most, I suppose," he replied. "I'm beginning to reconcile myself to it. I'm *not* reconciled to dying before my work is finished, though. I have a very strong will. There were occasions in the last year or so when I might have gone out. But my will forces me to go on because I've got unfinished work."

I asked him if he had any regrets.

"Oh, God, yes, baby! But I can't think about them now. So many things to regret. But there are, I believe, so very few things that one can change in one's life. There are very few acts of volition. I don't believe in individual guilt. . . . sometimes I wonder whether I even believe in collective guilt. And yet I do believe that the intelligent person, the moral individual, must avoid evil and cruelty and dishonesties. I once wrote that the only crime is deliberate cruelty. I still believe that. And I believe that one can try to pursue a path of virtue. That remains to us, I hope."

Over lunch we talked about his play being done in a Hudson Guild production. He was fighting with Shirley Knight, who was the play's star. I repeated to him the advice I had offered him a week before: Don't open the damn thing. You don't need it.

"Baby, I *won't* open it if the women [actresses] don't stop fighting! Olive and Miss Knight hate each other. Poor Olive is defenseless, Dot. Miss Knight resents the fact that Olive is from a theatrical family, and happens to reside in a welfare hotel, through no fault of her own. Dotson, these young actresses do not understand that one's financial position has no relationship to one's artistic gifts, unless it is an *inverse* relationship!" I asked him why an actress we both knew had been recently fired from the Spoleto Festival, where one of his plays was being staged.

"I asked the director why she had to go. 'A bitch can't play a bitch!' he declared. He's right, of course. These Southern theatre ladies. Such falseness. Such fear. You know, she always wanted a real man. She told me that herself. But all she ever married or knew were faggots. She is terrified of a straight man's touch," he said.

Tennessee had known the star in question since he met her in Hollywood when he was under contract to MGM in the forties. "Her first husband was very beautiful. Too beautiful, really. More beautiful than she. And she couldn't stand it. I was mad for his beauty. She couldn't stand not being able to control him, that people wanted him and not her. That's always been her way. To be with men more desirable than herself. She is the kind of bitch who doesn't care where you put your cock as long as she has you by the balls!"

Tennessee's conjunctivitis was bothering him terribly. His face was very red, resembling raw meat. He claimed the Manhattan Plaza pool was polluted, "worse than the East River!" because the management didn't provide soap in the showers, and thus the swimmers went into the water filthy. I thought his conjunctivitis was due to nerves. He was under the strain of a new production and it wasn't going well.

He wanted to go to Puerto Rico the next day, to get away from the cold rain and the feuding cast. He asked me if it was all right if Richard Zoerink went with him.

"He needs to get away, baby. He needs the sun. It's a terrible battle he's fighting." Richard was trying to quit drinking. "He needs a rest. And it's his birthday!"

I told Tennessee I thought it was a good idea.

"I wouldn't touch him, baby," he assured me, a little too piously. "I don't have sex anymore. It's not appropri-

ate to a gentleman of my age." He laughed. "I like to look
and to caress smooth skin. That's all. They all want you to
fuck them, you know. I just want to touch." He caressed
one hand with the other, and rolled his eyes. "I get lonely,
you know."

I said I understood.

"It's not easy. I have a few close friends, though. And
you can get by with a few. I have you and Richard, you
know. And as for sex? I don't feel I require it that much
anymore. I miss having a companion very much. I'll never
be without someone with me, although it'll just be someone who is fond of me and takes care of me, but it won't be
a sexual thing anymore."

Not much to ask, but he never really found a loving
companion again.

That night Tennessee, Richard, and I had dinner at a
friend's apartment uptown. Tennessee was in an expan-
sive mood, happy because he and Richard were flying off
to Puerto Rico in the morning. He had seen Truman Capote for lunch a few days before and told us about it.

"We went to Quo Vadis. He's very angry at Gore
[Vidal], and said that Gore was hateful. That he hated
Truman and he hated Norman [Mailer] and he hated me.
That was somewhat of a surprise. I said, 'I don't think
Gore hates me. Why would he hate me?' And he said,
'Because he isn't a real artist, and we are. We create art,
and he writes pulp, and he envies you and me and Norman because we can do what he can't. That's his dirty
secret. He knows he is second-rate, and isn't in our class,
and never will be. So he hates us.' I said I didn't think
Gore was second-rate, but I didn't think he was as good a
novelist as he thought he was. I find it very hard to make it
all the way through his books."

Tennessee went on to talk about the one time Truman came to Key West.

"It was two years ago. He had flown to Key West from Mexico, where he was to stay with Mrs. [Lee] Radziwill but left in a hurry because the mosquitoes were so terrible. So he came to Key West from the Yucatán. He had never been on the island before, and I suspect that he will never be there again. He was robbed the first night, losing all his credit cards, his address book, and about two thousand dollars. He said that he wasn't in his hotel room when the robbery occurred, but the police found no evidence of forced entry. I think he was cleaned out by some street boy he invited home for a private session!

"Truman came to Key West because when he sold excerpts of his book [Answered Prayers] to Esquire, he made one of the conditions of the contract that the editor of the magazine [Don Erickson] had to fly to Key West to pick up the manuscript. He did that because Hemingway used to make Arnold [Ginrich, the editor/founder of Esquire] come to Key West to edit his stories before they were published. Truman was not about to get one thing less than Hemingway.

"One night Truman, Jimmy Kirkwood, and a friend of Truman's, I, and some other men went to dinner. His friend was very drunk. The restaurant was full of tourists in double-knit suits, and since it was quite late, most of them were as tipsy as Truman's boyfriend. Some distance away, at a round table, sat three couples. Truman noticed them staring at us, and he said, 'Watch out! They'll be coming over for autographs!' And a few minutes later, one of the women at the table got up and came over, carrying a menu. She asked Truman to autograph the menu. He did. She left, and a few minutes later her husband came to our table and glared at Truman. 'Are you Truman Capote?' And Truman said, 'I was this morning!' And the man unzipped his pants, and pulled out his cock. He said, holding it in the palm of his hand, 'Can you put your signature on this?' And Truman looked down at his cock, and up again, and he said, 'I don't know about my *signature*. But I can *initial* it!' "

The next morning Tennessee and Richard flew off to San Juan, and I took a plane to Key West to stay at Tennessee's house.

Fifteen days later Richard and Tennessee came to Key West, arriving around 8 P.M., both giggling, giddy, and drunk. We went out to dinner at an Italian restaurant, and quickly Tennessee's mood soured. He became very depressed because his play had not received any New York reviews. He had received bad notices, certainly, but never before had a play of his been completely ignored.

"They say it's the Gelbs who've destroyed me at the *Times*," he said, beginning his familiar complaint about the "sinister Gelbs," and the New York *Times*, and the hatred Jewish literary types had for him.

"The New York *Times* hates me. They're almost as bad as *Time* magazine, which wishes me dead . . . Maybe I'm too old. Maybe when you get old you can't tell anymore if what you write is any good. Maybe it's all over."

We assured him that it wasn't over, and anyway fuck the New York *Times*.

He shrugged, and smiled sadly. "You go on"—he waved his hand in dismissal—"what else can you do?"

He thought a moment, and then remembered his other nemesis, Audrey Wood.

"Ever since my split with Audrey Wood there's been a holding pattern. I think she's the dominant figure in this. I think she has stock in the concern, ICM [International Creative Management, his literary agency], and she won't allow anything to happen until I'm dead, baby.

"People say I broke with her. That it was my fault. I didn't. Just the usual thing happened. An opening night. My nerves always go like spitfire then. We had a very good first preview [of *A Two Character Play*]. The second preview we had a bunch of sour old dames. They didn't get anything, and they hated it. It enraged me. I always lose my mind slightly when I get angry. Audrey was used to this. It happened time and time again. It shouldn't have surprised her at all. And I just turned to her after the performance and said, 'You must have been pleased by this audience,' because she hadn't been pleased by the enthusiastic, younger audience the night before. She got angry, and left town immediately with the greatest amount of publicity. And I realized that she had neglected me so totally during my seven years of terrible depression that any kind of professional relationship with her was no longer tenable.

"I don't hold grudges. So when I encountered her some time later at the Algonquin Hotel, I stretched out my hand to touch hers. She hissed like a snake! and drew back her hands as if I were a leper. Well, since then I know this woman hates me! She'd lost interest in me. I don't think you should lose interest in a person who's in deep depression. That's when your interest and concern should be most, if you're a true friend.

"And I think I had a great deal to do with making her career. She'd only sold *Room Service* to the Marx Brothers before I came along and got her Bill Inge and Carson Mc-

Cullers and . . . this sounds bitter," he acknowledged. "And I hold no animosity toward people. I hope I don't."

We went home, and Tennessee and Richard went swimming in the pool. I didn't. The water was too cold for me. Tennessee no longer heated the pool, since he was trying to save money.

A few nights later we had a strange dinner at a gay guesthouse. We were invited by a young actor from Atlanta who wanted to direct plays, and his young friend, Skyler, who is blond and handsome. There were seven of us at dinner, the actor, Skyler, Richard, Tennessee and I, and the two owners of the guesthouse, men in their thirties, dressed in boots and leather, an odd costume on a hot night. We ate outside by the pool. On the other side of the patio, lounging on a chair as if sunning, was a man completely naked except for a large dog collar around his neck. Where we ate was very dark, and you could barely see the food to eat it. There was something sinister about the place, a hostility in the air, as if a murder were about to happen. Or perhaps we were oversensitive to violence because only a few weeks before Frank Fontis had been murdered.

Every few minutes one of our obviously sadomasochistic hosts slipped from the table and went into the kitchen to snort cocaine. They said very little all evening, moving silently about like morticians at a funeral.

Tennessee responded to the threatening atmosphere by playing the invalid, whining about his many illnesses, his toothache, the antibiotics that alone kept him alive. And evil, that what he most talked about, how much he believed in the existence of evil. And about the pain of life, how life was always hurtful.

"There's not *that* much pain in life," Richard said.

Tennessee groaned, "What there is, baby, I've known."

Which sent Richard into Eliot, " '. . . I have known them all already . . .' "

While Tennessee sank back on the banquette, his eyes half-closed, listening to the actor beseech him to allow him to direct one of his plays (the actor was then employed as a waiter), one of our hosts, opposite me, started to sexually grope the other host. As I noted, both groper and gropee were dressed in S&M regalia, keys, bandanas, vials of amyl nitrate (poppers) dangling on necklaces made of steel chain. They had beards and very short hair. One kept repeating, "The stronger the more submissive, the stronger . . ." etc. as he lapped his pal's face, ears, and neck with his tongue like a dog. Then some naked man appeared and proceeded to pee in the swimming pool. Stood and peed.

Richard went to the bathroom inside and returned to report that its walls were papered with nude pictures of one of our hosts erect and engaging in various acts of sexual humiliation. "He isn't attractive," Richard said.

Finally, one of our by now coked-up hosts got abusive, demanding in foul language that we tip the serving girl, who wandered about the place with a look of mindless contentment on her face. Tennessee gave her ten bucks.

The next day we had lunch at Claire's Cafe on Duval Street, a rather pretty establishment all in white with blue tablecloths and overhead fans. We had clam chowder and quiche and a little white wine. It was good.

Richard complained that there was no sun in Key

West, the weather was consistently overcast, and there hadn't been any sun in San Juan either, and he felt cheated of a tan.

Tennessee, trying to cheer him up, said, "Some people look lovely when they're as pale as a shut-in. You're one of them."

Richard was to fly with him in a few days to Los Angeles, where Tennessee was scheduled to spend ten days overseeing the Long Beach production of *The Eccentricities of a Nightingale*. He promised Richard he would have sun there.

At the time Tennessee was working on two new plays, and at lunch he spoke about one of them.

"I call it *Tentworms*. It's about a married couple of retirement age. The husband is a professor at Harvard, a latent homosexual who is dying of cancer. They have a grand house in Newport, only this summer the husband wants to go somewhere more rustic, so they take a house on an island off the Cape [Cod]. It's infested with tentworms, and smoke pots burn constantly in a futile attempt to free the area of the pests. Some smoke gets into the house, and the wife, a bitch, complains loudly and often.

"She complains about everything. Mostly she complains about the thin, handsome young Harvard student her husband has hired as his secretary and whose attentions he invites."

Richard asked him if the wife complained about the secretary because she desired him too?

"Of course!" Tennessee replied. "At one point, she says, 'That young man stuffs his crotch with socks to make it bulge. You think it's so big it would stop a whore dead in her tracks. But it's a fake!' And her husband replies, indignantly, 'That's a slander and a lie!' She says, 'How would you know, have you investigated?' And he says, 'I'm allowed a certain license of a manual nature!' Haha. Oh, she is a mean one! There are only three characters, but she has conversations on the phone, often with doctors because she is working to get him confined in some remote hospital and out of the way. But the husband finally has his way with the young man, and declares himself . . . It'll be a statement about freedom and suppression . . . Gays must get a better image!" Tennessee declared. "All this public disgrace, these mad S and M fools," he said heatedly, remembering his experience from the night before at the guesthouse, "what does sadomasochism have to do with homosexuality? It's disgusting. A stop must be put to it at once!"

The next day, while we were at lunch at the Pier House hotel, Tennessee's worst fears about homosexuals displaying sexual license without concern for its effect on their image was confirmed.

We had lunch with Adriana Jackson, a new but dear friend of Tennessee's. I had known her for many years, and when she and her husband, Brooks, bought a weekend house in Key West, they grew close to Tennessee.

That morning Tennessee had been talking to Dakin, and the decision had been reached to put his mother in a nursing home. Now at lunch he was having second thoughts.

"My mother is a very cruel woman," he said to us, "as is any mother who forces her daughter to undergo a frontal lobotomy needlessly. She's ninety-four, and tough as hell. I don't think she should go into an old folks' home. Dakin does. It would be better if she died, don't you think? I'd rather die than end up in one of those homes. I want to die when I've lost my grip. But how do you know when it's time? Look at Hemingway. He went crazy and didn't know it. Or maybe he did, but not enough to do anything about it."

I reminded him that Hemingway had shot himself to death, suicide by anyone's definition, certainly. "He killed himself, and it was probably time. He was mad as a hatter at the end. Remember him trying to run into the whirling propeller of a plane in Rochester when he checked out of the Mayo Clinic? He wanted to die," I said.

Tennessee would have none of it. He had begun to write a play about Hemingway and Fitzgerald (Clothes for a Summer Hotel), was reading every book he could find on the two men, and considered himself an expert.

"I think she killed him."

"Who?" I asked.

"Mary. I think she killed him. She is mean enough to do it. It was convenient for her to do it. She couldn't take his craziness anymore. I think she did it."

"But Hemingway shot himself in the mouth!" I said.

Tennessee shrugged. "Who knows, really, baby? Only Mary knows for certain, and she's not saying."

I don't think he believed it himself. He was, as he often did, throwing out an idea that he might use in a play. I knew Mary Hemingway, and admired her. I was once at a dinner party at Peter Schub's apartment on Beekman Place. The dinner was in honor of Tony Snowdon, a client and friend of Peter's, who is a photographers' agent. Mary ate very little, and spent most of the evening sitting by herself in Peter's bedroom, drinking Scotch. Sensing she was lonely I went in and sat with her.

She said she was missing Hemingway. It was a week or two after the anniversary of his death. She spoke of how much she loved him, and how empty life was with him gone.

I tried to commiserate, saying that it must be terribly difficult and painful to lose both your lover and your best friend at the same time.

"Oh, we were never lovers," she suddenly said, correcting me. "We were very best friends. We loved to hunt and fish together, to be outdoors. We loved the same things best friends do. But we were never lovers. Mr. Hemingway was beyond that by then."

In the last years of his life, Tennessee developed a fixation about Hemingway, I think associating the writer's decline and his mental collapse with his own fears of senility and nonproductivity. One of the reasons why he was increasingly concerned with money was that he sensed that he was reaching a point where he couldn't make a living on what he was now able to write, and he feared surviving into old age depending on the mercy of others to make do, a patently absurd worry because he was worth millions. And always, of course, was the nagging suspicion that he might be going mad, like Hemingway, and not know it, and would end back in Barnes Hospital as an inmate in the violent ward. In the last few years of his life, he often asked me if I thought he was becoming senile. I assured him I didn't, but his anxiety grew, and with it an obsession for financial security.

In 1982, during the previews of *Clothes for a Summer Hotel*, we had dinner in New York at Elaine's restaurant with Margaux Hemingway and Bernardo Foucher, a man she would marry and later divorce. I had known Margaux for four or five years and had talked to Tennessee about her. He was keen to meet her, and so the dinner was arranged.

He complimented her on her beauty, and then talked about her grandfather Hemingway and his relationship with Zelda and Scott Fitzgerald. After praising Hemingway as a writer, "one of our country's greatest stylists, although his vision was dark and tormented," Tennessee said, "Your grandfather had a remarkable interest in and understanding of homosexuality, for a man who wasn't a homosexual."

"Grandpa wasn't a homosexual," Margaux replied, somewhat uncertainly. She seemed taken aback by the sudden turn in conversation, and a little wary as to where it was headed.

"Not a homosexual. But I think both Hemingway and Fitzgerald had *elements* of homosexuality in them. I make quite a bit of that in my play, *Clothes for a Summer Hotel*.

"Have you ever read 'A Simple Inquiry' by Hemingway?" he asked her. Margaux hadn't. "Well, it's about an Italian officer in the Alps during the First World War. And he's of course deprived of female companionship. He has an orderly, a very attractive young orderly. He desires the orderly. And he asks the boy, rather bluntly, 'Are you interested in girls?' The boy panics for a moment, and says, 'Oh, yes, I'm engaged to be married.' And the boy goes out of the room, and the Italian officer says, 'I wonder if that little sonofabitch was lying?'

"The final line in your grandfather's *Islands in the Stream*," Tennessee continued, adding evidence to his argument that Hemingway was a latent homosexual, "is one man saying I love you to another. I think it took your grandfather all his life to be able to write that line. It didn't mean that they'd had homosexual relations, although Gertrude Stein intimated that Hemingway had."

"I don't think Granddad was gay," Margaux reiterated.

"What does it matter? I don't think it matters," Tennessee, backing off.

"It doesn't," Margaux agreed. "I don't give a damn what two people do in bed, although I like to know about it!" She laughed.

Tennessee seized the opening. "You know what your grandfather said about Fitzgerald? He said, 'Fitzgerald was pretty. He had a mouth that troubled you when you first met him, and troubled you more later.' I think he may have been in love with Fitzgerald, or at the least sexually desired him. That was why he treated him so abominably in *A Moveable Feast,* ridiculing his sexual prowess and his innocence, quite cruelly, too.

"Fitzgerald played the female role in the Princeton Triangle Club, and there's a picture of him as a woman that's more feminine than any woman could look. Fitzgerald never had an affair with anybody but his wife. There was Sheilah Graham at the end, but did he sleep with her? I doubt it. Anyway, I don't think the sexuality of writers is all that interesting," he said, not quite truthfully. If Tennessee was interested in anything it was *everybody's* sexuality. He loved sexual gossip, especially that about other writers. "Their sexuality has no effect (on their work), I can tell you that. In very few instances does it have any effect on their ability to portray either sex. I am able to write of men as well as women, and I always project myself through whichever sex I'm writing about."

Margaux asked him if he had known Fitzgerald and her grandfather.

Tennessee told her about his meeting with Hemingway in Cuba, and about having drinks with him and

Tynan and George Plimpton at La Florida bar in Havana. Among the drinking party was a Dr. Marx, Castro's executioner, who happily invited them all to witness an execution the following morning in a stadium where a number of young male counterrevolutionaries were to be shot. Tennessee was shocked by the offer. Tynan wanted to go. Tennessee refused.

"I've written my new play about your grandfather and Fitzgerald. I think *Clothes* was the most difficult play, of all my plays, to write. Because of the documentation that I had to do. I had to spend four or five months reading everything there is about Fitzgerald and Zelda. There's a huge amount of material! Finally, when it was written, I had to cut an hour out of the play when it was on the road [for out-of-town tryouts]. José Quintero was in very fragile health, and after every opening, he had to flee. So I had to do it without any help or advice from anybody. To cut an hour out of it.

"And then I had to start rewriting it. The scene the critics objected to most violently was that between Fitzgerald and your grandfather. But that's an integral part of the play because each was a central figure in the life of the other. I thought the confrontation between them indispensable. Now I've rewritten the play again, and I've built up that scene, not so much in length of playing time, but in content, making it more pointed. I hope you and your friend will be able to see it," he said to Margaux and Bernardo.

They said they wanted to.

"Geraldine Page is marvelous as Zelda," Tennessee said, trying to sweeten the pot. "She moves back and forth in time in the play. It's a difficult role to pull off. Zelda's one great love affair was with this French aviator. It was her first infidelity to Scott, and probably her only one. It was aggressive because she was being liberated by infidelity from this very possessive love that Scott had for her. And for the first time she was experiencing erotic ecstasy. She'd never experienced that with Scott. She used to complain to poor Scott that he was sexually inadequate.

"Zelda frightened the aviator by the violence of her reactions. She went around the bend because of him. She tried to kill herself, swallowing the contents of a bottle of morphine or something. The aviator was frightened away.

"Zelda was also terribly anti-Semitic, like most Southern women, and a touch of it goes into the play . . ."

When the play opened on Broadway a few days later, it was severely attacked by the critics. Tennessee placed much of the blame on reviewers wanting to close the production because of Zelda's anti-Semitism.

"I think I just couldn't leave Zelda's anti-Semitism out," he continued, "and do a true portrait of her. I have her make a single anti-Semitic remark in the play, which is about Sheilah Graham, whose real name is Lili Sheil.

"In the theatre you hardly dare use the word Jew, and it's really a detriment to a very fine people that they're so frightened of any criticism whatsoever, although after the Holocaust they certainly have reason to be frightened. I have no feelings of anti-Semitism, but those feelings do exist in other people, and it's difficult to present a picture to the world as it truly is without on occasion allowing a voice to those sentiments."

I don't know what Margaux thought, but I agreed with him.

To return to our lunch years before in Key West, and Tennessee's sensitivity to the public image of gays. Curiously, he reacted to anti-gay bigotry in the same way that many Jews responded to anti-Semitism: with fear and out-rage. And he was no more about to tolerate homophobic slurs than Jews were about to let go unchallenged anti-Semitic swipes.

Around women, Tennessee was always very courtly, falling into a Victorian politeness, like a boy visiting a rich maiden aunt whose favor he desired and thus was on his very best behavior. He avoided using vulgar language, dressed with special care, and exaggerated any woman's sensitivity to male coarseness whether in speech, manners, or dress. In other words, he reacted in the ways taught him as a boy, that ladies were fragile creatures whose sensitivities might be violently offended by the merest of vulgarities, all princesses who could feel a pea under a mound of mattresses.

Adriana Jackson, who is a worldly, sophisticated Italian woman, and a countess to boot, was at this lunch the object of his excessive regard. He enjoyed playing the role of the protector of the frail sensibility of womankind. Adriana was quite capable of protecting herself.

At lunch, I mentioned having seen Jimmy Kirkwood on the street. Kirkwood, a splendid writer, had a house in Key West.

"What did he have to say, baby?" Tennessee asked.

"He asked me if I knew the difference between a blow job and lunch?"

"He *what?*" Tennessee was mortified by my language. He blushed for Adriana.

"I said, he asked me if I knew the difference between a blow job and lunch. I said I didn't. And he said, 'Then let me invite you to lunch!' "

All of us but Tennessee laughed.

I went on to tell a few more jokes, off-color ones, and

Tennessee sat and steamed, giving me dirty looks, interrupting to inform me that Adriana was not interested in such low humor. Adriana happily said she wanted to hear more.

We were sitting outside at an umbrella table on a deck at the restaurant at the Pier House Hotel, where we had club membership and use of the beach. We came here most days for lunch, bringing our swimsuits with us, and after lunch we swam in the bay off the hotel's tiny beach. Several hundred yards out the hotel had a floating raft anchored. You could swim to it and lie there and sun.

As we sat talking on the deck, we watched two young men swim out to the raft, climb aboard, and moments later remove their trunks and began sexual relations in full view of the beach and restaurant.

"Don't look, Adriana!" Tennessee declared, appalled by this homosexual lapse in public decency. "This is an outrage! Don't they know there are women here who are offended by such obscenity? It must be stopped!"

"I'm not offended, darling," Adriana said. "It is amusing, no? Those two trombas on the dock?"

"I am calling the manager! How can I bring ladies like yourself here if such offenses take place?" He went on venting his displeasure.

"*Basta! Basta!* [Enough! Enough!]" Adriana said, trying to calm his nearly hysterical fit.

Tennessee's loud protests finally caught the attention of the maître d', who came over and inquired what was bothering him.

Almost speechless with fury by now, Tennessee pointed at the raft and sputtered that someone must be dispatched forthwith to remove these vulgar exhibitionists from the floating platform.

A waiter was ordered to swim to the raft, since the two boys making love were defiantly oblivious to shouts from shore ordering them to desist.

The young waiter stripped to his jockey shorts. We watched him swim to the raft. He climbed aboard, stood a moment watching the activity of the two young men, then he pulled down his shorts and joined in the fun.

Tennessee stormed out of the Pier House in a godawful huff.

Until Tennessee died, Richard and I went every year to Key West to be with him, and we saw him elsewhere, in New York and London, Los Angeles and San Francisco, in the Hamptons, Puerto Rico, and other places. In 1978, when we rented a house in Princeton, New Jersey, he visited us there.

In September 1979, he came to Princeton to spend a week with us. It was a very large house on Bayard Lane in central Princeton, old and rather gloomy in appearance, known as the Scott house.

In some ways Tennessee's first visit was a disaster. I loved him and I wanted him with me, but there was a pathos to him now. His shyness was worse, except when he was drunk. He was given more easily to rages, and he was tired all the time. He couldn't seem to get enough sleep. For the first time I noticed that he was sleeping late in the day, then got up for a few hours to write. When I went upstairs to call him for cocktails, I would find him asleep at his writing table or on the bed. Worse, he couldn't shake his conviction that people hated him and wanted him dead. He had few close friends left, and he seemed unable to cope with daily life. He consumed a chilling variety of pills each day; he constantly lost things, from credit cards to eyeglasses to suits; his sense of regret, was now most fully focused on the years he was represented by Billy Barnes, who, he incorrectly came to believe had deliberately ruined Tennessee's career to advance his own; and he was still frightened of Billy and ICM, when it should have been the other way around. But I loved having Tennessee with me, whatever his condition, whatever the state of his heart. And he enjoyed the beauty of Princeton. Unhappily, he found most of the people who lived there not to his taste. But then, so did I.

As a general rule, Tennessee despised schoolteachers, as I have said before, and, being a college town, Princeton was populated mainly by schoolteachers and real estate agents, a depressingly conservative bunch.

Tennessee was afraid to return to Key West because his estranged boyfriend, Robert, had moved back into his house uninvited and wanted Tennessee to move out and give him the house.

"He thinks I should live with Miss Rose!" Tennessee had recently bought Miss Rose a big house near him in Key West, complete with pool, where she lived with a paid companion. "She's happy with her companion, a born-again Baptist who subjects my reputation to public prayers for my salvation!" But his chief worry was Robert, who was constantly on his mind, and he waited for Robert's bill of divorcement with trepidation. They had loved each other, and it was over, and they both knew it, but they couldn't agree on how to break it off amicably. Robert needed money, and I urged Tennessee to give it to him. I thought he deserved it. The problem was over what the settlement would be in actual dollars.

(Tennessee finally agreed to give Robert an allowance of two hundred fifty dollars a week for life.)

In Princeton, we were new residents, and Richard, my roommate, was very concerned that we not earn the reputation for wildness that we had quickly attained in other small towns and villages where we had had houses. I thought it was already too late as far as Princeton was concerned, although I don't think we had reached the nadir of Tennessee's community relations on Key West. The local gentry had not taken to firing on our house.

The three of us had dinner one night in the Garden Room at the Nassau Inn, with the director of the local theatre group, one Nagle Jackson, who had called Tennessee in Key West, suggesting that one of his plays might possibly be considered for production at the McCarter Theatre on campus. Tennessee swallowed the bait.

Mr. Jackson, whom I had not met until that night, struck me as prudish: at dinner he expressed shock when I first used the word "fuck" in conversation at table. His censorious attitude toward my language simply encouraged me to act worse. I told him Jimmy Kirkwood's blow-job joke. He pretended not to understand. Tennessee joined in with dirty jokes of his own, since by that early hour in the evening he had quickly sized up Jackson.

Jackson proceeded to lecture Tennessee on the nature of the American theatre, the art of the drama, complaining that Tennessee's frank and shocking portrayal of sexual attitudes and unnatural acts in his plays had done a great disservice to the moral reputation of the American theatre, whose cultural purity demanded the highest standards of "literary ethics." And Tennessee's *Memoirs*, with their explicit sexual confessions, certainly had harmed his reputation as a playwright and artist, and reflected badly on other, more "authentic" artists, who didn't display their private lives for publicity and personal gain. Tennessee might incorrectly believe, he continued, that cheap effects and locker-room language for the sake of shock would sell theatre tickets and books, but they sacrificed deeper values on the altar of success, such as receiving the attention and critical appreciation of that small and vitally important community of serious critics, academicians, and other "authentic" artists.

Later Jackson turned an unattractive shade of gray when we loudly and unsuccessfully tried to pick up the seventeen-year-old busboy because he had a wonderful, open face with beautiful eyes as gray and iniquitous as a threatening sky. The boy knew the score.

Our dinner guest protested that such conduct wasn't permitted in dear old Princeton, a town where the most asked question is: What will the neighbors think? And it did no good to explain that such solicitation was perfectly legal under the revised New Jersey criminal code and, what's more, was one of the compelling reasons we were in this godforsaken burg in the first place; it certainly wasn't for the chance of having dinner with teachers.

The following night Mrs. Liz Thayer, who lives in a house a block away from ours, gave a dinner party for Tennessee. Simple courtesy required our presence because she had kindly opened her heated pool to us during Tennessee's stay in Princeton, and we swam there every day.

When she asked whom Tennessee wanted to meet, he said, "Anyone attractive as long as they don't teach school. No academics, please!"

Well, she tried and failed. They were all academics except for a woman who spoke with a thick German accent and made no sense whatsoever, and a cartoonist from

New York. The group contained six homosexual teachers of the type that makes one deeply embarrassed to be homosexual.

After dinner the shit hit the fan.

The cartoonist sat at the dining table drawing Tennessee, who was drinking a brandy.

Tennessee: "Since you didn't ask my permission to draw me, may I be permitted to see what you have done?"

He took one look at the cartoon and went into a rage.

The picture was recognizable, but it was hideous: fat, clownish, with ugly tufts of hair sprouting from his head.

Tennessee stormed out of the place. I soon followed him, knowing he couldn't find his way home.

When I asked him why he bolted from the house, he declared, "Revolutionaries don't ever feel comfortable with the gentry!"

We were now out of the use of a terrific pool.

I had spent several years trying to get Tennessee to meet Patricia Kennedy Lawford, who ultimately did become one of his close friends. There was always one excuse or another why it couldn't be done. "The Kennedys don't need me in their lives," he admitted. "They are haunted enough!" The real reason was that he felt like a has-been, that he was of no use to Pat or her family, and that he would only be imposing himself where he was not wanted. It is difficult not to anticipate social rejection when you have lived through years of listening to the critics broadcast to the world that you are washed up, almost an embarrassment to your craft.

At a lunch that I finally arranged in Princeton, Tennessee talked to Pat about meeting President Kennedy.

"I met him through Gore Vidal," he told her, "at your family's estate in Palm Beach before he was President. Gore said he was invited to a lunch by Mr. Kennedy and would I like to come along? Of course I did, since I greatly admired your brother. He brought such vitality to our country's life, such hope and great style. He made thinking fashionable again.

"President Kennedy was a great gentleman, a really good, gentle man. On the way to see him we were caught in traffic. It was terrible. Gore Vidal isn't a particularly good driver, though he's a good writer at times. So we were an hour late for lunch with Mr. Kennedy, and he acted as if we were on time. His manners were so impeccable, and Jackie was a tremendous charmer, and still is, I presume, although I haven't seen her in a long time."

Pat asked him what he was working on, and he replied *Clothes for a Summer Hotel*, describing the plot to her, and offering to send her a copy of the rewritten script. Pat had worked in the theatre and produced a number of Broadway plays.

"José [Quintero, the director] wants Geraldine Page to play Zelda. But she's so fat now, and I don't see how she can lose enough weight to play both the young Zelda and the old. Maybe we should use two actresses for Zelda's different ages in the play."

Pat suggested Kim Stanley for the role.

"Unreliable," Tennessee replied. "She used to borrow pills from me, baby. She'd come to my place, and when she'd leave all the Valium would be gone! Of course, I'd call and ask her for Seconal from time to time, on Sundays, and she'd always get it for me. She had a special understanding with some pharmacy."

"What about Vanessa Redgrave?" Pat offered.

"Oh God, no! Can you imagine what the press would do with that? They'd kill the play before it opened, and if it did open the Jews wouldn't buy tickets; they'd *bomb* the place! She's PLO, not a popular thing to be in New York."

To play Fitzgerald, Tennessee wanted Jon Voight or Michael Moriarty.

Before she left, Tennessee asked Pat how her mother was feeling. He had heard she had been ill.

"My mother calls me every day and she is always asking if I know anyone older than she, and if I say I do, she wants to know how they are. Mother wants *specifics*, how healthy are they, can they still walk as well as she can." Pat laughed. "Mother is eighty-nine, and it's hard to find people much older to tell her about."

"My mother is ninety-one," Tennessee said. "She thinks there's a horse living in her room."

"Does your mother walk?"

"With a walker, yes," he replied. "She's had a number of small strokes, and her mind isn't totally functional, you know."

"I won't tell Mother that," Pat said.

They talked a long time about their two sisters, Pat's sister Rosemary, who was mentally retarded, and Miss Rose. There was a bond between Pat and Tennessee because they both shared the pain of mentally hurt sisters they loved. They spoke with intense interest about Rose and Rosemary, their intellectual levels and emotional vulnerability. Sad, and yet they took great pride in telling each other the small achievements of each of these sisters, seeing in their very survival, in the tiny, almost imperceptible advances in self-reliance and learning, the triumph of the human spirit.

Pat spoke about how Rosemary, despite her disability, cries and feels hurt, and laughs.

"Oh, Miss Rose feels all that, too. She even tries to pick out her own clothes," Tennessee boasted, "but when you take her shopping she always says she wears a size forty! She collects soap, you know. You can't take her anywhere without her stealing soap. She stuffs it in her handbag, and thinks no one knows. When she comes to visit me in Key West, she takes my soap. I'm always buying more . . . She's even learned to talk a little on the telephone. Until last year she would pick it up and hold it, not knowing that you are supposed to talk into the receiver. Now she can talk, not much, but a little. It makes me incredibly happy to hear her voice on the telephone, small and distant, oh so hesitant, but there."

For the next few days, Tennessee stayed in Princeton, refusing to go to New York. He was supposed to appear at a radio station to record a little drama written by someone else about William Faulkner. Colleen Dewhurst was scheduled to join him in the reading. Tennessee didn't want to do it. He procrastinated for days. At last he called the radio station, feigned a hoarseness that made his voice almost unintelligible, and complained of having a cold verging on pneumonia that prevented him from showing up.

I asked him why he was so reluctant to read the role of William Faulkner on a two-bit radio show.

"They're only paying two hundred and forty dollars, baby. *Slave wages.* And I don't know how Faulkner's voice *sounded.*"

"But you *knew* him."

"Baby, many people were acquainted with Mr. Faulkner, but he never *talked*. He never said a *word*. You had to *force* him to talk," Tennessee explained. "When they were making the movie of *Cat* he was always hanging around the set because he was in love with the script girl. So I saw him all the time, and he was usually drunk. But he never said much. I do remember he was partial to the word 'ain't.' He was continuously saying ain't, baby, even when some other word would do better. And he never looked you in the eye. He sat in the studio commissary at lunch staring down at the table. Silent as a cat about to pounce. Well, once he did look me in the eye. At lunch. And he had such sad eyes that I started to cry! He never looked me in the eye again!

"He was a lonely, unhappy man, with a wounded heart that nothing could mend. Some injuries to the soul are so great that nothing can repair the damage. He drank all the time, and he had his reasons. He was always falling in love with girls at a distance. Following them around like a homeless dog looking to be taken in. Watching them. Nothing came of it. The last woman he was in love with was Jean Stein. Her father was Jules Stein who owned MCA (which controls Universal Pictures). Faulkner was crazy about her, and he didn't know how to get her to marry him. He spent his time hanging around her in Los Angeles and New York, like some lovesick schoolboy.

One night Truman [Capote] came into Random House's offices. They were then located in an old mansion on Madison Avenue behind St. Patrick's Cathedral, and Bennett Cerf gave keys to writers he published so they could come at night and work in the empty offices when they needed to. Truman came in. It was about eleven at night, and the place was very dark. He heard sobbing coming from Bennett Cerf's office. The door was closed, and Truman thought someone was dying. He knocked on the door, and then opened it. Faulkner was lying on the sofa sobbing. He was very drunk. Truman said, 'What's the matter, Mr. Faulkner?' And Faulkner said, 'Jean [Stein] has just told me that her parents won't let me marry her because she's Jewish and I'm not. She won't see me anymore.' Faulkner said he wanted to die.

"Of course, I suspect Jean didn't want to marry him because he was a hell of a lot older than her, was a drunk, and she didn't look forward to spending her married life in Oxford, Mississippi, where about the only thing to do is to watch the cows go by!

"After Faulkner died, a professor at the university there asked me to come and give a lecture about Faulkner because he was a fellow Southerner who also wrote about the South. I think his greatest book is *Light in August*, and I love the character Joe Christmas. I wish I had created him. I told this professor that I don't give formal lectures anymore. I just give formal readings and I was not about to read from Faulkner's work. They should hire an actor for that.

"He asked me why I didn't give formal lectures anymore. And I said, 'Once I went to the University of Tennessee in Knoxville with a prepared lecture. When I got there I discovered I'd left the lecture at home. So I had to get up on stage and improvise, which infuriated the professors. They were outraged.' Knoxville, like other academic places, is very reactionary. I was not about to go down to Mississippi to lecture to the school there (the University of Mississippi) about Faulkner.

"The people there, his neighbors, the townspeople, even his family had no respect for him. They couldn't see his greatness. He was just the local drunk. You know, you see yourself as you're reflected in others. Other people are like mirrors, and if the mirrors are warped, like in a fun house, in time that is how you learn to see yourself. I think Faulkner came to believe that maybe he was just the town drunk, and he didn't care anymore, and he just upped and decided to end it. He killed himself with booze. He drank as much as he could in as short a time as he could until it killed him.

"So many writers are casualties. I think of poor Bill Inge. He was a tragic person. *Tragic.* The critics treated him very cruelly. They're brutal. I always thought he wrote two wonderful plays. *Come Back, Little Sheba* was a brilliant play. That's why I introduced him to Audrey Wood. And then he wrote a play in which a kid kills his mother, an enormously brilliant work. *Natural Affection,* or something like that.

"I met him in St. Louis. I came back there during the run of *Menagerie* in Chicago, and he interviewed me for a newspaper called the St. Louis *Times-Star.* He was the drama and music critic for it. He entertained me quite a bit the week I was there. We became friends. He came to Key West and visited me several times, the last time in the sixties after Frankie died. I was using drugs to lift my depression. Bill was abusing them because he couldn't bear life anymore. He drank all the time. He had these mad terrors, thinking people were poisoning his food. He refused to leave the house, even to swim, because hired killers were stalking the streets for him. Such despair. I had never seen a man driven to such violent terror before.

"At the end of his life, Barbara Baxley, with whom he attempted to have a heterosexual affair, and who was very, very fond of him, called me and said that Inge was in a desperate situation in California. 'He's sleeping with lots of barbiturates under his mattress. He only gets up to drink, and then he goes back to bed.'

"I said, 'He's on a suicide course.'

"She said, 'I know it. He commits himself voluntarily, and then lets himself out the next day.'

" 'Who's he with?'

" 'His sister,' she said. 'I want you to call his sister and tell her that she's got to commit him.'

"So after consulting Maureen Stapleton, who said I should, I did call his sister."

(On this one point Tennessee's memory was not wholly accurate. Barbara Baxley called him late at night at the Hotel Élysée. Maureen and I were with him when the call came. After he spoke with Baxley, and told us of her request, Maureen urged him to call Inge's sister. At first he was afraid to. He feared she might want him to fly to the Coast to get Inge to a hospital, and he was frightened of Inge when he was crazed with drugs. Maureen called Inge's sister, talked to her a moment, and then insisted Tennessee take the phone. He did.)

"I told his sister what Barbara had told me, and she said, 'Yes, that's just how it is.' She was talking in a whisper. I said, 'I can hardly hear you. Why are you whispering like that?'

"She answered, 'Because I never know whether he's up or down.'

"I said, 'Just listen, then. Get him into the hospital. Don't have him commit himself. *You* commit him. Otherwise he's going to kill himself.' "

Ironically, unknowingly, Tennessee was giving to his sister Dakin's reasons for having committed Tennessee to

Barnes Hospital: he thought if he didn't, his brother would kill himself.

"Well, a month later in Rome I read a headline in the Rome *Daily American* that Bill Inge was dead. He had asphyxiated himself by running the motor on his car in a closed garage.

"Fitzgerald, Hemingway, Hart Crane. Inge . . . oh, the debris!" he said, his voice breaking. "The *wreckage*. The *wreckage!* Toward the end of an American writer's life it's just dreadful. Hemingway's last years were a nightmare. Faulkner's one unending misery. Edna St. Vincent Millay walked into the sea to die. Fitzgerald's end was not much better, although it was less dramatic . . . Once they become known, everybody wants a piece of them."

The night before Tennessee was to leave Princeton to return to New York, he, Richard, and I went to see the movie *Casablanca.* He laughed throughout it.

On leaving the theatre, I said, "Let's go home and have a few drinks, and then I'll make us a nice chicken." All I knew how to cook was chicken, and after days of eating Perdue's birds at every meal, Tennessee was complaining about sprouting pinfeathers.

On the way home we drove past a French restaurant on Witherspoon Street.

"Baby, look!" Tennessee exclaimed, like a man lost in the desert spotting an oasis. "A French restaurant. We can go there for dinner."

"But Dotson's making chicken," Richard protested loyally.

Pause.

Tennessee, petulant like a child: "Oh, do we *have* to go

home and eat Dotson's old *chicken*, when we can be sitting in that lovely French restaurant?"

We ate at the restaurant, Tennessee bounding from the car and through the door before I could change my mind.

We had martinis and ordered a splendid wine. Not having to face another stewed hen, Tennessee was delighted to be alive. We told jokes, some of them rather lame. A typical example: How do you get a meal on Air India? You go to First Class and you beg! But Tennessee laughed loudly at the weakest lines.

I said to him, "You're in an awfully good mood suddenly."

"Baby, you know, with advancing age I find humor more and more interesting. Black humor, especially. My present play, the one I'm starting to work on, I call a Gothic comedy. My humor is Gothic in theatre. I make some serious, even tragic observations about society, but I make them through the medium of comedy."

I asked him to tell Richard the story about his funniest adventure, a tale I had heard many times and which he loved telling.

"I was alone in Miami," he began. "Frank hadn't arrived yet from Miami. I was staying in Miami until he got there and took me to Key West.

"It was night, and I was lonely. I walked out on to Biscayne Boulevard. There's a park along there frequented by rentable companions of both sexes. This young vagrant was lolling on a bench. I think he was mentally retarded, poor child. I struck up a conversation with him. He seemed not too bright, but personable. I said I was alone, would he like to accompany me to my hotel? He said he would. Well, once he got under the streetlight I saw he'd never be able to go through a hotel lobby because his clothes were so dilapidated. So I suggested that we go out by the pool where I had a cabaña.

"We got out there, and he suddenly jerked my wallet out of my pocket. I had only seven dollars in it, though. Then he tried to get my wristwatch off. It had a very simple clasp upon it, but he couldn't manage to get it unclasped. Finally he gave up on that. I wasn't frightened at all for some reason. I was wearing a ring with three diamonds and he couldn't get that off either. It was a tight fit. So I said, 'Now this is a very silly situation! I've got hundreds of dollars in my room. You sit down here and rest, and I'll be down in a little while with a large sum of money for you.' I'd realized by this time that he was a moron.

"Well, I went back to my room in the hotel, locked the door, and went to bed. And at half-hour intervals all night, the phone would ring and he'd say, 'I'm still waiting.' I finally said, 'Baby, go see a doctor. You really think I was coming back down with a hundred dollars for you?' I liked the poor kid by that time.

"It's the funniest adventure I ever had. 'I'm still waiting!' He might still be."

That night Tennessee slept badly. My bedroom was across the hall from his, and I heard him get up and pace the room. From time to time he said something too muffled to be discernible to me.

Around five in the morning, he knocked on my bedroom door and came in, the room lit by a faint dawn.

"I can't sleep, baby. I'll have to stay with you."

He sat down on the bed, and I asked him what was troubling his sleep.

"There's an old woman who keeps knocking on the window pane," he told me. His room was on the third floor in the tower. The window had no shade. "She peers in at me, all white with these desperate eyes. When I try to sleep, she keeps rapping. I have told her many times to leave me be. Baby, I think you ought to reconsider your decision to live in Princeton when the village has an elderly Peeping Tom climbing ladders to stranger's windows."

I laughed. "It must be Mrs. Scott."

He asked who that was.

I told him that when I rented the house the landlady told me, after I had signed the lease and she had cashed the deposit check, that the house was haunted by a harmless ghost, one Mrs. Scott. It seems that when Mrs. Scott and her husband had built the house in the nineteenth century, she insisted on an enormous staircase for one reason: when she died she didn't want her body lowered out of an upper window because the staircase was too narrow to permit transit of a dead body in a coffin. Unfortunately, Mrs. Scott heard the call to glory at her sister's house, some blocks away, and the act that all her considerable modesty and sense of decorum cried out against took place: she was lowered in a sheet from an upper window into a coffin awaiting her below. Ever since then she has haunted her old house, unable to find peace.

Tennessee asked me if I believed the story.

I told him I didn't much believe in ghosts, but it was undeniable that doors swung open and closed for no apparent reason, that objects you put in their familiar places would later inexplicably, unexpectedly appear where they didn't belong. Who knows?

He thought a moment. "I have seen death. I have always thought death would come to me as my grandmother's ghost, her presence. I have felt her presence all my life when I was in trouble and frightened. And now I've seen her. She must be warning me. But of what?"

On March 26, 1981, Tennessee's last Broadway play, *Clothes for a Summer Hotel*, opened at the Cort Theatre. It was his sixty-ninth birthday. Kurt and Jill Vonnegut, Norris and Norman Mailer, Jerzy Kosinski, and other friends attended—by the middle of the first act we all knew it was a commercial failure. I had been to a preview, and I spent much of the play with Tennessee at a bar across the street from the theatre. He said very little.

After the curtain came down, Pat Lawford and I walked through the chilly night to the cast party at a restaurant on Third Avenue. It took us some time to find him; we finally did, sitting on a bar stool next to Maria St. Just, as far from the door as he could get, half hidden in the semidarkness. He tried to smile when he saw us. The first reviews were a disaster, and worse was to come. The notices on his last opening night in New York were among the cruelest he had ever received. When we greeted him, he already sensed that his life as a writer for the Broadway theatre was over, and with it, much that made him want to live.

Pat and I told him how wonderful the play was, and he knew we were exaggerating our appreciation of it, as friends do on an opening night. I had rarely seen him

unhappier, you could read forboding in his eyes. It was as
if he were condemned.

Pat and I huddled together.

"We've got to do something to help him. He needs to
know people love him. Let's get some of his friends together at my place and try to cheer him up," Pat suggested, very worried about him.

We went back to Tennessee, and Pat said how proud
she was of him, and how proud she was of his play, and
she would love to give a dinner party in his honor on
Wednesday night? Could he come?

Tennessee beamed with delight, and said that he
would be happy to come.

Pat has a lovely duplex apartment on the East River.
And the night of the party there were flowers everywhere,
and in the foyer was an immense balloon, about five feet
high, on which was written: HURRAY FOR TENNES-
SEE!

At the dinner, in addition to me, were Philip Kingsley, Richard Zoerink, Eli Wallach, Vass Voglis, Jan Cush-
ing, and Boaty Nielson. We had all been coached before-
hand to do our best to cheer Tennessee up.

He arrived with Maria. He was dressed in a beautifully cut gray suit. He seemed nervous, depressed, and
unsure of himself. We stood in Pat's drawing room, its
french doors and windows overlooking the water and the
lights on the other shore. It was a cold, clear night.

Everyone avoided mentioning the play and the terrible reviews. Suddenly about ten minutes after he arrived,
Tennessee bolted across the room and pulled open the
french doors. He ran out on to the balcony, seven floors
above the ground, and tried to crawl over the railing and
hurl himself to his death. Eli grabbed him and pulled him

back, and Tennessee laughed his manic laugh, and pretended it was all a joke.

During dinner we had a lot to drink, and gradually Tennessee's mood brightened with the liquor and the company of his friends. We sat for hours at the table, Tennessee seated at Pat's right, and when he got nervous or suddenly a look of fright came over him, some darkness momentarily shadowing his mind, he would take her hand and kiss it, and tell her how beautiful she was. Or he would caress her hair.

"We're all doomed," he said several times, laughing. "Doomed. Dying ducks in a winter freeze." As he spoke this gloom, he cackled.

Eli Wallach interrupted, trying to change the subject. He told stories about actors he knew, Yul Brynner for one. And Tennessee snapped out of his depression.

Eli talked about his long friendship with Tennessee, about how he had met his wife, Anne Jackson, through Tennessee, and how at every major turning point in their lives and career Tennessee figured.

"I love the tragic vision of your plays, but most of all I love your humor. If you'll permit me, Tennessee, I want to recite a marvelous poem you wrote, a poem that shows the humor you bring to all of life. It's entitled, 'Life Story':

After you've been to bed together for the first time,
without the advantage or disadvantage of any prior
    acquaintance,
the other party very often says to you,
Tell me about yourself, I want to know all about you,
what's your story? And you think maybe they really and
    truly do

sincerely want to know your life story, and so you light up
a cigarette and begin to tell it to them, the two of you
lying together in completely relaxed positions
like a pair of rag dolls a bored child dropped on a bed.

You tell them your story, or as much of your story
as time or a fair degree of prudence allows, and they say,
        Oh, oh, oh, oh, oh,
each time a little more faintly, until the oh
is just an audible breath, and then of course

there's some interruption. Slow room service comes up
with a bowl of melting ice cubes, or one of you rises to pee
and gaze at himself with mild astonishment in the bathroom
        mirror.
And then, the first thing you know, before you've had time
to pick up where you left off with your enthralling life story,
they're telling you *their* life story, exactly as they'd intended
        to all along,

and you're saying, Oh, oh, oh, oh, oh,
each time a little more faintly, the vowel at last becoming
no more than an audible sigh,

as the elevator, halfway down the corridor and a turn to
        the left,
draws one last, long, deep breath of exhaustion
and stops breathing forever. Then?

Well, one of you falls asleep
and the other one does likewise with a lighted cigarette
        in his mouth,
and that's how people burn to death in hotel rooms.

When he finished reciting the poem, we laughed and
applauded, Tennessee joining in.

"Tennessee," Eli said, "do you know what this is?" Eli

pointed to a ring he was wearing. "It is an actor's ring. It has two faces, and when you turn the ring the face of tragedy becomes the face of comedy, two sides of the same reality. I have had it most of my life, and there is nothing I own that I cherish and value more than this ring. It has brought me luck. And there is no one else I would give it to, no man I love more, than you."

He took off the ring, and put it on Tennessee's finger. At first Tennessee protested that he couldn't accept the gift, and then he did, with tears in his eyes.

Eli then raised his wineglass, and said, "I want you to stand with me and toast not only the greatest living playwright, but the greatest playwright. Period."

We stood and saluted him one last time.

"Eli," Tennessee said, 'thank you, baby. I don't know how true what you say is, or whether it matters if it is. It's nice to hear it from a friend. They say my days as a playwright, with any hope of being produced, are over. But my writing goes on. I don't want to die until my work is finished. But what a man wants, and what he is given, aren't often the same. I have done my best, for what it's worth." Tennessee paused, drawing his fingers gently down his cheeks. "All my life I have cared about the sufferings of people. Maybe that's all that really matters."

CHAPTER · EIGHT

Life is a series of burned-out sites.
Nobody escapes the bonfire:
if you live—you burn.

—ANDREI VOZNESENSKY

I SAW TENNESSEE OFTEN during the following two years, mainly in New York and Key West, but also in Chicago and on the Coast. He never really recovered his confidence after *Clothes for A Summer Hotel,* which closed after only fourteen performances and lost about a half a million dollars, twenty thousand of which Tennessee had put in to keep it going. And whether out of habit or need, he soon returned to Key West and began rewriting *Clothes,* trying to salvage what he could not let go.

He left Key West for the last time in December 1982, and he fled suddenly, unexpectedly.

Leoncia McGee, his longtime housekeeper, heard a taxi being called by Tennessee. She asked, "Where are you going, Mr. Tom?"

"To New York, Lee."

She remembered how sad he seemed when she recalled that day.

"When are you coming home, Mr. Tom?"

"I won't ever be coming home again," he said.

He handed her a check covering her weekly salary,

and he said that for the rest of her life her salary would be sent to her each week from New York.

Later she told me that Tennessee had been very quiet all week, unlike himself, enveloped by a sadness he could not defeat.

"Before Mr. Tom went away from the house alone, he came back into the kitchen and handed me another check, one for a thousand dollars. 'What's this for?' I asked Mr. Tom. 'For Christmas,' he said.

"I walked with him to the front door, and before he left he kissed me on the cheek, a thing he never done before. That's when I knew he wasn't coming back. He kissed me, and he was traveling alone, and he never done them things before."

On February 24, 1983, I was to have dinner with Tennessee and Jon Uker in New York. He was staying at the Hotel Élysée (or "The Easy Lay," as he called it), in town to oversee a semiprofessional production of his play, *Vieux Carré*, at a tiny theatre on the far West Side. It was a part-time company, much like those which had first produced his earliest plays in St. Louis long ago. He was once again rewriting the play, determined still to make the critics and the public realize the beauty of this drama about his early years as a starving young writer barely surviving in a rooming house in the French Quarter.

Jon Uker, his paid companion, was a young actor he had met through me a few years before. Jon, like most actors, couldn't get theatrical work, and so Tennessee hired him from time to time to stay with him. He was paid two hundred and fifty dollars a week, essentially to keep Tennessee alive. Tennessee, at seventy-two, was in bad health, fatigued and often disoriented, melancholy, nearly blind, and ineffably lonely. He suffered from a loneliness like a growing wound, unstanchable, a wound he no longer could heal nor tried to disguise.

On the afternoon of the twenty-fourth, he called me in Princeton. I had to fly to San Francisco the next day, and so I told him that I couldn't make dinner, but I would see him as soon as I returned in about three days. He seemed very tired, but he was optimistic about the show-case production of his play. He asked about Pat and Richard, and then we said good-bye.

On February 25, 1983, sometime before dawn, Tennessee Williams died in his two-room suite at the Hotel Élysée. He had gone to bed around midnight. Jon was in the living room when he said good-night.

On the bedstand were scattered his many pills, and among them was the plastic cap from an eyedrop bottle. He used drops because of glaucoma. Also beside his bed was a small triptych showing the Virgin and Child, an object he carried with him when he traveled.

He took two Seconals just before he went to sleep.

Sometime before morning he woke, and half-asleep in the darkness, he searched to find another Seconal to help him back to sleep. By mistake, he picked up the plastic bottle cap and put it in his mouth. It stuck in his throat and, choking, he gagged loudly. Trying to summon help, he toppled out of bed, knocking over the nightstand. It made a crash that Jon heard in the other room. He ignored it.

Tennessee choked to death.

Today I remember how he smiled, how he reached for his wineglass, his hand making an extraordinarily elegant arch as it reached the cold surface; his fingers, one by one, slowly touching it and then lifting it. It was a gesture unique to him, and whenever I saw it, it brought to mind such memories—good times, laughter, pranks, outrageous camping. And the kindliness of his nature. All those who met him when they were young and came to know him well will tell you what I do: that they never knew anyone kinder. He was the net under the wire for us.

"I don't think people are responsible for what they do," Tennessee said. "And yet, knowing that, I believe the moral person must try to avoid evil and cruelty and dishonesty as best he can. That remains to us."

His greatness is that he tried to do that harder and longer than any other artist.

When he died, he was working, naturally, on the rewrite of a new play, *In Masks Outrageous and Austere*. I do not know if he ever finished it, but he talked a lot about it, and I read scenes from it. Or rather I would start to read a scene, and he would grab it from me impatiently and say, "Baby, you don't know how to read!" Then he would sit back, reach for his wine, and in his deep voice with its Mississippi drawl, read what he had written, cackling with laughter at the most sorrowful passages.

I can hear him reading now as I can hear him padding about his house in the middle of the night and knocking at my door before daybreak and asking me to come and sit with him awhile because he cannot sleep, he is frightened, and will I stay with him until it is light? I can feel myself holding him, listening to him breathe after he has taken yet another Seconal to sleep, listening to make sure the breaths are deep enough and long enough to signal that sleep has come and I can slip away knowing he is safe. He said many times, "Death doesn't like crowds. It comes to you when you're alone."

AFTERWORD

The morning Tennessee died, I came into New York to catch an afternoon flight to San Francisco where I was to appear on a television talk show to discuss the plight of runaway children. Before going to the airport, I stopped by *Parade* magazine's offices to pick up my mail. It was around noon, and the place was largely empty. Gida Ingrassia, Walter Anderson's editorial assistant, handed me a dozen telephone messages; one was from National Public Radio, another from Pat Lawford. I called Pat first.

"Are you sitting down?" she asked.

"Why?"

"I have some terrible news. Mary [her housekeeper] heard on the radio that Tennessee was dead," Pat said. "She told me about an hour ago."

I went cold. My immediate reaction was denial. "It couldn't be true," I said. "I talked to him last night. He was in great shape. Mary must have heard wrong."

"I'm so sorry, Dotson, but I think it's true. Can I do anything for you?"

I said no, I'd be all right.

It was lunchtime, and there were few people at the office. I asked the people I could find if they had heard anything about Tennessee Williams. They said no.

I called National Public Radio, whose studios are near *Parade*'s offices. They asked if I could come by in half an hour and be interviewed. The woman I talked to, a secretary, didn't know what they wanted to interview me about. I should have caught on then, but I didn't. I put the possibility of his death entirely out of mind. I had been through so many false calls with him, had watched him play dead so often and listened to him talk about his coming demise as a ploy for sympathy that it had become a joke, a party game, something to laugh about. Inexplicably, I came to believe that I would die before him, and he would go on forever.

On the way to the radio studios I stopped at the bar at the Harley Hotel on Forty-second Street and had a double martini. I asked the bartender if he had heard anything about Tennessee Williams. He said no. I relaxed.

At National Public Radio I was ushered into a small recording studio. Opposite me sat the producer who would do the interview. He said, "What are your feelings on the death of your friend, Tennessee Williams?"

I said nothing. He repeated the question. Then I knew it was true. I made a few remarks, and I left.

I walked for hours around midtown Manhattan. It was a gray day, and I walked four or five times past the Hotel Élysée, but I couldn't bring myself to go inside and inquire about my friend.

I canceled my flight and went back to Princeton.

When I got home Richard was crying. There was a pile of phone messages from news organizations, TASS among them, wanting a statement. I took the phone off the hook.

On the evening news I saw pictures of his body being carried out of the Élysée in a rubber sack. I felt disembodied, like I was outside my body watching me watching the news.

The next morning, in the newspapers, I learned that his remains were on display at Frank Campbell's funeral home. One thing he had wanted was that there would be no public viewing of his body. That was the first of his wishes to be disregarded. There was more to come.

On June 21, 1972, Tennessee was staying in a suite at the Hotel Élysée. That night we had dinner together at Gino's on Lexington Avenue. When we got back to the hotel Tennessee talked about how he wanted to be buried. He wanted to add a codicil to his will stating how he wanted his remains disposed of, and where. We needed a witness. I called Tom Ligeon, a young actor who was a friend of mine. Tom came to the hotel, and Tennessee wrote out the codicil in longhand on hotel stationery.

"I, Thomas Lanier (Tennessee) Williams, being in sound mind upon this subject, and having declared this wish repeatedly to my close friends—do hereby state my desire to be buried at sea. More specifically, I wish to be buried at sea at as close a possible point as the American poet Hart Crane died by choice in the sea; this would be ascernatible [sic], this geographic point, by the various books (biographical) upon his life and death. I wish to be sewn up in a canvas sack and dropped overboard, as stated above, as close as possible to where Hart Crane was given by himself to the great mother of life which is the sea: the Caribbean, specifically, if that fits the geography of his death. Otherise [sic]—whereever [sic] fits it.

"This is my irrevocable testament concerning the disposal of my remains. I wish my obxquies [sic] to be conductee [sic] by my revolutionary comrades in the what I regard as the true sense of revolution: those desiring freedom from an imperialistic and militaristic regime. I should like the Episcopalian burial service to be read."

(signed) Tennessee Williams
Dotson Rader
Tom Ligeon

The next morning we took the codicil to his lawyer, Floria Lasky, and had it added to his will.

A few years later, talking to Dick Cavett on PBS, Tennessee said, "Personally, I intend to be buried at sea. I want to be put in a sack and dropped overboard."

In two books of his that he gave to me, he wrote, "To the Big Dot, Bury me at sea! Love, Tenn." And on a poster for *Small Craft Warnings* he wrote the same thing.

He spoke often to me about it, and as he got older his burial in the waters off Key West became an obsession, and I was commissioned to carry it through.

When I learned that he was to be buried in St. Louis next to his mother, I called Eastman and Eastman, his new attorneys, to protest. I was informed, somewhat unpleasantly, that Dakin had decided on interment in St. Louis, and that the services would be Catholic. They denied that any codicil concerning his burial existed, and in any case I had no standing in law to intervene. Dakin was completely in charge.

Disgusted, I flew to San Diego and decided to go on to Mexico, anywhere out of the country far enough so I couldn't be found. I was bitter and knew greater grief than I had ever known, and I wanted out. And I was appalled by the movie stars and critics coming forward to tell of their admiration for Tennessee, what close friends they had been to him, how they had stood by him to the wretched end. I knew otherwise. Even the New York *Times* played its part. It wrote that America's greatest playwright, *after* Eugene O'Neill, had died.

Two years before he died, Tennessee wrote a new will. He left his estate, its value estimated at ten million dollars, to the University of the South and to Harvard. The University of the South because his grandfather had gone there. I haven't a clue as to why Harvard was in the will, unless the lawyers who drew it up were Harvard alumni.

A few months after he died, Leoncia McGee, his housekeeper in Key West, stopped receiving her monthly checks.

The day before his funeral Lorraine Garland, a friend of mine from Princeton, and I went to a travel agent in San Diego. I wanted to go somewhere in Mexico for a couple of weeks. He suggested Mazatlán, where I had never been, telling us we didn't need hotel reservations. There are plenty of rooms, he assured us.

When we arrived in Mazatlán, a city on the Mexican coast across the Gulf from Baja, we couldn't find a room. Every hotel on the beach was booked. After about six hours we convinced the manager of a hotel to give us a room. It would be for only one night, he said.

The hotel was the Camino Real.

After we checked in, I went alone to the bar. It was called Lafitte, like the bar in New Orleans (Lafitte in Exile) that had been our favorite.

I sat down next to another American. I ordered a drink. He said, "It's terrible about Tennessee Williams. You know, it's ironic to be here in Mazatlán."

I asked him why.

"Well, Mazatlán is the town that the father in *The Glass Menagerie* ran away to."

And then I remembered, it was also the place where

Tennessee went to lick his wounds after the failure of *Battle of Angels.*

In running from his death, I had unintentionally found my way to his sometime hiding place, the refuge he had found as a young playwright just before success would find him. The irony wasn't lost on me. There is no escaping him, I thought, and there never will be.